Get the eBooks FREE!

(PDF, ePub, Kindle, and liveBook all included)

We believe that once you buy a book from us, you should be able to read it in any format we have available. To get electronic versions of this book at no additional cost to you, purchase and then register this book at the Manning website.

Go to https://www.manning.com/freebook and follow the instructions to complete your pBook registration.

That's it!
Thanks from Manning!

Get Programming with Go

Get Programming with

Go

Nathan Youngman
Roger Peppé

MANNING
Shelter Island

Acquisition editor: Michael Stephens
Development editors: Jenny Stout, Marina Michaels
Technical development editors: Matthew Merkes, Joel Kotarski
Review editor: Aleksandar Dragosavljević
Project editor: David Novak
Copyeditor: Corbin Collins
Proofreaders: Melody Dolab, Elizabeth Martin
Technical proofreader: Christopher Haupt
Typesetter: Dottie Marsico
Graphics: Olga Shalakhina, Erick Zelaya, April Milne
Cover designer: Monica Kamsvaag

M Manning Publications Co.
    20 Baldwin Road
    PO Box 761
    Shelter Island, NY 11964

ISBN 9781617293092
Printed in the United States of America

  2 3 4 5 6 7 8 9 10 – DP – 23 22 21 20 19 18

Contents

Unit 7

CONCURRENT PROGRAMMING

Preface

Everything changes and nothing remains still.

—Heraclitus

While traveling Europe in 2005, Nathan heard rumblings of a new web framework called Ruby on Rails. Returning to Alberta in time to celebrate Christmas, he found a copy of *Agile Web Development with Rails* (Pragmatic Bookshelf, 2005) at the computer bookstore downtown. Over the next two years, he transitioned his career from Cold-Fusion to Ruby.

At university in York, England, Roger was introduced to the radical simplicity of Bell Labs Research UNIX and the Plan 9 OS produced by the same group, which included Go authors Rob Pike and Ken Thompson. Roger became a fan and later worked with the Inferno system, which used its own language, Limbo, a close ancestor of Go.

In November 2009, Go was announced as an open source project. Roger immediately saw its potential and started using it, making contributions to its standard library and ecosystem. He remains delighted by Go's success, now programs in Go full time, and runs a local Go meetup.

Nathan watched Rob Pike's tech talk announcing Go but didn't give Go a serious look until 2011. When a coworker spoke highly of Go, Nathan decided to read through a rough cut of *The Go Programming Language Phrasebook* (Addison-Wesley Professional, 2012) over Christmas break. Over the next few years, he went from using Go on hobby projects and blogging about Go (nathany.com) to organizing a local Go meetup (edmontongo.org) and writing Go at work.

There's no end to learning in the world of computer science, where the tools and techniques are continuously changing and improving. Whether you have a degree in computer science or are just starting out, teaching yourself new skills is important. We hope this book serves you well as you learn the Go programming language.

Acknowledgments

What a privilege it has been to write this book and help you learn Go. Thank you for reading!

These pages represent the efforts of many individuals, not merely the authors on the cover.

First and foremost, we would like to thank our editors Jennifer Stout and Marina Michaels for providing valuable feedback and for continuing to push us little by little over the finish line. Also, thank you to Joel Kotarski and Matt Merkes for your spot-on technical editing, Christopher Haupt for technical proofing, and copyeditor Corbin Collins for improving our grammar and style. Our thanks go to Bert Bates and to series editors Dan Maharry and Elesha Hyde for the conversations and guidelines that helped shape *Get Programming with Go*.

We would like to thank Olga Shalakhina and Erick Zelaya for the wonderful illustrations, Monica Kamsvaag for the cover design, April Milne for sprucing up our figures, and Renée French for giving Go the lighthearted mascot that we all love. A special thank you goes to Dan Allen for creating AsciiDoctor, the tool used to write this book, and for his ongoing support.

This book wouldn't be a reality without Marjan Bace, Matko Hrvatin, Mehmed Pasic, Rebecca Rinehart, Nicole Butterfield, Candace Gillhoolley, Ana Romac, Janet Vail, David Novak, Dottie Marsico, Melody Dolab, Elizabeth Martin, and the whole crew at Manning for getting *Get Programming with Go* into the hands of readers.

Thanks also to Aleksandar Dragosavljević for getting this book to reviewers, and to all the reviewers for providing valuable feedback, including Brendan Ward, Charles Kevin, Doug Sparling, Esther Tsai, Gianluigi Spagnuolo, Jeff Smith, John Guthrie, Luca Campobasso, Luis Gutierrez, Mario Carrion, Mikaël Dautrey, Nat Luengnaruemitchai, Nathan Farr, Nicholas Boers, Nicholas Land, Nitin Gode, Orlando Sánchez, Philippe Charrière, Rob Weber, Robin Percy, Steven Parr, Stuart Woodward, Tom Goodheard,

Ulises Flynn, and William E. Wheeler. We'd also like to thank all the early access readers who provided feedback through the forums.

Finally, we would like to thank Michael Stephens for suggesting the crazy idea of writing a book, and the Go community for creating a language and ecosystem that we're excited to write about!

Nathan Youngman

Naturally, I need to thank my parents, without whom I wouldn't be here today. Both of my parents encouraged me to pursue my interest in computer programming from an early age, providing books and courses and access to computers.

In addition to the official reviewers, I would like to thank Matthias Stone for providing feedback on early drafts, and Terry Youngman for helping me brainstorm ideas. I also want to thank the Edmonton Go community for cheering me on, and my employer, Mark Madsen, for providing the flexibility to make this endeavor feasible.

More than anyone else, I want to thank Roger Peppé for coming alongside me as coauthor. He shortened the long road ahead by writing unit 7, and gave the project a much needed bump in momentum.

Roger Peppé

Most of all, I'd like to thank my wife, Carmen, for her forbearance and support as I worked on this book when we could have been out walking in the hills.

Many thanks also to Nathan Youngman and Manning for their trust in taking me on as coauthor and for their patience during the final stages of this book.

About this book

Who should read this book

Go is suitable for programmers with a wide range of skill levels—a necessity for any large project. Being a relatively small language, with minimal syntax and few conceptual hurdles, Go could be the next great language for beginners.

Unfortunately, many resources for learning Go presume a working knowledge of the C programming language. *Get Programming with Go* exists to fill the gap for scripters, hobbyists, and newcomers looking for a direct path to Go. To make it easier to get started, every code listing and exercise in this book can run inside the Go Playground (play .golang.org), so there's nothing to install!

If you've ever used a scripting language like JavaScript, Lua, PHP, Perl, Python, or Ruby, you're ready to learn Go. If you've used Scratch or Excel formulas, or written HTML, you're not alone in choosing Go as your first "real" programming language (see the video "A Beginner's Mind" featuring Audrey Lim at youtu.be/fZh8uCInEfw). Mastering Go will take patience and effort, but we hope *Get Programming with Go* is a helpful resource in your quest.

How this book is organized: A roadmap

Get Programming with Go gradually explains the concepts needed to use Go effectively and provides a plethora of exercises to hone your skills. This is a beginner's guide to Go, intended to be read from cover to cover, with each lesson building on the last. It isn't a complete specification (golang.org/ref/spec) of every language feature, but it covers most of the language and touches on advanced topics like object-oriented design and concurrency.

Whether you go on to write massively *concurrent* web services or small scripts and simple tools, this book will help you establish a solid foundation.

- Unit 1 brings together *variables, loops,* and *branches* to build tiny apps, from greet-ings to rocket launches.
- Unit 2 explores *types* for both text and numbers. Decode secret messages with ROT13, investigate the destruction of the Arianne 5 rocket, and use big numbers to calculate how long light takes to reach Andromeda.
- Unit 3 uses *functions* and *methods* to build a fictional weather station on Mars with sensor readouts and temperature conversions.
- Unit 4 demonstrates how to use *arrays* and *maps* while terraforming the solar sys-tem, tallying up temperatures, and simulating Conway's Game of Life.
- Unit 5 introduces concepts from *object-oriented* languages in a distinctly non-object-oriented language. Use *structures* and methods to navigate the surface of Mars, satisfy *interfaces* to improve output, and embed structures in one another to create even bigger structures!
- Unit 6 digs into the nitty-gritty. Here, you use *pointers* to enable mutation, over-come the knights who say nil, and learn how to handle errors without panicking.
- Unit 7 introduces Go's *concurrency* primitives, enabling communication between thousands of running tasks while constructing assembly lines in a gopher factory.
- The appendix provides our solutions for the exercises, but coming up with your own solutions is what makes programming fun!

About the code

All code is in a `fixed-width font` to separate it from ordinary text. Code annotations accompany many of the listings, highlighting important concepts.

You can download the source code for all listings from the Manning website (www.manning.com/books/get-programming-with-go). The download also includes solutions for all the exercises in this book. If you prefer to browse the source code online, you can find it in the GitHub repository at github.com/nathany/get-programming-with-go.

Although you could copy and paste code from GitHub, we encourage you to type in the examples yourself. You'll get more out of the book by typing the examples, fixing typos, and experimenting with the code.

Book forum

The purchase of *Get Programming with Go* includes free access to a private web forum run by Manning Publications where you can make comments about the book, ask technical questions, share your solutions to exercises, and receive help from the authors and from other users. To access the forum and subscribe to it, point your web browser to forums.manning.com/forums/get-programming-with-go. You can learn more about Manning's forums and the rules of conduct at forums.manning.com/ forums/about.

Manning's commitment to our readers is to provide a venue where a meaningful dialogue between individual readers and between readers and the authors can take place. It's not a commitment to any specific amount of participation on the part of the authors, whose contribution to the forum remains voluntary (and unpaid). We suggest you try asking the authors some challenging questions lest their interest stray! The forum and the archives of previous discussions will be accessible from the publisher's website as long as the book is in print.

About the authors

 NATHAN YOUNGMAN is a self-taught web developer and lifelong learner. He serves as organizer for the Edmonton Go meetup, mentor with Canada Learning Code, and paparazzi of VIP gopher plushies.

 ROGER PEPPÉ is a Go contributor, maintains a number of open source Go projects, runs the Newcastle upon Tyne Go meetup, and currently works on Go cloud infrastructure software.

Getting started

Traditionally, the first step to learning a new programming language is to set up the tools and environment to run a simple "Hello, world" application. With the Go Playground, this age-old endeavor is reduced to a single click.

With that out of the way, you can begin learning the syntax and concepts needed to write and modify a simple program.

GET READY, GET SET, GO

After reading lesson 1, you'll be able to

- Know what sets Go apart
- Visit the Go Playground
- Print text to the screen
- Experiment with text in any natural language

Go is the contemporary programming language of *cloud computing*. Amazon, Apple, Canonical, Chevron, Disney, Facebook, General Electric, Google, Heroku, Microsoft, Twitch, Verizon, and Walmart are among the companies adopting Go for serious projects (see thenewstack.io/who-is-the-go-developer/ and golang.org/wiki/GoUsers). Much of the infrastructure underlying the web is shifting to Go, driven by companies like CloudFlare, Cockroach Labs, DigitalOcean, Docker, InfluxData, Iron.io, Let's Encrypt, Light Code Labs, Red Hat CoreOS, SendGrid, and organizations like the Cloud Native Computing Foundation.

Go excels in the data center, but its adoption extends beyond the workplace. Ron Evans and Adrian Zankich created Gobot (gobot.io), a library to control robots and hardware. Alan Shreve created the development tool ngrok (ngrok.com) as a project to learn Go, and has since turned it into a full-time business.

The community of people who have adopted Go call themselves *gophers*, in honor of Go's lighthearted mascot (figure 1.1). Programming is challenging, but with Go and this book, we hope you discover the joy of coding.

Figure 1.1   Go gopher mascot designed by Renée French

In this lesson, you'll experiment with a Go program in your web browser.

Consider this   If you tell a digital assistant, "Call me a cab," does it dial a taxi company? Or does it assume you changed your name to *a cab*? Natural languages like English are full of ambiguity.

Clarity is paramount in programming languages. If the language's grammar or syntax allows for ambiguity, the computer may not do what you say. That rather defeats the point of writing a program.

Go isn't a perfect language, but it strives for clarity more so than any other language we've used. As you go through this lesson, there will be some abbreviations to learn and jargon to overcome. Not everything will be clear at first glance, but take the time to appreciate how Go works to reduce ambiguity.

1.1   What is Go?

Go is a *compiled* programming language. Before you run a program, Go uses a *compiler* to translate your code into the 1s and 0s that machines speak. It compiles all your code into a single *executable* for you to run or distribute. During this process, the Go compiler can catch typos and mistakes.

Not all programming languages employ this approach. Python, Ruby, and several other popular languages use an *interpreter* to translate one statement at a time as a program is running. That means bugs may be lurking down paths you haven't tested.

On the other hand, interpreters make the process of writing code fast and interactive, with languages that are dynamic, carefree, and fun. Compiled languages have a reputation for being static, inflexible robots that programmers are forced to appease, and compilers are derided for being slow. But does it need to be this way?

> We wanted a language with the safety and performance of statically compiled languages such as C++ and Java, but the lightness and fun of dynamically typed interpreted languages such as Python.
>
> —Rob Pike, *Geek of the Week*
> (see mng.bz/jr8y)

Go is crafted with a great deal of consideration for the *experience* of writing software. Large programs compile in seconds with a single command. The language omits features that lead to ambiguity, encouraging code that is predictable and easily understood. And Go provides a lightweight alternative to the rigid structure imposed by classical languages like Java.

> Java omits many rarely used, poorly understood, confusing features of C++ that in our experience bring more grief than benefit.
>
> —James Gosling, *Java: an Overview*

Each new programming language refines ideas of the past. In Go, using memory efficiently is easier and less error-prone than earlier languages, and Go takes advantage of every core on multicore machines. Success stories often cite improved efficiency as a reason for switching to Go. Iron.io was able to replace 30 servers running Ruby with 2 servers using Go (see mng.bz/Wevx and mng.bz/8yo2). Bitly has "seen consistent, measurable performance gains" when rewriting Python apps in Go, and subsequently replaced its C apps with a Go successor (see mng.bz/EnYl).

Go provides the enjoyment and ease of interpreted languages, with a step up in efficiency and reliability. As a small language, with only a few simple concepts, Go is relatively quick to learn. These three tenets form the motto for Go:

> Go is an open source programming language that enables the production of **simple**, **efficient**, and **reliable** software at scale.
>
> —Go Brand Book

TIP   When searching the internet for topics related to Go, use the keyword golang, which stands for Go language. The -lang suffix can be applied to other programming languages as well: Ruby, Rust, and so on.

Quick check 1.1   What are two benefits of the Go compiler?

 ## 1.2   The Go Playground

The quickest way to get started with Go is to navigate to play.golang.org. At the Go Playground (figure 1.2) you can edit, run, and experiment with Go without needing to install anything. When you click the Run button, the playground will compile and execute your code on Google servers and display the result.

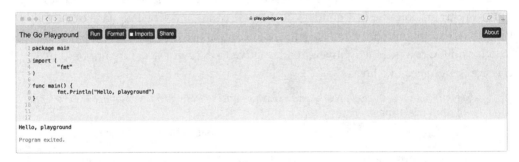

Figure 1.2   The Go Playground

If you click the Share button, you'll receive a link to come back to the code you wrote. You can share the link with friends or bookmark it to save your work.

QC 1.1 answer   Large programs compile in seconds, and the Go compiler can catch typos and mistakes before running a program.

NOTE You can use the Go Playground for every code listing and exercise in this book. Or, if you're already familiar with a text editor and the command line, you can download and install Go on your computer from golang.org/dl/.

Quick check 1.2 What does the Run button do in The Go Playground?

 ## 1.3 Packages and functions

When you visit the Go Playground, you'll see the following code, which is as good a starting point as any.

Listing 1.1 Hello, playground: playground.go

```go
package main          ← Declares the package
                        this code belongs to
import (
    "fmt"             ← Makes the fmt (format)
)                       package available for use

func main() {         ←——————— Declares a function named main
    fmt.Println("Hello, playground")   ← Prints Hello, playground
}                                         to the screen
```

Though short, the preceding listing introduces three keywords: package, import, and func. Each keyword is reserved for a special purpose.

The package keyword declares the package this code belongs to, in this case a package named main. All code in Go is organized into *packages*. Go provides a standard library comprised of packages for math, compression, cryptography, manipulating images, and more. Each package corresponds to a single idea.

The next line uses the import keyword to specify packages this code will use. Packages contain any number of *functions*. For example, the math package provides functions like Sin, Cos, Tan, and Sqrt (square root). The fmt package used here provides functions for *formatted* input and output. Displaying text to the screen is a frequent operation, so this package name is abbreviated fmt. Gophers pronounce fmt as "FŌŌMT!," as though it were written in the large explosive letters of a comic book.

QC 1.2 answer The Run button will compile and then execute your code on Google servers.

The `func` keyword declares a function, in this case a function named `main`. The *body* of each function is enclosed in curly braces {}, which is how Go knows where each function begins and ends.

The `main` *identifier* is special. When you run a program written in Go, execution begins at the `main` function in the `main` package. Without `main`, the Go compiler will report an error, because it doesn't know where the program should start.

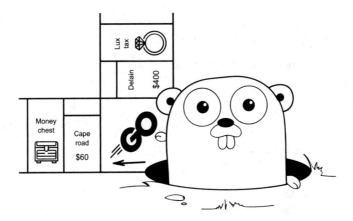

To print a *line* of text, you can use the `Println` function (`ln` is an abbreviation for line). `Println` is prefixed with `fmt` followed by a dot because it is provided by the `fmt` package. Every time you use a function from an imported package, the function is prefixed with the package name and a dot. When you read code written in Go, the package each function came from is immediately clear.

Run the program in the Go Playground to see the text *Hello, playground*. The text enclosed in quotes is echoed to the screen. In English, a missing comma can change the meaning of a sentence. Punctuation is important in programming languages too. Go relies on quotes, parentheses, and braces to understand the code you write.

Quick check 1.3

  1   Where does a Go program start?
  2   What does the `fmt` package provide?

QC 1.3 answer

  1   A program starts at the `main` function in the `main` package.
  2   The `fmt` package provides functions for formatted input and output.

1.4   The one true brace style

Go is picky about the placement of curly braces {}. In listing 1.1, the opening brace { is on the same line as the `func` keyword, whereas the closing brace } is on its own line. This is the *one true brace style*—there is no other way. See mng.bz/NdE2.

To understand why Go became so strict, you need to travel back in time to the birth of Go. In those early days, code was littered with semicolons. Everywhere. There was no escaping them; semicolons followed every single statement like a lost puppy. For example:

```
fmt.Println("Hello, fire hydrant");
```

In December of 2009, a group of ninja gophers expelled semicolons from the language. Well, not exactly. Actually, the Go compiler inserts those adorable semicolons on your behalf, and it works perfectly. Yes, perfectly, but in exchange you must follow the *one true brace style*.

If you put an opening brace on a separate line from the `func` keyword, the Go compiler will report a syntax error:

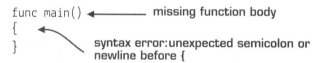

```
func main()            missing function body
{
}                      syntax error:unexpected semicolon or
                       newline before {
```

The compiler isn't upset with you. A semicolon was inserted in the wrong place and it got a little confused.

> **TIP** As you work through this book, it's a good idea to type the code listings yourself. You may see a syntax error if you mistype something, and that's okay. Being able to read, understand, and correct errors is an important skill, and perseverance is a valuable trait.

 **Summary**

- With the Go Playground you can start using Go without installing anything.
- Every Go program is made up of functions contained in packages.
- To print text on the screen, use the fmt package provided by the standard library.
- Punctuation is just as important in programming languages as it is in natural languages.
- You used 3 of the 25 Go keywords: package, import, and func.

Let's see if you got this...

For the following exercise, modify the code in the Go Playground and click the Run button to see the result. If you get stuck, refresh your web browser to get back the original code.

Experiment: playground.go

- Change the text printed to the screen by modifying what appears between quotes. Have the computer greet you by name.
- Display two lines of text by writing a second line of code within the body {} of the main function. For example:

```
fmt.Println("Hello, world")
fmt.Println("Hello, 世界")
```

- Go supports characters of every language. Print text in Chinese, Japanese, Russian, or Spanish. If you don't speak those languages, you can use Google Translate (translate.google.com) and copy/paste text into the Go Playground.

Use the Share button to get a link to your program and share it with other readers by posting it on the *Get Programming with Go* forums (forums.manning.com/forums/get-programming-with-go).

Compare your solution to the code listing in the appendix.

Imperative programming

Most computer programs are a series of steps, like the directions for your mom's stroganoff. Tell a computer precisely *how* to accomplish a task, and it can do all sorts of things. Writing down these instructions is known as *imperative* programming. If only computers could cook!

In unit 1, you'll review Go fundamentals and start learning the syntax Go uses to instruct your computer. Each lesson builds up the knowledge you'll need to tackle your first challenge: an app that lists ticket prices for a vacation to Mars.

A GLORIFIED CALCULATOR

After reading lesson 2, you'll be able to

- Teach a computer to do your math
- Declare variables and constants
- See how declaration and assignment differ
- Use the standard library to generate pseudorandom numbers

Computer programs are capable of a great many things. In this lesson you'll write programs to solve mathematical problems.

Consider this   Why write a program when you could just use a calculator?

Well, have you memorized the speed of light or how long it takes Mars to orbit the sun? Code can be saved and read later, serving as both a calculator and a reference. A program is an executable document that can be shared and modified.

2.1   Performing calculations

There are days when we think it would be nice to be younger and weigh a little less. In this regard, Mars has a lot to offer. Mars takes 687 Earth days to travel around the sun, and its weaker gravitational force means everything weighs approximately 38% of what it does on Earth.

To calculate how young and light Nathan would be on Mars, we wrote a small program, shown in listing 2.1. Go provides the same arithmetic *operators* as other programming languages: +, -, *, /, and % for addition, subtraction, multiplication, division, and modulus respectively.

> **TIP**   The modulus operator (%) obtains the remainder of dividing two whole numbers (for example, 42 % 10 is 2).

Listing 2.1   Hello Mars: mars.go

```go
// My weight loss program.         A comment for
package main                       human readers

import "fmt"

// main is the function where it all begins.
func main() {
    fmt.Print("My weight on the surface of Mars is ")
    fmt.Print(149.0 * 0.3783)           Prints 56.3667
    fmt.Print(" lbs, and I would be ")
    fmt.Print(41 * 365 / 687)        Prints 21
    fmt.Print(" years old.")
}
```

> **NOTE**   Though listing 2.1 displays weight in pounds, the chosen unit of measurement doesn't impact the weight calculation. Whichever unit you choose, the weight on Mars is 37.83% of the weight on Earth.

The code in the preceding listing begins with a comment. When Go sees a double slash //, it ignores everything until the end of the line. Computer programming is all about communication. Code communicates your instructions to a computer, and when written well, it communicates your intentions to other people. Comments are just for us. They don't affect how a program runs.

The preceding listing calls the Print function several times to display a sentence on a single line. Alternatively, you can pass a list of *arguments* separated by commas. An argument to Println can be text, a number, or a mathematical *expression*:

```
fmt.Println("My weight on the surface of Mars is", 149.0*0.3783, "lbs, and
➥I would be", 41*365.2425/687, "years old.")
```

Prints My weight on the surface of Mars is 56.3667 lbs, and I would be 21.79758733624454 years old.

> **Quick check 2.1** Type and run listing 2.1 in the Go Playground at play.golang.org. How much would you weigh on Mars? How old would you be? Replace Nathan's age (41) and weight (149.0) with your own.

TIP After modifying your code, click the Format button in the Go Playground. It will automatically reformat the indentation and spacing of your code without changing what it does.

 ## 2.2 Formatted print

The Print and Println functions have a sibling that gives more control over output. By using Printf, shown in the following listing, you can insert values anywhere in the text.

Listing 2.2 Printf: fmt.go

```
fmt.Printf("My weight on the surface of Mars is %v lbs,", 149.0*0.3783)
fmt.Printf(" and I would be %v years old.\n", 41*365/687)
```

Prints My weight on the surface of Mars is 56.3667 lbs,

Prints and I would be 21 years old.

Unlike Print and Println, the first argument to Printf is always text. The text contains the *format verb* %v, which is substituted for the *value* of the expression provided by the second argument.

> **NOTE**   We'll introduce more format verbs (other than %v) as needed in upcoming lessons. For a complete reference, see the online documentation at golang.org/pkg/fmt/.

The Println function automatically moves to the next line, but Printf and Print don't. Whenever you want to move to a new line, place \n in the text.

If multiple format verbs are specified, the Printf function will substitute multiple values in order:

```
fmt.Printf("My weight on the surface of %v is %v lbs.\n", "Earth", 149.0)
```

Prints My weight on the surface of Earth is 149 lbs.

In addition to substituting values anywhere in a sentence, Printf can help you align text. Specify a width as part of the format verb, such as %4v to pad a value to a width of 4 characters. A positive number pads with spaces to the left, and a negative number pads with spaces to the right:

```
fmt.Printf("%-15v $%4v\n", "SpaceX", 94)
fmt.Printf("%-15v $%4v\n", "Virgin Galactic", 100)
```

The preceding code displays the following output:

```
SpaceX          $  94
Virgin Galactic $ 100
```

Quick check 2.2
1 How do you print a new line?
2 What does Printf do when it encounters the %v format verb?

QC 2.2 answer
1 Use \n anywhere in the text you're printing to insert a new line or use fmt.Println().
2 The %v is substituted for a value from the following arguments.

2.3   Constants and variables

The calculations in listing 2.1 are performed on *literal* numbers. It isn't clear what the numbers mean, particularly values like 0.3783. Programmers sometimes refer to unclear literal numbers as *magic numbers*. Constants and variables can help by providing descriptive names.

After seeing the benefits of living on Mars, our next question is how long the trip will take. Traveling at the speed of light would be ideal. Light travels at a *constant* speed in the vacuum of space, which makes the math easy. On the other hand, the distance between Earth and Mars *varies* significantly, depending on where the planets are in their orbits around the Sun.

The following listing introduces two new keywords, const and var, for declaring constants and variables respectively.

Listing 2.3   Traveling at the speed of light: lightspeed.go

```go
// How long does it take to get to Mars?
package main

import "fmt"

func main() {
    const lightSpeed = 299792 // km/s
    var distance = 56000000   // km

    fmt.Println(distance/lightSpeed, "seconds")      ⟵ Prints 186 seconds

    distance = 401000000
    fmt.Println(distance/lightSpeed, "seconds")      ⟵ Prints 1337 seconds
}
```

Type listing 2.3 into the Go Playground and click Run. Light speed is pretty convenient; you probably wouldn't hear anyone asking, "Are we there yet?"

The first calculation is based on Mars and Earth being nearby, with distance declared and assigned an initial value of 56,000,000 km. Then the distance variable is assigned a new value of 401,000,000 km, with the planets on opposite sides of the Sun, though plotting a course directly through the Sun could be problematic.

> **NOTE**   The lightSpeed constant can't be changed. If you try to assign it a new value, the Go compiler will report the error "cannot assign to lightSpeed."

NOTE   Variables must be declared before you can use them. Go will report an error if you assign a value to a variable that hasn't been declared with var—for example, speed = 16. This restriction can help catch mistakes, such as accidentally assigning a value to distence when you intended to type distance.

Quick check 2.3

1   The SpaceX Interplanetary Transport System lacks a warp drive, but it will coast to Mars at a respectable 100,800 km/h. An ambitious launch date of January 2025 would place Mars and Earth 96,300,000 km apart. How many days would it take to reach Mars? Modify listing 2.3 to find out.

2   There are 24 hours in one Earth day. To give 24 a descriptive name in your program, which keyword would you use?

 ## 2.4   Taking a shortcut

There may not be any shortcuts to visit Mars, but Go provides a few keystroke-saving shortcuts.

2.4.1   Declare multiple variables at once

When you declare variables or constants, you can declare each one on its own line like this:

```
var distance = 56000000
var speed = 100800
```

Or you can declare them as a group:

```
var (
    distance = 56000000
    speed = 100800
)
```

QC 2.3 answer

1   Spaceships don't travel in a straight line, but as an approximation, the trip would take 39 days.

```
const hoursPerDay = 24
var speed = 100800      // km/h
var distance = 96300000 // km

fmt.Println(distance/speed/hoursPerDay, "days")
```

2   The const keyword because the value doesn't change while the program is running.

Yet another option is to declare multiple variables on a single line:

```
var distance, speed = 56000000, 100800
```

Before you declare multiple variables as a group or on a single line, consider whether or not the variables are related. Always keep in mind the readability of your code.

Quick check 2.4 What single line of code would declare both the number of hours in a day and the minutes per hour?

2.4.2   Increment and assignment operators

There are a few shortcuts to perform assignment with other operations. The last two lines of the following listing are equivalent.

Listing 2.4 Assignment operators: shortcut.go

```
var weight = 149.0
weight = weight * 0.3783
weight *= 0.3783
```

Incrementing by one has an additional shortcut, as shown in the following listing.

Listing 2.5 Increment operator

```
var age = 41
age = age + 1      ◀─── happy birthday!
age += 1
age++
```

You can decrement with count-- or shorten other operations like price /= 2 in the same way.

> **NOTE** In case you're wondering, Go does not support the prefix increment ++count like C and Java.

QC 2.4 answer
```
const hoursPerDay, minutesPerHour = 24, 60
```

Quick check 2.5   Write the shortest line of code to subtract two pounds from a variable named weight.

 ## 2.5   Think of a number

Think of a number between 1 and 10.

Got it? Okay.

Now have your computer "think" of a number between 1 and 10. Your computer can generate pseudorandom numbers using the rand package. They're called *pseudorandom* because they're more or less random, but not truly random.

The code in listing 2.6 will display two numbers between 1–10. Passing 10 to Intn *returns* a number from 0–9, to which you add 1 and assign the result to num. The num variable can't be a Go constant because it's the result of a function call.

> **NOTE**   If you forget to add 1, you'll get a number between 0–9. Because we want a number between 1–10, that's an example of an off-by-one error, a classic programming mistake.

Listing 2.6 Random numbers: rand.go

```
package main

import (
    "fmt"
    "math/rand"
)

func main() {
    var num = rand.Intn(10) + 1
    fmt.Println(num)

    num = rand.Intn(10) + 1
    fmt.Println(num)
}
```

QC 2.5 answer
```
weight -= 2
```

The *import path* for the rand package is math/rand. The Intn function is prefixed with the package name rand, but the import path is longer.

> **TIP** To use a new package, it must be listed as an import. The Go Playground can add import paths for you. First ensure the Imports checkbox is checked and then click the Format button. The Go Playground will determine which packages are being used and update your import paths.

> **NOTE** Every time you run listing 2.6, the same two pseudorandom numbers are displayed. It's rigged! In the Go Playground, time stands still and results are cached, but these numbers are good enough for our purposes.

> **Quick check 2.6** The distance between Earth and Mars varies from nearby to opposite sides of the sun. Write a program that generates a random distance from 56,000,000 to 401,000,000 km.

 ## Summary

- The Print, Println, and Printf functions display text and numbers on the screen.
- With Printf and the %v *format verb*, values can be placed anywhere in the displayed text.
- Constants are declared with the const keyword and can't be changed.
- Variables are declared with var and can be assigned new values while a program is running.
- The math/rand import path refers to the rand package.
- The Intn function in the rand package generates pseudorandom numbers.
- You used 5 of the 25 Go keywords: package, import, func, const, and var.

Let's see if you got this...

Experiment: malacandra.go

> *Malacandra is much nearer than that: we shall make it in about twenty-eight days.*
> —C.S. Lewis, *Out of the Silent Planet*

QC 2.6 answer

```
// a random distance to Mars (km)
var distance = rand.Intn(345000001) + 56000000
fmt.Println(distance)
```

Malacandra is another name for Mars in *The Space Trilogy* by C. S. Lewis. Write a program to determine how fast a ship would need to travel (in km/h) in order to reach Malacandra in 28 days. Assume a distance of 56,000,000 km.

Compare your solution to the code listing in the appendix.

LOOPS AND BRANCHES

After reading lesson 3, you'll be able to

- Have your computer make choices with `if` and `switch`
- Repeat code with `for` loops
- Use conditions for looping and branching

Computer programs rarely read from beginning to end like a novel. Programs are more like Choose Your Own Adventure books or interactive fiction. They take different paths under certain conditions or repeat the same steps until a condition is met.

If you're familiar with the `if`, `else`, and `for` keywords found in many programming languages, this lesson will serve as a speedy introduction to Go's syntax.

Consider this   When Nathan was young, his family would play *Twenty Questions* to pass the time on long trips. One person would think of something, and everyone else tried to guess what it was. Questions could only be answered with yes or no. A question like "How big is it?" would invite a blank stare. Instead, a common question was "Is it larger than a toaster?"

Computer programs operate on yes/no questions. Given some condition (such as *larger than a toaster*), a CPU can either continue down a path or jump (`JMP`) to somewhere else in the program. Complex decisions need to be broken down into smaller, simpler conditions.   ‖➡

(continued)

Consider the clothes you're wearing today. How did you pick each article of clothing? Which variables were involved, such as the weather forecast, planned activity, availability, fashion, randomness, and so on? How would you teach a computer to get dressed in the morning? Write down several questions with a yes or no answer.

 ## 3.1 True or false

When you read Choose Your Own Adventure books, you'll come across choices like this:

If you walk outside the cave, turn to page 21.

—Edward Packard, *The Cave of Time*

Do you walk outside the cave? In Go, your answer can be either `true` or `false`, two constants that are already declared. You can use them like this:

```
var walkOutside = true
var takeTheBluePill = false
```

> **NOTE** Some programming languages have a loose definition of truth. In Python and JavaScript the absence of text ("") is considered false, as is the number zero. In Ruby and Elixir the same values are considered true. In Go, the only true value is `true` and the only false value is `false`.

True and false are *Boolean* values, so named after 19th century mathematician George Boole. Several functions in the standard library return a Boolean value. For example, the following listing uses the `Contains` function from the `strings` package to ask if the `command` variable contains the text "outside". It does contain that text, so the result is `true`.

Listing 3.1 A function that returns a Boolean value: contains.go

```go
package main
import (
    "fmt"
    "strings"
)
func main() {
    fmt.Println("You find yourself in a dimly lit cavern.")
```

```
    var command = "walk outside"
    var exit = strings.Contains(command, "outside")

    fmt.Println("You leave the cave:", exit)
}
```
← Print You leave the cave: true

Quick check 3.1

1 Emerging from the cave, your eyes meet the blinding midday sun. How do you declare a Boolean variable named wearShades?
2 There is a sign near the cave entrance. How can you determine if the command contains the word "read"?

 ## 3.2 Comparisons

Another way to arrive at a true or false value is by comparing two values. Go provides the comparison operators shown in table 3.1.

Table 3.1 Comparison operators

==	Equal	!=	Not equal
<	Less than	>	Greater than
<=	Less than or equal	>=	Greater than or equal

You can use the operators in table 3.1 to compare text or numbers, as shown in the following listing.

Listing 3.2 Comparing numbers: compare.go

```
fmt.Println("There is a sign near the entrance that reads 'No Minors'.")

var age = 41
var minor = age < 18

fmt.Printf("At age %v, am I a minor? %v\n", age, minor)
```

QC 3.1 answer

1 var wearShades = true
2 var read = strings.Contains(command, "read")

The previous listing will produce this output:

```
There is a sign near the entrance that reads 'No Minors'.
At age 41, am I a minor? false
```

> **NOTE** JavaScript and PHP have a special *threequals* operator for strict equality. In those languages "1" == 1 is true (lax), but "1" === 1 is false (strict). Go only has a single equality operator, which doesn't allow direct comparison of text with numbers. Lesson 10 demonstrates how to convert numbers to text and vice versa.

Quick check 3.2   Which is greater, an "apple" or a "banana"?

 ## 3.3   Branching with if

A computer can use Boolean values or comparisons to choose between different paths with an if statement, as shown in the following listing.

Listing 3.3 Branching: if.go

```
package main

import "fmt"

func main() {
    var command = "go east"

    if command == "go east" {
        fmt.Println("You head further up the mountain.")
    } else if command == "go inside" {
        fmt.Println("You enter the cave where you live out the rest of your
life.")
    } else {
        fmt.Println("Didn't quite get that.")
    }
}
```

If command is equal to "go east"

Otherwise, if command is equal to "go inside"

Or, if anything else

QC 3.2 answer   The banana is clearly greater.

```
fmt.Println("apple" > "banana")
```
Prints false

The previous listing will produce the following output:

```
You head further up the mountain.
```

Both else if and else are optional. When there are several paths to consider, you can repeat else if as many times as needed.

> **NOTE** Go reports an error if you accidentally use assignment (=) when equality (==) is intended.

> **Quick check 3.3** Adventure games are divided up into rooms. Write a program that uses if and else if to display a description for each of three rooms: cave, entrance, and mountain. When writing your program, ensure the curly braces {} are placed according to the one true brace style as shown in listing 3.3.

3.4 Logical operators

In Go the logical operator || means *or*, and the logical operator && means *and*. Use logical operators to check multiple conditions at once. See figures 3.1 and 3.2 for how these operators are evaluated.

QC 3.3 answer

```
package main

import "fmt"

func main() {
    var room = "cave"

    if room == "cave" {
        fmt.Println("You find yourself in a dimly lit cavern.")
    } else if room == "entrance" {
        fmt.Println("There is a cavern entrance here and a path to the east.")
    } else if room == "mountain" {
        fmt.Println("There is a cliff here. A path leads west down the mountain.")
    } else {
        fmt.Println("Everything is white.")
    }
}
```

	false	true
false	false	true
true	true	true

Figure 3.1   True if either a `||` b is true (or)

	false	true
false	false	false
true	false	true

Figure 3.2   True if both a `&&` b are true (and)

The code in listing 3.4 determines whether 2100 will be a leap year. The rules for determining a leap year are as follows:

- Any year that is evenly divisible by 4 but not evenly divisible by 100
- Or any year that is evenly divisible by 400

NOTE   Recall that modulus (%) obtains the remainder of dividing two whole numbers. A remainder of zero indicates that a number is evenly divisible by another.

Listing 3.4   Leap year determination: leap.go

```
fmt.Println("The year is 2100, should you leap?")

var year = 2100
var leap = year%400 == 0 || (year%4 == 0 && year%100 != 0)
if leap {
    fmt.Println("Look before you leap!")
} else {
    fmt.Println("Keep your feet on the ground.")
}
```

The previous listing will produce the following output:

```
The year is 2100, should you leap?
Keep your feet on the ground.
```

As with most programming languages, Go uses *short-circuit logic*. If the first condition is true (the year is evenly divisible by 400), there's no need to evaluate what follows the || operator, so it is ignored.

The && operator is just the opposite. The result is false unless both conditions are true. If the year isn't evenly divisible by 4, there's no need to evaluate the next condition.

The *not* logical operator (!) flips a Boolean value from false to true or vice versa. The following listing displays a message if the player doesn't have a torch or if the torch isn't lit.

Listing 3.5   The not operator: torch.go

```
var haveTorch = true
var litTorch = false

if !haveTorch || !litTorch {
    fmt.Println("Nothing to see here.")
}
```

→ Prints Nothing to see here.

Quick check 3.4

1 Using pen and paper, substitute 2000 into the leap year expression from listing 3.4. Evaluate all the modulus operators to find the remainders (use a calculator if need be). Then evaluate the == and != conditions to true or false. Finally, evaluate the logical operators && and then ||. Was 2000 a leap year?

2 Would you have saved time if you had used short-circuit logic to evaluate 2000%400 == 0 to true first?

QC 3.4 answer

1 Yes, the year 2000 was a leap year:
```
2000%400 == 0 || (2000%4 == 0 && 2000%100 != 0)
0 == 0 || (0 == 0 && 0 != 0)
true || (true && false)
true || (false)
true
```

2 Yes, evaluating and writing down the later half of the equation did take time. Computers are much faster, but short-circuit logic still saves time.

3.5   Branching with switch

When comparing one value to several others, Go provides the `switch` statement, which you can see in the following listing.

Listing 3.6 The `switch` **statement: concise-switch.go**

```
fmt.Println("There is a cavern entrance here and a path to the east.")
var command = "go inside"

switch command {                          Compares cases
case "go east":                           to command
    fmt.Println("You head further up the mountain.")    A comma-
case "enter cave", "go inside":                         separated list of
    fmt.Println("You find yourself in a dimly lit cavern.")  possible values
case "read sign":
    fmt.Println("The sign reads 'No Minors'.")
default:
    fmt.Println("Didn't quite get that.")
}
```

The previous listing will produce the following output:

```
There is a cavern entrance here and a path to the east.
You find yourself in a dimly lit cavern.
```

> **NOTE**   You can also use the `switch` statement with numbers.

Or you can use the `switch` statement with conditions for each case, much like using `if…else`. One unique feature of `switch` is the `fallthrough` keyword, which is used to execute the body of the next `case`, as shown in the next listing.

Listing 3.7 The switch statement: switch.go

```
var room = "lake"
                          Expressions are
switch {                  in each case.
case room == "cave":
    fmt.Println("You find yourself in a dimly lit cavern.")
case room == "lake":
    fmt.Println("The ice seems solid enough.")
    fallthrough
case room == "underwater":                Falls through to
                                          the next case
```

```
    fmt.Println("The water is freezing cold.")
}
```

The previous listing will produce the following output:

```
The ice seems solid enough.
The water is freezing cold.
```

> **NOTE** Falling through happens by default in C, Java, and JavaScript, whereas Go takes a safer approach, requiring an explicit `fallthrough` keyword.

Quick check 3.5 Modify listing 3.7 to use the more concise form of `switch`, as every comparison is with `room`.

 ## 3.6 Repetition with loops

Rather than type the same code multiple times, the `for` keyword repeats code for you. Listing 3.8 loops around until `count` equals 0.

Before each iteration, the expression `count > 0` is evaluated to produce a Boolean value. If the value is `false` (`count = 0`), the loop terminates—otherwise, it runs the body of the loop (the code between { and }).

QC 3.5 answer

```
switch room {
case "cave":
    fmt.Println("You find yourself in a dimly lit cavern.")
case "lake":
    fmt.Println("The ice seems solid enough.")
    fallthrough
case "underwater":
    fmt.Println("The water is freezing cold.")
}
```

Listing 3.8 A countdown loop: countdown.go

```go
package main

import (
    "fmt"
    "time"
)

func main() {
    var count = 10                      ← Declares and initializes
    for count > 0 {                     ← A condition
        fmt.Println(count)
        time.Sleep(time.Second)
        count--                         ← Decrements count;
    }                                     otherwise it will
    fmt.Println("Liftoff!")               loop forever
}
```

An *infinite* loop doesn't specify a for condition, but you can still break out of a loop at any time. The following listing orbits a 360° circle and stops randomly.

Listing 3.9 To infinity and beyond: infinity.go

```go
var degrees = 0
for {
    fmt.Println(degrees)
    degrees++
    if degrees >= 360 {
        degrees = 0
        if rand.Intn(2) == 0 {
            break
        }
    }
}
```

> **NOTE** The for loop has other forms that will be introduced in lessons 4 and 9.

Quick check 3.6 Not every launch goes smoothly. Implement a countdown where every second there's a 1 in 100 chance that the launch fails and the countdown stops.

 Summary

- Booleans are the only values that can be used in conditions.
- Go provides branching and repetition with if, switch, and for.
- You used 12 of the 25 Go keywords: package, import, func, var, if, else, switch, case, default, fallthrough, for, and break.

Let's see if you got this...

Experiment: guess.go

Write a guess-the-number program. Make the computer pick random numbers between 1–100 until it guesses your number, which you declare at the top of the program. Display each guess and whether it was too big or too small.

QC 3.6 answer

```
var count = 10

for count > 0 {
    fmt.Println(count)
    time.Sleep(time.Second)
    if rand.Intn(100) == 0 {
        break
    }
    count--
}
if count == 0 {
    fmt.Println("Liftoff!")
} else {
    fmt.Println("Launch failed.")
}
```

VARIABLE SCOPE

After reading lesson 4, you'll be able to

- Know the benefits of variable scope
- Use a shorter way to declare variables
- See how variable scoping interacts with `for`, `if`, and `switch`
- Know when to use a wide or narrow scope

In the course of running a program, many variables are used briefly and then discarded. This is facilitated by the *scoping rules* of the language.

> **Consider this** How many things can you keep in your head at once?
>
> It has been suggested that our short-term memory is limited to about seven items, with a seven-digit phone number being an excellent example.
>
> Computers can store many values in their short-term or Random Access Memory (RAM), but remember that code is read not only by computers, but also by humans. As such, code should be kept as simple as possible.
>
> If any variable in a program could change at any time, and be accessed from anywhere, keeping track of everything in a large program could become quite hectic. Variable scope helps by allowing you to focus on the relevant variables in a given function or portion of code without concerning yourself with the rest.

4.1   Looking into scope

When a variable is declared, it comes into *scope*, or to put it another way, the variable becomes visible. Your program can access the variable so long as it's in scope, but once a variable is no longer in scope, attempts to access it will report an error.

One benefit of variable scope is that you can reuse the same name for different variables. Can you imagine if every variable in your program had to have a unique name? If so, try to imagine a slightly bigger program.

Scoping also helps while reading through code because you don't need to keep all the variables in your head. Once a variable goes out of scope, you can stop thinking about that variable.

In Go, scopes tend to begin and end along the lines of curly braces {}. In the following listing, the main function begins a scope, and the for loop begins a nested scope.

Listing 4.1 Scoping rules: scope.go

```go
package main

import (
    "fmt"
    "math/rand"
)
func main() {
    var count = 0
    for count < 10 {            A new scope begins.
        var num = rand.Intn(10) + 1
        fmt.Println(num)

        count++            This scope ends.
    }
}
```

The count variable is declared within the *function scope* and is visible until the end of the main function, whereas the num variable is declared within the scope of the for loop. After the loop ends, the num variable goes out of scope.

The Go compiler will report an error for any attempt to access num after the loop. You can access the count variable after the for loop ends because it's declared outside of the loop, though there really is no reason to. In order to confine count to the scope of a loop, you'll need a different way to declare variables in Go.

Quick check 4.1

1   How does variable scope benefit you?
2   What happens to a variable when it goes out of scope? Modify listing 4.1 to access num after the loop and see what happens.

 ## 4.2   Short declaration

Short declaration provides an alternative syntax for the var keyword. The following two lines are equivalent:

```
var count = 10
count := 10
```

It may not seem like much, but saving three characters makes short declaration far more popular than var. More importantly, short declaration can go places where var can't.

The following listing demonstrates a variant of the for loop that combines initialization, a condition, and a post statement that decrements count. When using this form of for loops, the provided order is significant: initialize, condition, post.

Listing 4.2 A condensed countdown: loop.go

```
var count = 0

for count = 10; count > 0; count-- {
    fmt.Println(count)
}
fmt.Println(count)
```
← count remains in scope.

QC 4.1 answer

1   The same variable name can be used in multiple places without any conflicts. You only need to think about the variables that are currently in scope.
2   The variable is no longer visible or accessible. The Go compiler reports an undefined: num error.

Without short declaration, the count variable must be declared outside of the loop, which means it remains in scope after the loop ends.

By using short declaration, the count variable in the next listing is declared and initialized as part of the for loop and falls out of scope once the loop ends. If count were accessed outside of the loop, the Go compiler would report an undefined: count error.

Listing 4.3 Short declaration in a `for` loop: short-loop.go

```
for count := 10; count > 0; count-- {
    fmt.Println(count)
}
```
count is no
longer in scope.

> **TIP**   For the best readability, declare variables near where they are used.

Short declaration makes it possible to declare a new variable in an if statement. In the following listing the num variable can be used in any branch of the if statement.

Listing 4.4 Short declaration in a `if` statement: short-if.go

```
if num := rand.Intn(3); num == 0 {
    fmt.Println("Space Adventures")
} else if num == 1 {
    fmt.Println("SpaceX")
} else {
    fmt.Println("Virgin Galactic")
}
```
num is no longer
in scope.

Short declaration can also be used as part of a switch statement, as the following listing shows.

Listing 4.5 Short declaration in a `switch` statement: short-switch.go

```
switch num := rand.Intn(10); num {
case 0:
    fmt.Println("Space Adventures")
case 1:
    fmt.Println("SpaceX")
case 2:
    fmt.Println("Virgin Galactic")
default:
    fmt.Println("Random spaceline #", num)
}
```

4.3   Narrow scope, wide scope

The code in the next listing generates and displays a random date—perhaps a departure date to Mars. It also demonstrates several different scopes in Go and shows why considering scope when declaring variables is important.

Listing 4.6 Variable scoping rules: scope-rules.go

```go
package main

import (
    "fmt"
    "math/rand"
)
var era = "AD"                                          ← era is available throughout
                                                          the package.
func main() {
    year := 2018                                        ← era and year
                                                          are in scope.
    switch month := rand.Intn(12) + 1; month {          ← era, year, and month
    case 2:                                               are in scope.
        day := rand.Intn(28) + 1                        ← era, year, month, and
        fmt.Println(era, year, month, day)                day are in scope.
    case 4, 6, 9, 11:
        day := rand.Intn(30) + 1                        ← It's a new day.
        fmt.Println(era, year, month, day)
    default:
        day := rand.Intn(31) + 1                        ←
        fmt.Println(era, year, month, day)
    }                                                   ← month and day
}                                                         are out of scope.
```

year is no longer in scope.

The era variable is declared outside of the main function in the *package scope*. If there were multiple functions in the main package, era would be visible from all of them.

> **NOTE** Short declaration is not available for variables declared in the package scope, so era can't be declared with era := "AD" at its current location.

The year variable is only visible within the main function. If there were other functions, they could see era but not year. The *function scope* is narrower than the package scope. It begins at the func keyword and ends with the terminating brace.

The month variable is visible anywhere within the switch statement, but once the switch statement ends, month is no longer in scope. The scope begins at the switch keyword and ends with the terminating brace for switch.

Each case has its own scope, so there are three independent day variables. As each case ends, the day variable declared within that case goes out of a scope. This is the only situation where there are no braces to indicate scope.

The code in listing 4.6 is far from perfect. The narrow scope of month and day results in code duplication (Println, Println, Println). When code is duplicated, someone may revise the code in one place, but not the other (such as deciding not to print the era, but forgetting to change one case). Sometimes code duplication is justified, but it's considered a *code smell*, and should be looked at.

To remove the duplication and simplify the code, the variables in listing 4.6 should be declared in the wider function scope, making them available after the switch statement for later work. It's time to refactor! *Refactoring* means modifying the code without modifying the code's behavior. The code in the following listing still displays a random date.

Listing 4.7 Random date refactored: random-date.go

```
package main

import (
    "fmt"
    "math/rand"
)

var era = "AD"

func main() {
    year := 2018
    month := rand.Intn(12) + 1
    daysInMonth := 31
```

```
    switch month {
    case 2:
        daysInMonth = 28
    case 4, 6, 9, 11:
        daysInMonth = 30
    }

    day := rand.Intn(daysInMonth) + 1
    fmt.Println(era, year, month, day)
}
```

Though a narrower scope often reduces the mental overhead, listing 4.6 demonstrates that constraining variables too tightly can result in *less* readable code. Take it on a case-by-case basis, refactoring until you can't improve the readability any further.

> **Quick check 4.3**　What's one way to recognize that variables are scoped too tightly?

 ## Summary

- An opening curly brace { introduces a new scope that ends with a closing brace }.
- The case and default keywords also introduce a new scope even though no curly braces are involved.
- The location where a variable is declared determines which scope it's in.
- Not only is shortcut declaration shorter, you can take it places where var can't go.
- Variables declared on the same line as a for, if, or switch are in scope until the end of that statement.
- A wide scope is better than a narrow scope in some situations—and vice versa.

Let's see if you got this...

Experiment: random-dates.go

Modify listing 4.7 to handle leap years:

- Generate a random year instead of always using 2018.
- For February, assign daysInMonth to 29 for leap years and 28 for other years.
  Hint: you can put an if statement inside of a case block.
- Use a for loop to generate and display 10 random dates.

QC 4.3 answer　If code is being duplicated due to where variables are declared.

CAPSTONE: TICKET TO MARS

Welcome to the first challenge. It's time to take everything covered in unit 1 and write a program on your own. Your challenge is to write a ticket generator in the Go Playground that makes use of variables, constants, `switch`, `if`, and `for`. It should also draw on the `fmt` and `math/rand` packages to display and align text and to generate random numbers.

When planning a trip to Mars, it would be handy to have ticket pricing from multiple spacelines in one place. Websites exist that aggregate ticket prices for airlines, but so far nothing exists for spacelines. That's not a problem for you, though. You can use Go to teach your computer to solve problems like this.

Start by building a prototype that generates 10 random tickets and displays them in a tabular format with a nice header, as follows:

```
Spaceline        Days Trip type  Price
=======================================
Virgin Galactic    23 Round-trip $  96
Virgin Galactic    39 One-way    $  37
```

```
SpaceX              31 One-way    $  41
Space Adventures    22 Round-trip $ 100
Space Adventures    22 One-way    $  50
Virgin Galactic     30 Round-trip $  84
Virgin Galactic     24 Round-trip $  94
Space Adventures    27 One-way    $  44
Space Adventures    28 Round-trip $  86
SpaceX              41 Round-trip $  72
```

The table should have four columns:

- The spaceline company providing the service
- The duration in days for the trip to Mars (one-way)
- Whether the price covers a return trip
- The price in millions of dollars ☹

For each ticket, randomly select one of the following spacelines: Space Adventures, SpaceX, or Virgin Galactic.

Use October 13, 2020 as the departure date for all tickets. Mars will be 62,100,000 km away from Earth at the time.

Randomly choose the speed the ship will travel, from 16 to 30 km/s. This will determine the duration for the trip to Mars and also the ticket price. Make faster ships more expensive, ranging in price from $36 million to $50 million. Double the price for round trips.

When you're done, post your solution to the *Get Programming with Go* forums at forums.manning.com/forums/get-programming-with-go. If you get stuck, feel free to ask questions on the forums, or take a peek at the appendix for our solution.

Types

The text `"Go"` and the number `28487` are both represented with the same zeros and ones on an x86 computer (`0110111101000111`). The *type* establishes what those bits and bytes mean. One is a *string* of two characters, the other is a 16-bit *integer* (2 bytes). The string type is used for multilingual text, and 16-bit integers are one of many numeric types.

Unit 2 covers the primitive types that Go provides for text, characters, numbers, and other simple values. When appropriate, these lessons reveal the benefits and drawbacks to help you select the most appropriate type.

REAL NUMBERS

After reading lesson 6, you'll be able to

- Use two types of real numbers
- Understand the memory-versus-precision trade-off
- Work around rounding errors in your piggy bank

Computers store and manipulate real numbers like 3.14159 using the IEEE-754 floating-point standard. *Floating-point* numbers can be very large or incredibly small: think galaxies and atoms. With such versatility, programming languages like JavaScript and Lua get by using floating-point numbers exclusively. Computers also support *integers* for whole numbers, the subject of the next lesson.

Consider this   Imagine a carnival game with three cups. The nearest cup is worth $0.10 to $1.00, the next is worth $1 to $10, and the farthest cup is worth $10 to $100. Choose one cup and toss as many as 10 coins. If landing four coins in the middle cup is worth $4, how would you win $100?

To represent many possible real numbers with a fixed amount of space, a floating-point number is like choosing 1 of 2,048 cups and placing anywhere from one to several trillion coins in it. Some bits represent a cup or *bucket*, and other bits represent the coins or *offset* within that bucket.

⫸

(continued)

One cup may represent very tiny numbers, and another represent huge numbers. Though every cup fits the same number of coins, some cups represent a smaller range of numbers more precisely than others, which represent a larger range of numbers with less precision.

6.1   Declaring floating-point variables

Every variable has a type. When you declare and initialize a variable with a real number, you're using a floating-point type. The following three lines of code are equivalent, because the Go compiler will infer that days is a float64, even if you don't specify it:

```
days := 365.2425          Short declaration
var days = 365.2425       (covered in lesson 4)
var days float64 = 365.2425
```

It's valuable to know that days has a float64 type, but it's superfluous to specify float64. You, me, and the Go compiler can all infer the type of days by looking at the value to the right. Whenever the value is a number with a decimal point, the type will be float64.

> **TIP** The golint tool provides hints for coding style. It discourages the clutter with the following message:
>
> ```
> "should omit type float64 from declaration of var days;
> it will be inferred from the right-hand side"
> ```

If you initialize a variable with a whole number, Go won't know you want floating-point unless you explicitly specify a floating-point type:

```
var answer float64 = 42
```

Quick check 6.1   What type is inferred for answer := 42.0?

QC 6.1 answer   Real numbers are inferred as float64.

6.1.1   Single precision floating-point numbers

Go has two floating-point types. The default floating-point type is float64, a 64-bit floating-point type that uses eight bytes of memory. Some languages use the term *double precision* to describe the 64-bit floating-point type.

The float32 type uses half the memory of float64 but offers less precision. This type is sometimes called *single precision*. To use float32, you must specify the type when declaring a variable. The following listing shows float32 in use.

Listing 6.1   64-bit vs. 32-bit floating-point: pi.go

```
var pi64 = math.Pi
var pi32 float32 = math.Pi      Prints 3.141592653589793

fmt.Println(pi64)       Prints 3.1415927
fmt.Println(pi32)
```

When working with a large amount of data, such as thousands of vertices in a 3D game, it may make sense to sacrifice precision for memory savings by using float32.

> **TIP**   Functions in the math package operate on float64 types, so prefer float64 unless you have a good reason to do otherwise.

Quick check 6.2   How many bytes of memory does a single precision float32 use?

6.1.2   The zero value

In Go, each type has a default value, called the *zero value*. The default applies when you declare a variable but don't initialize it with a value, as you can see in the next listing.

Listing 6.2   Declaring a variable without a value: default.go

```
var price float64       Prints 0
fmt.Println(price)
```

The previous listing declares price with no value, so Go initializes it with zero. To the computer, it's identical to the following:

```
price := 0.0
```

QC 6.2 answer   A float32 uses 4 bytes (or 32 bits).

To the programmer, the difference is subtle. When you declare price := 0.0, it's like saying the price is free. Not specifying a value for price, as in listing 6.2, hints that the real value is yet to come.

Quick check 6.3   What is the zero value for a float32?

6.2   Displaying floating-point types

When using Print or Println with floating-point types, the default behavior is to display as many digits as possible. If that's not what you want, you can use Printf with the %f formatting verb to specify the number of digits, as the following listing shows.

Listing 6.3 Formatted print for floating-point: third.go

```
third := 1.0 / 3
fmt.Println(third)       ←———— Prints 0.3333333333333333
fmt.Printf("%v\n", third)   ↙
fmt.Printf("%f\n", third)    ←———— Prints 0.333333
fmt.Printf("%.3f\n", third)  ←———— Prints 0.333
fmt.Printf("%4.2f\n", third) ←———— Prints 0.33
```

The %f verb formats the value of third with a width and with precision, as shown in figure 6.1.

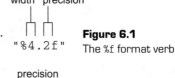

Figure 6.1
The %f format verb

Precision specifies how many digits should appear after the decimal point; two digits for %.2f, for example, as shown in figure 6.2.

Figure 6.2   Output formatted with a width of 4, precision of 2

Width specifies the minimum number of characters to display, including the decimal point and the digits before and after the decimal (for example, 0.33 has a width of 4). If the width is larger than the number of characters needed, Printf will pad the left with spaces. If the width is unspecified, `Printf` will use the number of characters necessary to display the value.

To left-pad with zeros instead of spaces, prefix the width with a zero, as in the following listing.

Listing 6.4 Zero padding: third.go

```
fmt.Printf("%05.2f\n", third)  ◀——————  Prints 00.33
```

Quick check 6.4

1 Type listing 6.3 into the body of a main function in the Go playground. Try different values for the width and precision in the `Printf` statement.

2 What is the width and precision of 0015.1021?

 ## 6.3   Floating-point accuracy

In mathematics, some rational numbers can't be accurately represented in decimal form. The number 0.33 is only an approximation of ⅓. Unsurprisingly, a calculation on approximate values has an approximate result:

⅓ + ⅓ + ⅓ = 1

0.33 + 0.33 + 0.33 = 0.99

Floating-point numbers suffer from rounding errors too, except floating-point hardware uses a binary representation (using only 0s and 1s)

QC 6.4 answer

1 ```
   third := 1.0 / 3
   fmt.Printf("%f\n", third)   ◀—————— Prints 0.333333
   fmt.Printf("%7.4f\n", third) ◀—————— Prints 0.3333
   fmt.Printf("%06.2f\n", third) ◀—————— Prints 000.33
   ```

2  The width is 9 and the precision is 4, with zero padding "%09.4f".
   ```

instead of decimal (using 1–9). The consequence is that computers can accurately represent ⅓ but have rounding errors with other numbers, as the following listing illustrates.

Listing 6.5   Floating-point inaccuracies: float.go

```
third := 1.0 / 3.0
fmt.Println(third + third + third)   ⟵——— Prints 1

piggyBank := 0.1
piggyBank += 0.2
fmt.Println(piggyBank)   ⟵——— Prints 0.30000000000000004
```

As you can see, floating-point isn't the best choice for representing money. One alternative is to store the number of cents with an integer type, which is covered in the next lesson.

On the other hand, even if your piggyBank were off by a penny, well, it isn't mission critical. As long as you've saved enough for the trip to Mars, you're happy. To sweep the rounding errors under the rug, you can use Printf with a precision of two digits.

To minimize rounding errors, we recommend that you perform multiplication before division. The result tends to be more accurate that way, as demonstrated in the temperature conversion examples in the next two listings.

Listing 6.6   Division first: rounding-error.go

```
celsius := 21.0
fmt.Print((celsius/5.0*9.0)+32, "° F\n")    Prints 69.80000000000001° F
fmt.Print((9.0/5.0*celsius)+32, "° F\n")
```

Listing 6.7   Multiplication first: temperature.go

```
celsius := 21.0
fahrenheit := (celsius * 9.0 / 5.0) + 32.0
fmt.Print(fahrenheit, "° F")   ⟵——— Prints 69.8° F
```

Quick check 6.5   What is the best way to avoid rounding errors?

QC 6.5 answer   Don't use a floating-point.

6.4   Comparing floating-point numbers

In listing 6.5, the `piggyBank` contained 0.30000000000000004, rather than the desired 0.30. Keep this in mind any time you need to compare floating-point numbers:

```
piggyBank := 0.1
piggyBank += 0.2
fmt.Println(piggyBank == 0.3)  ⟵──── Prints false
```

Instead of comparing floating-point numbers directly, determine the absolute difference between two numbers and then ensure the difference isn't too big. To take the absolute value of a `float64`, the `math` package provides an `Abs` function:

```
fmt.Println(math.Abs(piggyBank-0.3) < 0.0001)  ⟵──── Prints true
```

> **TIP** The upper bound for a floating-point error for a single operation is known as the machine epsilon, which is 2^{-52} for `float64` and 2^{-23} for `float32`. Unfortunately, floating-point errors accumulate rather quickly. Add 11 dimes ($0.10 each) to a fresh `piggyBank`, and the rounding errors exceed 2^{-52} when compared to $1.10. That means you're better off picking a tolerance specific to your application—in this case, 0.0001.

> **Quick check 6.6** If you add 11 dimes ($0.10 each) to an empty `piggyBank` of type `float64`, what is the final balance?

 Summary

- Go can infer types for you. In particular, Go will infer `float64` for variables initialized with real numbers.
- Floating-point types are versatile but not always accurate.
- You used 2 of Go's 15 numeric types (`float64`, `float32`).

QC 6.6 answer

```
piggyBank := 0.0
for i := 0; i < 11; i++ {
    piggyBank += 0.1
}
fmt.Println(piggyBank)
```
⟵ Prints
1.0999999999999999

Let's see if you got this...

Experiment: piggy.go

Save some money to buy a gift for your friend. Write a program that randomly places
nickels ($0.05), dimes ($0.10), and quarters ($0.25) into an empty piggy bank until it con-
tains at least $20.00. Display the running balance of the piggy bank after each deposit,
formatting it with an appropriate width and precision.

WHOLE NUMBERS

After reading lesson 7, you'll be able to

- Use 10 types of whole numbers
- Choose the right type
- Use hexadecimal and binary representations

Go offers 10 different types for whole numbers, collectively called *integers*. Integers don't suffer from the accuracy issues of floating-point types, but they can't store fractional numbers and they have a limited range. The integer type you choose will depend on the range of values needed for a given situation.

Consider this How many numbers can you represent with two tokens?

If the tokens are individually identifiable by position, there are four possible permutations. Both tokens, neither token, one token, or the other token. You could represent four numbers.

Computers are based on bits. A bit can either be off or on—0 or 1. Eight bits can represent 256 different values. How many bits would it take to represent the number 4,000,000,000?

7.1   Declaring integer variables

Five integer types are *signed,* meaning they can represent both positive and negative whole numbers. The most common integer type is a signed integer abbreviated `int`:

```
var year int = 2018
```

The other five integer types are *unsigned,* meaning they're for positive numbers only. The abbreviation for unsigned integer is `uint`:

```
var month uint = 2
```

When using type inference, Go will always pick the `int` type for a literal whole number. The following three lines are equivalent:

```
year := 2018
var year = 2018
var year int = 2018
```

> **TIP** As with the floating-point types in lesson 6, it's preferable to not specify the `int` type when it can be inferred.

> **Quick check 7.1** If your glass is half full, which integer type would you use to represent the number of milliliters of water in your glass?

7.1.1   Integer types for every occasion

Integers, whether signed or unsigned, come in a variety of sizes. The size affects their minimum and maximum values and how much memory they consume. There are eight architecture-independent types suffixed with the number of bits they need, as summarized in table 7.1.

> **QC 7.1 answer** The `uint` type (unsigned integer) is for positive integers only.

Table 7.1 Architecture-independent integer types

Type	Range	Storage
int8	–128 to 127	8-bit (one byte)
uint8	0 to 255	
int16	–32,768 to 32,767	16-bit (two bytes)
uint16	0 to 65535	
int32	–2,147,483,648 to 2,147,483,647	32-bit (four bytes)
uint32	0 to 4,294,967,295	
int64	–9,223,372,036,854,775,808 to 9,223,372,036,854,775,807	64-bit (eight bytes)
uint64	0 to 18,446,744,073,709,551,615	

That's a lot of types to choose from! Later in this lesson, we'll show some examples where specific integer types make sense, along with what happens if your program exceeds the available range.

There are two integer types not listed in table 7.1. The int and uint types are optimal for the target device. The Go Playground, Raspberry Pi 2, and older mobile phones provide a 32-bit environment where both int and uint are 32-bit values. Any recent computer will provide a 64-bit environment where int and uint will be 64-bit values.

> **TIP** If you're operating on numbers larger than two billion, and if the code could be run on older 32-bit hardware, be sure to use int64 or uint64 instead of int and uint.

> **NOTE** Although it's tempting to think of int as an int32 on some devices and an int64 on other devices, these are three distinct types. The int type isn't an alias for another type.

> **Quick check 7.2**   Which integer types support the value –20,151,021?

7.1.2   Knowing your type

If you're ever curious about which type the Go compiler inferred, the Printf function provides the %T format verb to display a variable's type, as shown in the following listing.

QC 7.2 answer   The int32, int64, and int types would work.

Listing 7.1 Inspect a variable's type: inspect.go

```
year := 2018
fmt.Printf("Type %T for %v\n", year, year)
```
← Prints Type int for 2018

Instead of repeating the variable twice, you can tell Printf to use the first argument [1] for the second format verb:

```
days := 365.2425
fmt.Printf("Type %T for %[1]v\n", days)
```
← Prints Type float64 for 365.2425

> **Quick check 7.3**   Which types does Go infer for text between quotes, a whole number, a real number, and the word true (without quotes)? Expand listing 7.1 to declare variables with different values and run the program to see which types Go infers.

 ## 7.2   The uint8 type for 8-bit colors

In Cascading Style Sheets (CSS), colors on screen are specified as a red, green, blue triplet, each with a range of 0–255. It's the perfect situation to use the uint8 type, an 8-bit unsigned integer able to represent values from 0–255:

```
var red, green, blue uint8 = 0, 141, 213
```

Here are the benefits of uint8 instead of a regular int for this case:

- With a uint8, the variables are restricted to the range of valid values, eliminating over four billion incorrect possibilities compared to a 32-bit integer.
- If there are a lot of colors to store sequentially, such as in an uncompressed image, you could achieve considerable memory savings by using 8-bit integers.

QC 7.3 answer

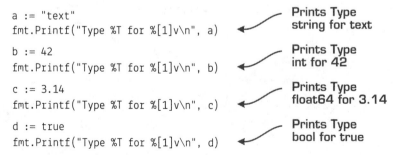

```
a := "text"
fmt.Printf("Type %T for %[1]v\n", a)
```
← Prints Type string for text

```
b := 42
fmt.Printf("Type %T for %[1]v\n", b)
```
← Prints Type int for 42

```
c := 3.14
fmt.Printf("Type %T for %[1]v\n", c)
```
← Prints Type float64 for 3.14

```
d := true
fmt.Printf("Type %T for %[1]v\n", d)
```
← Prints Type bool for true

Hexadecimal in Go

Colors in CSS are specified in hexadecimal instead of decimal. *Hexadecimal* represents numbers using 6 (*hexa-*) more digits than decimal's 10. The first 10 digits are the same 0 through 9, but they're followed by A through F. A in hexadecimal is equivalent to 10 in decimal, B to 11, and so on up to F, which is 15.

Decimal is a great system for 10-fingered organisms, but hexadecimal is better suited to computers. A single hexadecimal digit consumes four bits, called a *nibble*. Two hexadecimal digits require precisely eight bits, or one *byte*, making hexadecimal a convenient way to specify values for a uint8.

The following table shows some hexadecimal numbers and their equivalent numbers in decimal.

Hexadecimal and decimal values

Hexadecimal	Decimal
A	10
F	15
10	16
FF	255

To distinguish between decimal and hexadecimal, Go requires a 0x prefix for hexadecimal. These two lines of code are equivalent:

```
var red, green, blue uint8 = 0, 141, 213
var red, green, blue uint8 = 0x00, 0x8d, 0xd5
```

To display numbers in hexadecimal, you can use the %x or %X format verbs with Printf:

```
fmt.Printf("%x %x %x", red, green, blue)      ◄──────  Prints 0 8d d5
```

To output a color that would feel at home in a .css file, the hexadecimal values need some padding. As with the %v and %f format verbs, you can specify a minimum number of digits (2) and zero padding with %02x:

```
fmt.Printf("color: #%02x%02x%02x;", red, green, blue)   ◄
```
Prints color #008dd5;

Quick check 7.4   How many bytes are required to store a value of type uint8?

 ## 7.3   Integers wrap around

Integers are free of the rounding errors that make floating-point inaccurate, but all integer types have a different problem: a limited range. When that range is exceeded, integer types in Go *wrap around*.

An 8-bit unsigned integer (uint8) has a range of 0–255. Incrementing beyond 255 will wrap back to 0. The following listing increments both signed and unsigned 8-bit integers, causing them to wrap around.

Listing 7.2 Integers wrap around: integers-wrap.go

```
var red uint8 = 255
red++
fmt.Println(red)          ←——— Prints 0

var number int8 = 127
number++
fmt.Println(number)    ←——— Prints –128
```

7.3.1   Looking at the bits

To understand why integers wrap, take a look at the bits. The %b format verb will show you the bits for an integer value. Like other format verbs, %b can be zero padded to a minimum length, as you can see in this listing.

Listing 7.3 Display the bits: bits.go

```
var green uint8 = 3                 Prints 00000011
fmt.Printf("%08b\n", green)   ←——
green++                             Prints 00000100
fmt.Printf("%08b\n", green)   ←——
```

QC 7.4 answer   An 8-bit (unsigned) integer only requires a single byte.

Quick check 7.5 Use the Go Playground to experiment with the wrapping behavior of integers:

1. In listing 7.2, the code increments red and number by 1. What happens when you add a larger number to either variable?
2. Go the other way. What happens if you decrement red when it's 0 or number when it's equal to –128?
3. Wrapping applies to 16-bit, 32-bit, and 64-bit integers too. What happens if you declare a uint16 assigned to the maximum value of 65535 and then increment it by 1?

TIP The math package defines math.MaxUint16 as 65535 and similar min/max constants for each architecture-independent integer type. Remember that int and uint could be either 32-bit or 64-bit, depending on the underlying hardware.

In listing 7.3, incrementing green causes the 1 to be carried, leaving zeros to the right. The result is 00000100 in binary, or 4 in decimal, as shown in figure 7.1.

```
      1 1
  00000011
+ 00000001
  00000100
```

Figure 7.1 Carrying the 1 in binary addition

QC 7.5 answer

1.
```
// add a number larger than one
var red uint8 = 255
red += 2
fmt.Println(red)        ◄──────  Prints 1

var number int8 = 127
number += 3
fmt.Println(number)     ◄──────  Prints -126
```

2.
```
// wrap the other way
red = 0
red--
fmt.Println(red)        ◄──────  Prints 255

number = -128
number--
fmt.Println(number)     ◄──────  Prints 127
```

3.
```
// wrapping with a 16-bit unsigned integer
var green uint16 = 65535
green++
fmt.Println(green)      ◄──────  Prints 0
```

The same thing happens when incrementing 255, with one critical difference: with only eight bits available, the 1 that's carried has nowhere to go, so the value of blue is left as 0, as shown in the next listing and illustrated in figure 7.2.

Listing 7.4 The bits when integers wrap: bits-wrap.go

```
var blue uint8 = 255          ⟵ Prints 11111111
fmt.Printf("%08b\n", blue)
blue++                        ⟵ Prints 00000000
fmt.Printf("%08b\n", blue)
```

Wrapping may be what you want in some situations, but not always. The simplest way to avoid wrapping is to use an integer type large enough to hold the values you expect to store.

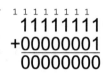

```
 1 1 1 1 1 1 1 1
 11111111
+00000001
 00000000
```

Figure 7.2 Where should the carry go?

> **Quick check 7.6** Which format verb lets you look at the bits?

7.3.2 Avoid wrapping around time

On Unix-based operating systems, time is represented as the number of seconds since January 1, 1970 UTC (Coordinated Universal Time). In the year 2038, the number of seconds since January 1, 1970 will exceed two billion, the capacity of an int32.

Thankfully, int64 can support dates well beyond 2038. This is a situation where int32 or int simply won't do. Only the int64 and uint64 integer types are able to store numbers well beyond two billion on all platforms.

The code in listing 7.5 uses the Unix function from the time package. It accepts two int64 parameters, corresponding to the number of seconds and the number of nanoseconds since January 1, 1970. Using a suitably large value (over 12 billion) demonstrates that dates beyond 2038 work just fine in Go.

QC 7.6 answer The %b format verb outputs integers in base 2.

Listing 7.5 64-bit integers: time.go

```go
package main

import (
    "fmt"
    "time"
)

func main() {
    future := time.Unix(12622780800, 0)
    fmt.Println(future)
}
```

Prints 2370-01-01
00:00:00 +0000 UTC
in the Go Playground

> **Quick check 7.7** Which integer type should you choose to avoid wrapping?

Summary

- The most common integer types are `int` and `uint`, but some situations call for smaller or larger types.
- Integer types need to be chosen carefully to avoid wrapping around, unless wrapping is what you want.
- You looked at 10 more of the 15 numeric types in Go (`int`, `int8`, `int16`, `int32`, `int64`, `uint`, `uint8`, `uint16`, `uint32`, `uint64`).

Let's see if you got this...

Experiment: piggy.go

Write a new piggy bank program that uses integers to track the number of cents rather than dollars. Randomly place nickels (5¢), dimes (10¢), and quarters (25¢) into an empty piggy bank until it contains at least $20.

Display the running balance of the piggy bank after each deposit in dollars (for example, $1.05).

> **TIP** If you need to find the remainder of dividing two numbers, use modulus (%).

QC 7.7 answer Use an integer type large enough to hold the values you expect to store.

BIG NUMBERS

After reading lesson 8, you'll be able to

- Save your zero key by specifying an exponent
- Use Go's `big` package for really big numbers
- Use big constants and literal values

Computer programming is full of trade-offs. Floating-point types can store numbers of any size, but they lack precision and accuracy at times. Integers are accurate but have a limited range. What if you need a really big, accurate number? This lesson explores two alternatives to the native `float64` and `int` types.

Consider this CPUs are optimized for integer and floating-point math, but other numeric representations are possible. When you need to go big, Go has you covered.

What are some situations where integers are too small, floating-point too imprecise, or another numeric type would be more suitable?

8.1 Hitting the ceiling

If you haven't realized it yet, 64-bit integers are mind-bogglingly big—much bigger than their 32-bit counterparts.

For some perspective, the nearest star, Alpha Centauri, is 41.3 trillion kilometers away. A trillion: that's one followed by 12 zeros, or 10^{12}. Rather than painstakingly typing every zero, you can write such numbers in Go with an exponent, like so:

```
var distance int64 = 41.3e12
```

An int32 or uint32 can't contain such a large number, but an int64 doesn't break a sweat. Now you can go about your business, perhaps calculating how many days it would take to travel to Alpha Centauri, a task tackled in the following listing.

Listing 8.1 Days to Alpha Centauri: alpha.go

```
const lightSpeed = 299792 // km/s
const secondsPerDay = 86400

var distance int64 = 41.3e12
fmt.Println("Alpha Centauri is", distance, "km away.")

days := distance / lightSpeed / secondsPerDay
fmt.Println("That is", days, "days of travel at light speed.")
```

Prints Alpha Centauri is 41300000000000 km away

Prints That is 1594 days of travel at light speed

As big as 64-bit integers are, there's something bigger: space. The Andromeda Galaxy is 24 quintillion (10^{18}) kilometers away. Even the largest unsigned integer (uint64) can only contain numbers up to 18 quintillion. Attempting to declare a variable beyond 18 quintillion reports an overflow error:

```
var distance uint64 = 24e18
```

24000000000000000000 overflows uint64

But don't panic—there are still a few options. You could use floating-point math. That's not a bad idea, and you already know how floating-point works. But there's another way. The next section takes a look at Go's big package.

> **NOTE** If a variable doesn't have an explicit type, Go will infer float64 for numbers containing exponents.

Quick check 8.1   The distance between Mars and Earth ranges from 56,000,000 km to 401,000,000 km. Express these two values as integers with the exponent (e) syntax.

 ## 8.2   The big package

The big package provides three types:

- big.Int is for big integers, when 18 quintillion isn't enough.
- big.Float is for arbitrary-precision floating-point numbers.
- big.Rat is for fractions like ⅓.

> **NOTE**   Your code can declare new types too, but we'll come back to that in lesson 13.

The big.Int type can happily store and operate on the distance to Andromeda Galaxy, a mere 24 quintillion kilometers.

Opting to use big.Int requires that you use it for everything in your equation, even the constants you had before. The NewInt function takes an int64 and returns a big.Int:

```
lightSpeed := big.NewInt(299792)
secondsPerDay := big.NewInt(86400)
```

NewInt isn't going to help for a number like 24 quintillion. It won't fit in an int64, so instead you can create a big.Int from a string:

```
distance := new(big.Int)
distance.SetString("24000000000000000000", 10)
```

After creating a new big.Int, set its value to 24 quintillion by calling the SetString method. The number 24 quintillion is in base 10 (decimal), so the second argument is 10.

> **NOTE**   Methods are similar to functions. You'll learn all about them in lesson 13. The new built-in function is for pointers, which are covered in lesson 26.

With all the values in place, the Div method performs the necessary division so the result can be displayed, as shown in the following listing.

QC 8.1 answer

```
var distance int = 56e6
distance = 401e6
```

Listing 8.2 Days to Andromeda Galaxy: andromeda.go

```go
package main

import (
    "fmt"
    "math/big"
)

func main() {
    lightSpeed := big.NewInt(299792)
    secondsPerDay := big.NewInt(86400)

    distance := new(big.Int)
    distance.SetString("24000000000000000000", 10)
    fmt.Println("Andromeda Galaxy is", distance, "km away.")

    seconds := new(big.Int)
    seconds.Div(distance, lightSpeed)

    days := new(big.Int)
    days.Div(seconds, secondsPerDay)

    fmt.Println("That is", days, "days of travel at light speed.")
}
```

> Prints Andromeda Galaxy is 24000000000000000000 km away.

> Prints That is 926568346 days of travel at light speed.

As you can see, these big types are more cumbersome to work with than the native int and float64 types. They're also slower. Those are the trade-offs for being able to accurately represent numbers of any size.

> **Quick check 8.2** What are two ways to make a big.Int with the number 86,400?

QC 8.2 answer

Construct a big.Int with the NewInt function:

```go
secondsPerDay := big.NewInt(86400)
```

Or use the SetString method:

```go
secondsPerDay := new(big.Int)
secondsPerDay.SetString("86400", 10)
```

8.3   Constants of unusual size

Constants can be declared with a type, just like variables. And just like variables, a `uint64` constant can't possibly contain a number like 24 quintillion:

```
const distance uint64 = 24000000000000000000
```
Constant
24000000000000000000
overflows uint64

It gets interesting when you declare a constant without a type. For variables, Go uses type inference to determine the type, and in the case of 24 quintillion, overflows the `int` type. Constants are different. Rather than infer a type, constants can be *untyped*. The following line doesn't cause an overflow error:

```
const distance = 24000000000000000000
```

Constants are declared with the `const` keyword, but every literal value in your program is a constant too. That means unusually sized numbers can be used directly, as shown in the following listing.

Listing 8.3 Literals of unusual size: constant.go

```
fmt.Println("Andromeda Galaxy is", 24000000000000000000/299792/86400, "light days away.")
```

     Prints Andromeda Galaxy is
          926568346 light days away.

Calculations on constants and literals are performed during compilation rather than while the program is running. The Go compiler is written in Go. Under the hood, untyped numeric constants are backed by the `big` package, enabling all the usual operations with numbers well beyond 18 quintillion, as shown in the following listing.

Listing 8.4 Constants of unusual size: constant.go

```
const distance = 24000000000000000000
const lightSpeed = 299792
const secondsPerDay = 86400

const days = distance / lightSpeed / secondsPerDay

fmt.Println("Andromeda Galaxy is", days, "light days away.")
```

**Prints Andromeda
Galaxy is 926568346
light days away.**

Constant values can be assigned to variables so long as they fit. An int can't contain 24 quintillion, but 926,568,346 fits just fine:

```
km := distance
days := distance / lightSpeed / secondsPerDay
```

Constant
24000000000000000000
overflows int.

926568346
fits into an int.

There's a caveat to constants of unusual size. Though the Go compiler utilizes the big package for untyped numeric constants, constants and big.Int values aren't interchangeable. Listing 8.2 displayed a big.Int containing 24 quintillion, but you can't display the distance constant due to an overflow error :

```
fmt.Println("Andromeda Galaxy is", distance, "km away.")
```

Constant
24000000000000000000
overflows int.

Very large constants are certainly useful, but they aren't a replacement for the big package.

Quick check 8.3   When are calculations on constants and literals performed?

 **Summary**

- When the native types can't go the distance, the big package has you covered.
- Big things are possible with constants that are untyped, and all numeric literals are untyped constants too.
- Untyped constants must be converted to typed variables when passed to functions.

Let's see if you got this...

Experiment: canis.go

Canis Major Dwarf is the closest known galaxy to Earth at 236,000,000,000,000,000 km from our Sun (though some dispute that it is a galaxy). Use constants to convert this distance to light years.

QC 8.3 answer   The Go compiler simplifies equations containing constants and literals during compilation.

MULTILINGUAL TEXT

After reading lesson 9, you'll be able to

- Access and manipulate individual letters
- Cipher and decipher secret messages
- Write your programs for a multilingual world

From `"Hello, playground"` at the beginning, you've been using text in your programs. The individual letters, digits, and symbols are called *characters*. When you *string* together characters and place them between quotes, it's called a *literal string*.

> **Consider this** You know computers represent numbers with 1s and 0s. If you were a computer, how would you represent the alphabet and human language?
>
> If you said with numbers, you're right. Characters of the alphabet have numeric values, which means you can manipulate them like numbers.
>
> It's not entirely straightforward, though. The characters from every written language and countless emoji add up to thousands of characters. There are some tricks to representing text in a space-efficient and flexible manner.

 ## 9.1   Declaring string variables

Literal values wrapped in quotes are inferred to be of the type string, so the following three lines are equivalent:

```
peace := "peace"
var peace = "peace"
var peace string = "peace"
```

If you declare a variable without providing a value, it will be initialized with the zero value for its type. The *zero value* for the string type is an empty string (""):

```
var blank string
```

9.1.1   Raw string literals

String literals may contain *escape sequences*, such as the \n mentioned in lesson 2. To avoid substituting \n for a new line, you can wrap text in backticks (`) instead of quotes ("), as shown in the following listing. Backticks indicate a *raw* string literal.

Listing 9.1 Raw string literals: raw.go

```
fmt.Println("peace be upon you\nupon you be peace")
fmt.Println(`strings can span multiple lines with the \n escape sequence`)
```

The previous listing displays this output:

```
peace be upon you
upon you be peace
strings can span multiple lines with the \n escape sequence
```

Unlike conventional string literals, raw string literals can span multiple lines of source code, as shown in the next listing.

Listing 9.2 Multiple-line raw string literals: raw-lines.go

```
fmt.Println(`
    peace be upon you
    upon you be peace`)
```

Running listing 9.2 will produce the following output, including the tabs used for indentation:

```
        peace be upon you
        upon you be peace
```

Literal strings and raw strings both result in strings, as the following listing shows.

Listing 9.3 String type: raw-type.go

```
fmt.Printf("%v is a %[1]T\n", "literal string")      ←── Prints literal string
fmt.Printf("%v is a %[1]T\n", `raw string literal`)  ←──   is a string
                                                      └── Prints raw string
                                                          literal is a string
```

> **Quick check 9.1** For the Windows file path C:\go, would you use a string literal or a raw string literal, and why?

 9.2   Characters, code points, runes, and bytes

The Unicode Consortium assigns numeric values, called *code points*, to over one million unique characters. For example, 65 is the code point for the capital letter A, and 128515 is a smiley face ☺.

To represent a single Unicode code point, Go provides rune, which is an alias for the int32 type.

QC 9.1 answer Use a raw string literal `C:\go` because "C:\go" fails with an unknown escape sequence error.

A `byte` is an alias for the `uint8` type. It's intended for binary data, though `byte` can be used for English characters defined by ASCII, an older 128-character subset of Unicode.

Type aliases

An alias is another name for the same type, so `rune` and `int32` are interchangeable. Though `byte` and `rune` have been in Go from the beginning, Go 1.9 introduced the ability to declare your own type aliases. The syntax looks like this:

```
type byte = uint8
type rune = int32
```

Both `byte` and `rune` behave like the integer types they are aliases for, as shown in the following listing.

Listing 9.4 `rune` **and** `byte`: **rune.go**

```
var pi rune = 960
var alpha rune = 940
var omega rune = 969                              Prints 960 940 969 33
var bang byte = 33

fmt.Printf("%v %v %v %v\n", pi, alpha, omega, bang)
```

To display the characters rather than their numeric values, the `%c` format verb can be used with `Printf`:

```
fmt.Printf("%c%c%c%c\n", pi, alpha, omega, bang)  ◄─────  Prints πάω!
```

> **TIP** Any integer type will work with `%c`, but the `rune` alias indicates that the number 960 represents a character.

Rather than memorize Unicode code points, Go provides a character literal. Just enclose a character in single quotes `'A'`. If no type is specified, Go will infer a `rune`, so the following three lines are equivalent:

```
grade := 'A'
var grade = 'A'
var grade rune = 'A'
```

The `grade` variable still contains a numeric value, in this case 65, the code point for a capital `'A'`. Character literals can also be used with the `byte` alias:

```
var star byte = '*'
```

9.3   Pulling the strings

A puppeteer manipulates a marionette by pulling on strings, but strings in Go aren't susceptible to manipulation. A variable can be assigned to a different string, but strings themselves can't be altered:

```
peace := "shalom"
peace = "salām"
```

Your program can access individual characters, but it can't alter the characters of a string. The following listing uses square brackets [] to specify an index into a string, which accesses a single byte (ASCII character). The index starts from zero.

Listing 9.5   Indexing into a string: index.go

```
message := "shalom"
c := message[5]
fmt.Printf("%c\n", c)   ←——— Prints m
```

Strings in Go are *immutable*, as they are in Python, Java, and JavaScript. Unlike strings in Ruby and character arrays in C, you can't modify a string in Go:

```
message[5] = 'd'   ◄────── Cannot assign to message[5]
```

> **Quick check 9.3** Write a program to print each byte (ASCII character) of "shalom", one character per line.

 ## 9.4   Manipulating characters with Caesar cipher

One effective method of sending secret messages in the second century was to shift every letter, so 'a' becomes 'd', 'b' becomes 'e', and so on. The result might pass for a foreign language:

> *L fdph, L vdz, L frqtxhuhg.*
> —Julius Caesar

It turns out that manipulating characters as numeric values is really easy with computers, as shown in the following listing.

Listing 9.6 Manipulate a single character: caesar.go

```
c := 'a'
c = c + 3
fmt.Printf("%c", c)   ◄────── Prints d
```

QC 9.3 answer

```
message := "shalom"
for i := 0; i < 6; i++ {
    c := message[i]
    fmt.Printf("%c\n", c)
}
```

The code in listing 9.6 has one problem, though. It doesn't account for all the messages about xylophones, yaks, and zebras. To address this need, the original Caesar cipher wraps around, so `'x'` becomes `'a'`, `'y'` becomes `'b'`, and `'z'` becomes `'c'`. With 26 characters in the English alphabet, it's a simple matter:

```
if c > 'z' {
    c = c - 26
}
```

To *decipher* this Caesar cipher, subtract 3 instead of adding 3. But then you need to account for `c < 'a'` by adding 26. What a pain.

> **Quick check 9.4**   What is the result of the expression `c = c - 'a' + 'A'` if c is a lowercase `'g'`?

9.4.1   A modern variant

ROT13 (rotate 13) is a 20th century variant of Caesar cipher. It has one difference: it adds 13 instead of 3. With ROT13, ciphering and deciphering are the same convenient operation.

Let's suppose, while scanning the heavens for alien communications, the SETI Institute received a transmission with the following message:

```
message := "uv vagreangvbany fcnpr fgngvba"
```

We suspect this `message` is actually English text that was ciphered with ROT13. Call it a hunch. Before you can crack the code, there's one more thing you need to know. This `message` is 30 characters long, which can be determined with the built-in `len` function:

```
fmt.Println(len(message))
```
◀——— Prints 30

> **NOTE**   Go has a handful of built-in functions that don't require an import statement. The `len` function can determine the length for a variety of types. In this case, `len` returns the length of a `string` in bytes.

QC 9.4 answer   The letter is converted to uppercase:
```
c := 'g'
c = c - 'a' + 'A'
fmt.Printf("%c", c)
```
◀——— Prints G

The following listing will decipher a message from space. Run it in the Go Playground to find out what the aliens are saying.

Listing 9.7   ROT13 cipher: rot13.go

```
message := "uv vagreangvbany fcnpr fgngvba"        Iterates through each
                                                    ASCII character
for i := 0; i < len(message); i++ {
    c := message[i]
    if c >= 'a' && c <= 'z' {          Leaves spaces
        c = c + 13                     and punctuation
        if c > 'z' {                   as they are
            c = c - 26
        }
    }
    fmt.Printf("%c", c)
}
```

Note that the ROT13 implementation in the previous listing is only intended for ASCII characters (bytes). It will get confused by a message written in Spanish or Russian. The next section looks at a solution for this issue.

Quick check 9.5

1 What does the built-in `len` function do when passed a string?
2 Type listing 9.7 into the Go Playground. What does the message say?

9.5   Decoding strings into runes

Strings in Go are encoded with UTF-8, one of several encodings for Unicode code points. UTF-8 is an efficient variable length encoding where a single code point may use 8 bits, 16 bits, or 32 bits. By using a variable length encoding, UTF-8 makes the transition from ASCII straightforward, because ASCII characters are identical to their UTF-8 encoded counterparts.

QC 9.5 answer

1 The `len` function returns the length of a string in bytes.
2 hi international space station

NOTE   UTF-8 is the dominant character encoding for the World Wide Web. It was invented in 1992 by Ken Thompson, one of the designers of Go.

The ROT13 program in listing 9.7 accessed the individual bytes (8-bit) of the `message` string without accounting for characters that are multiple bytes long (16-bit or 32-bit). This is why it works fine for English characters (ASCII), but produces garbled results for Russian and Spanish. You can do better, *amigo*.

The first step to supporting other languages is to decode characters to the `rune` type before manipulating them. Fortunately, Go has functions and language features for decoding UTF-8 encoded strings.

The `utf8` package provides functions to determine the length of a string in runes rather than bytes and to decode the first character of a string. The `DecodeRuneInString` function returns the first character and the number of bytes the character consumed, as shown in listing 9.8.

NOTE   Unlike many programming languages, functions in Go can return multiple values. Multiple return values are discussed in lesson 12.

Listing 9.8 The `utf8` package: **spanish.go**

```
package main

import (
    "fmt"
    "unicode/utf8"
)

func main() {
    question := "¿Cómo estás?"
    fmt.Println(len(question), "bytes")            ⟵ Prints 15 bytes
    fmt.Println(utf8.RuneCountInString(question), "runes")  ⟵ Prints 12 runes
    c, size := utf8.DecodeRuneInString(question)
    fmt.Printf("First rune: %c %v bytes", c, size) ⟵ Prints First rune: ¿ 2 bytes
}
```

The Go language provides the `range` keyword to iterate over a variety of collections (covered in unit 4). It can also decode UTF-8 encoded strings, as shown in the following listing.

Listing 9.9 Decoding runes: spanish-range.go

```
question := "¿Cómo estás?"

for i, c := range question {
    fmt.Printf("%v %c\n", i, c)
}
```

On each iteration, the variables i and c are assigned to an index into the string and the code point (rune) at that position.

If you don't need the index, the blank identifier (an underscore) allows you to ignore it:

```
for _, c := range question {
    fmt.Printf("%c ", c)    ◄──────  Prints ¿ C ó m o   e s t á s ?
}
```

- -

Quick check 9.6

1 How many runes are in the English alphabet "abcdefghijklmnopqrstuvwxyz"? How many bytes?
2 How many bytes are in the rune '¿'?

 **Summary**

- Escape sequences like \n are ignored in raw string literals (`).
- Strings are immutable. Individual characters can be accessed but not altered.
- Strings use a variable length encoding called UTF-8, where each character consumes 1–4 bytes.
- A byte is an alias for the uint8 type, and rune is an alias for the int32 type.
- The range keyword can decode a UTF-8 encoded string into runes.

Let's see if you got this...

QC 9.6 answer

1 There are 26 runes and 26 bytes in the English alphabet.
2 There are 2 bytes in the rune '¿'.

Experiment: caesar.go

Decipher the quote from Julius Caesar:

> *L fdph, L vdz, L frqtxhuhg.*
> —Julius Caesar

Your program will need to shift uppercase and lowercase letters by –3. Remember that 'a' becomes 'x', 'b' becomes 'y', and 'c' becomes 'z', and likewise for uppercase letters.

Experiment: international.go

Cipher the Spanish message "Hola Estación Espacial Internacional" with ROT13. Modify listing 9.7 to use the range keyword. Now when you use ROT13 on Spanish text, characters with accents are preserved.

CONVERTING BETWEEN TYPES

After reading lesson 10, you'll be able to

- Convert between numeric, string, and Boolean types

Previous lessons covered Booleans, strings, and a dozen different numeric types. If you have variables of different types, you must convert the values to the same type before they can be used together.

Consider this   Say you're at the grocery store with a shopping list from your spouse. The first item is milk, but should you get cow's milk, almond, or soy? Should it be organic, skim, 1%, 2%, whole, evaporated, or condensed? How many gallons? Do you call your spouse to ask or just pick something?

Your spouse may get annoyed if you keep calling to ask for each detail. Iceberg or romaine lettuce? Russet or red potatoes? Oh, and was that 5 lbs. or 10? On the other hand, if you "think for yourself" and return with chocolate milk and french fries, that may not go over so well.

If your spouse is a programmer and you're a compiler in this scenario, what do you think Go's approach would be?

10.1 Types don't mix

A variable's *type* establishes the behavior that's appropriate for it. Numbers can be added, strings can be joined. To join two strings together, use the plus operator:

```
countdown := "Launch in T minus " + "10 seconds."
```

If you try to join a number to a string, the Go compiler will report an error:

```
countdown := "Launch in T minus " + 10 + " seconds."
```
Invalid operation: mismatched types string and int

Mixing types in other languages

When presented with two or more different types, some programming languages make a best effort to guess the programmer's intentions. Both JavaScript and PHP can subtract 1 from the string "10":

```
"10" - 1
```
9 in JavaScript and PHP

The Go compiler rejects "10" - 1 with a mismatched types error. In Go, you first need to convert "10" to an integer. The Atoi function in the strconv package will do the conversion, but it will return an error if the string doesn't contain a valid number. By the time you handle errors, the Go version is four lines long, which isn't exactly convenient.

That said, if "10" is user input or came from an external source, the JavaScript and PHP versions should check whether it's a valid number too.

In languages that *coerce* types, the code's behavior is less predictable to anyone who hasn't memorized a myriad of implicit behaviors. The plus operator (+) in both Java and JavaScript coerces numbers to strings to be joined, whereas PHP coerces the values to numbers and does the math:

```
"10" + 2
```
"102" in JavaScript or Java, 12 in PHP

Once again, Go would report a mismatched types error.

Another example of mismatched types occurs when attempting a calculation with a mix of integer and floating-point types. Real numbers like 365.2425 are represented with a floating-point type, and Go infers that whole numbers are integers:

```
age := 41
marsDays := 687         age and marsDays are integers.
earthDays := 365.2425
fmt.Println("I am", age*earthDays/marsDays, "years old on Mars.")
    earthDays is a                        Invalid operation:
    floating point type.                  mismatched types
```

If all three variables were integers, the calculation would succeed, but then earthDays would need to be 365 instead of the more accurate 365.2425. Alternatively, the calculation would succeed if age and marsDays were floating-point types (41.0 and 687.0 respectively). Go doesn't make assumptions about which you'd prefer, but you can explicitly convert between types, which is covered in the next section.

Quick check 10.1   What is "10" - 1 in Go?

10.2 Numeric type conversions

Type conversion is straightforward. If you need the integer age to be a floating-point type for a calculation, wrap the variable with the new type:

```
age := 41
marsAge := float64(age)
```

Variables of different types don't mix, but with type conversion, the calculation in the following listing works.

Listing 10.1 Mars age: mars-age.go

```
age := 41
marsAge := float64(age)

marsDays := 687.0                        Prints I am
earthDays := 365.2425                     21.797587336244543
                                          years old on Mars.
marsAge = marsAge * earthDays / marsDays
fmt.Println("I am", marsAge, "years old on Mars.")
```

QC 10.1 answer   A compiler error: invalid operation: "10" - 1 (mismatched types string and int)

You can convert from a floating-point type to an integer as well, though the digits after the decimal point will be truncated without any rounding:

```
fmt.Println(int(earthDays))  ◀────  Prints 365
```

Type conversions are required between unsigned and signed integer types, and between types of different sizes. It's always safe to convert to a type with a larger range, such as from an `int8` to an `int32`. Other integer conversions come with some risks. A `uint32` could contain a value of 4 billion, but an `int32` only supports numbers to just over 2 billion. Likewise, an `int` may contain a negative number, but a `uint` can't.

There's a reason why Go requires type conversions to be explicitly stated in the code. Every time you use a type conversion, consider the possible consequences.

> **Quick check 10.2**
>   1   What code would convert the variable `red` to an unsigned 8-bit integer?
>   2   What is the result of the comparison `age > marsAge`?

 ## 10.3 Convert types with caution

In 1996, the unmanned Arianne 5 rocket veered off its flight path, broke up, and exploded just 40 seconds after launch. The reported cause was a type conversion error from a `float64` to an `int16` with a value that exceeded 32,767—the maximum value an `int16` can hold. The unhandled failure left the flight control system without orientation data, causing it to veer off course, break apart, and ultimately self-destruct.

We haven't seen the Arianne 5 code, nor are we rocket scientists, but let's look at how Go handles the same type conversion. If the value is in range, as in the following listing, no problem.

QC 10.2 answer
  1   The type conversion would be `uint8(red)`.
  2   Mismatched types `int` and `float64`

```
var bh float64 = 32767
var h = int16(bh)          To-do: add
fmt.Println(h)             rocket science
```

If the value of bh is 32,768, which is too big for an int16, the result is what we've come to expect of integers in Go: it wraps around, becoming the lowest possible number for an int16, –32768.

The Ada language used for the Arianne 5 behaves differently. The type conversion from float64 to int16 with an out-of-range value caused a software exception. According to the report, this particular calculation was only meaningful prior to liftoff, so Go's approach may have been better in this instance, but usually it's best to avoid incorrect data.

To detect whether converting a type to int16 will result in an invalid value, the math package provides min/max constants:

```
if bh < math.MinInt16 || bh > math.MaxInt16 {
    // handle out of range value
}
```

> **NOTE**　These min/max constants are untyped, allowing the comparison of bh, a floating-point value, to MaxInt16. Lesson 8 talks more about untyped constants.

Quick check 10.3　What code will determine if the variable v is within the range of an 8-bit unsigned integer?

QC 10.3 answer

```
v := 42
if v >= 0 && v <= math.MaxUint8 {          Prints
    v8 := uint8(v)                         converted: 42
    fmt.Println("converted:", v8)
}
```

10.4 String conversions

To convert a rune or byte to a string, you can use the same type conversion syntax as numeric conversions, as shown in the next listing. This gives the same result using the %c format verb introduced in lesson 9 to display runes and bytes as characters.

Listing 10.3 Converting rune to string: rune-convert.go

```
var pi rune = 960
var alpha rune = 940
var omega rune = 969
var bang byte = 33
                                                        Prints πάω!
fmt.Print(string(pi), string(alpha), string(omega), string(bang))
```

Converting a numeric code point to a string works the same with any integer type. After all, rune and byte are just aliases for int32 and uint8.

To convert digits to a string, each digit must be converted to a code point, starting at 48 for the 0 character, through 57 for the 9 character. Thankfully, the Itoa function in the strconv (string conversion) package does this for you, as shown in the next listing.

Listing 10.4 Integer to ASCII: itoa.go

```
countdown := 10

str := "Launch in T minus " + strconv.Itoa(countdown) + " seconds."
fmt.Println(str)
```
        Prints Launch in T
        minus 10 seconds.

> **NOTE** Itoa is short for integer to ASCII. Unicode is a superset of the old ASCII standard. The first 128 code points are the same, which includes digits (used here), English letters, and common punctuation.

Another way to convert a number to a string is to use Sprintf, a cousin of Printf that returns a string rather than displaying it:

```
countdown := 9
str := fmt.Sprintf("Launch in T minus %v seconds.", countdown)
fmt.Println(str)
```
        Prints Launch in T
        minus 9 seconds.

To go the other way, the strconv package provides the Atoi function (ASCII to integer). Because a string may contain gibberish or a number that's too big, the Atoi function may return an error:

```
countdown, err := strconv.Atoi("10")
if err != nil {
    // oh no, something went wrong
}
fmt.Println(countdown)    ◄─────── Prints 10
```

A nil value for err indicates that no error occurred and everything is A-OK. Lesson 28 navigates the perilous topic of errors.

> **Quick check 10.4** Name two functions that can convert an integer to a string.

Types are static

In Go, once a variable is declared, it has a type and the type cannot be changed. This is known as *static typing*, which is easier for the compiler to optimize, so your programs run fast. But attempting to use a variable with a value of a different type will cause the Go compiler to report an error:

```
var countdown = 10
countdown = 0.5                                    Error: countdown
countdown = fmt.Sprintf("%v seconds", countdown)   can only store
                                                   integers.
```

Languages such as JavaScript, Python, and Ruby use *dynamic typing* instead of static typing. In those languages, each value has an associated type, and variables can hold values of any type. They would allow the type of countdown to change as the program executes.

Go does have an escape hatch for situations where the type is uncertain. For example, the Println function will accept both strings and numeric types. Lesson 12 explores the Println function in more detail.

QC 10.4 answer Both Itoa and Sprintf will convert a whole number to a string.

10.5 Converting Boolean values

The Print family of functions displays the Boolean values true and false as text. As such, the next listing uses the Sprintf function to convert the Boolean variable launch to text. If you want to convert to numeric values or different text, a humble if statement works best.

Listing 10.5 Converting a Boolean to a string: launch.go

```
launch := false

launchText := fmt.Sprintf("%v", launch)
fmt.Println("Ready for launch:", launchText)          Prints Ready for
                                                      launch: false
var yesNo string
if launch {
    yesNo = "yes"
} else {
    yesNo = "no"
}                                                     Prints Ready for
                                                      launch: no
fmt.Println("Ready for launch:", yesNo)
```

The inverse conversion requires less code because you can assign the result of a condition directly to a variable, as in the following listing.

Listing 10.6 Converting a string to a Boolean: tobool.go

```
yesNo := "no"

launch := (yesNo == "yes")                            Prints Ready for
fmt.Println("Ready for launch:", launch)              launch: false
```

The Go compiler will report an error if you attempt to convert a Boolean with string(false), int(false), or similar, and likewise for bool(1) or bool("yes").

> **NOTE** In programming languages without a dedicated bool type, the values 1 and 0 often stand in for true and false, respectively. Booleans in Go don't have a numeric equivalent.

> **Quick check 10.5**　How would you convert a Boolean to an integer, with 1 for true and 0 for false?

Summary

- Conversion between types is explicit to avoid ambiguity.
- The `strconv` package provides functions for converting strings to and from other types.

Let's see if you got this...

Experiment: input.go

Write a program that converts strings to Booleans:

- The strings "true", "yes", or "1" are `true`.
- The strings "false", "no", or "0" are `false`.
- Display an error message for any other values.

> **TIP**　The `switch` statement accepts multiple values per `case`, as covered in lesson 3.

QC 10.5 answer　With a humble `if` statement:

```
launch := true

var oneZero int
if launch {
    oneZero = 1
} else {
    oneZero = 0
}
fmt.Println("Ready for launch:", oneZero)
```

Prints Ready for launch: 1

CAPSTONE: THE VIGENÈRE CIPHER

The Vigenère cipher (see en.wikipedia.org/wiki/Vigenere_cipher) is a 16th century variant of the Caesar cipher. For this challenge, you will write a program to decipher text using a keyword.

Before describing the Vigenère cipher, allow us to reframe the Caesar cipher, which you've already worked with. With the Caesar cipher, a plain text message is ciphered by shifting each letter ahead by three. The direction is reversed to decipher the resulting message.

Assign each English letter a numeric value, where A = 0, B = 1, all the way to Z = 25. With this in mind, a shift by 3 can be represented by the letter D (D = 3).

To decipher the text in table 11.1, start with the letter L and shift it by D. Because L = 11 and D = 3, the result of 11–3 is 8, or the letter I. Should you need to decipher the letter A, it should wrap around to become X, as you saw in lesson 9.

Table 11.1 Caesar cipher

L	F	D	P	H	L	V	D	Z	L	F	R	Q	T	X	H	U	H	G
D	D	D	D	D	D	D	D	D	D	D	D	D	D	D	D	D	D	D

The Caesar cipher and ROT13 are susceptible to what's called *frequency analysis*. Letters that occur frequently in the English language, such as E, will occur frequently in the ciphered text as well. By looking for patterns in the ciphered text, the code can be cracked.

To thwart would-be code crackers, the Vigenère cipher shifts each letter based on a repeating keyword, rather than a constant like 3 or 13. The keyword repeats until the end of the message, as shown for the keyword GOLANG in table 11.2.

Now that you know what the Vigenère cipher is, you may notice that Vigenère with the keyword D is equivalent to the Caesar cipher. Likewise, ROT13 has a keyword of N (N = 13). Longer keywords are needed to be of any benefit.

Table 11.2 Vigenère cipher

C	S	O	I	T	E	U	I	W	U	I	Z	N	S	R	O	C	N	K	F	D
G	O	L	A	N	G	G	O	L	A	N	G	G	O	L	A	N	G	G	O	L

Experiment: decipher.go

Write a program to decipher the ciphered text shown in table 11.2. To keep it simple, all characters are uppercase English letters for both the text and keyword:

```
cipherText := "CSOITEUIWUIZNSROCNKFD"
keyword := "GOLANG"
```

- The strings.Repeat function may come in handy. Give it a try, but also complete this exercise without importing any packages other than fmt to print the deciphered message.
- Try this exercise using range in a loop and again without it. Remember that the range keyword splits a string into runes, whereas an index like keyword[0] results in a byte.

  TIP You can only perform operations on values of the same type, but you can convert one type to the other (string, byte, rune).

- To wrap around at the edges of the alphabet, the Caesar cipher exercise made use of a comparison. Solve this exercise without any if statements by using modulus (%).

> **TIP**   If you recall, modulus gives the remainder of dividing two numbers. For example, 27 % 26 is 1, keeping numbers within the 0–25 range. Be careful with negative numbers, though, as -3 % 26 is still -3.

After you complete the exercise, take a look at our solution in the appendix. How do they compare? Use the Go Playground's Share button and post a link to your solution in the Get Programming with Go forum.

Ciphering text with Vigenère isn't any more difficult than deciphering text. Just add letters of the keyword to letters of a plain text message instead of subtracting.

Experiment: cipher.go

To send ciphered messages, write a program that ciphers plain text using a keyword:

```
plainText := "your message goes here"
keyword := "GOLANG"
```

Bonus: rather than write your plain text message in uppercase letters with no spaces, use the `strings.Replace` and `strings.ToUpper` functions to remove spaces and uppercase the string before you cipher it.

Once you've ciphered a plain text message, check your work by deciphering the ciphered text with the same keyword.

Use the keyword `"GOLANG"` to cipher a message and post it to the forums for Get Programming with Go at forums.manning.com/forums/get-programming-with-go.

> **NOTE**   Disclaimer: Vigenère cipher is all in good fun, but don't use it for important secrets. There are more secure ways to send messages in the 21st century.

Building blocks

Programming is the breaking of one big impossible task into several very small possible tasks.

—Jazzwant

Functions are the building blocks of computer programs. You can call on functions like Printf to format and display values. The pixels that end up on your screen are delivered by layers of functions in Go and your operating system.

You can write functions too. Functions help you organize your code, reuse functionality, and think about a problem in smaller pieces.

Not only that, by learning how to declare functions and methods in Go, you'll be equipped to explore the rich functionality provided by the standard library and documented at golang.org/pkg.

FUNCTIONS

After reading lesson 12, you'll be able to

- Identify the parts of a function declaration
- Write reusable functions to build up larger programs

This lesson begins by examining the standard library documentation for functions that were used in earlier lessons.

Once you're familiar with the syntax for declaring functions, you'll write functions for a weather station program. The Rover Environmental Monitoring Station (REMS) gathers weather data on the surface of Mars. You'll write functions that could conceivably be part of a REMS program, such as converting temperatures.

> **Consider this**   Make a sandwich. It sounds simple, but many steps are involved. Wash the lettuce, slice a tomato, and so on. Maybe you go so far as to harvest the grain, grind it into flour, and bake the bread, or maybe those functions are provided by a farmer and a baker.
>
> Break down the process with a function for each step. Then later, if you need tomato slices for a pizza, that function can be reused.
>
> What is something else from your daily life that you can break down into functions?

12.1 Function declarations

The Go package documentation at golang.org/pkg lists the functions that are declared in every package of the standard library. There are a lot of handy functions—more than this book can possibly cover.

To use these functions in your own project, you'll often need to read the function declaration in the documentation to know how to call the function. After scrutinizing the declarations for `Intn`, `Unix`, `Atoi`, `Contains`, and `Println`, you'll be able to apply your newfound knowledge when exploring other functions on your own, and when writing functions yourself.

You used the `Intn` function in lesson 2 to generate pseudorandom numbers. Navigate to golang.org/pkg and the `math/rand` package to find the `Intn` function. You can also use the search box to find `Intn`.

The declaration for `Intn` from the `rand` package looks like this:

```
func Intn(n int) int
```

As a refresher, here's an example of using the `Intn` function:

```
num := rand.Intn(10)
```

In figure 12.1 the parts of the declaration are identified, as is the syntax to call the `Intn` function. The `func` keyword lets Go know this is a function declaration. Then comes the function name, `Intn`, which begins with a capital letter.

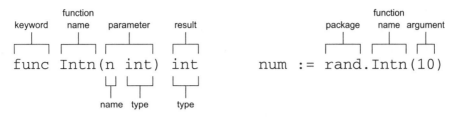

Figure 12.1 The Intn function declaration and calling the Intn function

In Go, the functions, variables, and other identifiers that begin with an uppercase letter are *exported* and become available to other packages. The rand package contains functions that begin with a lowercase letter too, but they're not accessible from the main package.

The Intn function accepts a single *parameter*, which is surrounded by parentheses. The parameter is a variable name followed by a type, consistent with variable declarations:

```
var n int
```

When calling the Intn function, the integer 10 is passed as a single *argument*, also surrounded by parentheses. The argument corresponds to the single parameter Intn expects. If no argument is passed, or if the argument isn't of type int, the Go compiler reports an error.

> **TIP** Parameter and argument are terms from mathematics, with a subtle distinction. A function accepts parameters and is invoked with arguments, though at times people may use the terms interchangeably.

The Intn function returns a single result, a pseudorandom integer of type int. The result is passed back to the caller, where it's used to initialize the newly declared variable num.

The Intn function only accepts a single parameter, but functions can accept multiple parameters with a comma-separated list. If you recall from lesson 7, the Unix function from the time package accepts two int64 parameters, corresponding to the number of seconds and the number of nanoseconds since January 1, 1970. The declaration from the documentation looks like this:

```
func Unix(sec int64, nsec int64) Time
```

Here's the example of calling the Unix function with two arguments, corresponding to the sec and nsec parameters respectively:

```
future := time.Unix(12622780800, 0)
```

The result returned by Unix is of the type Time. Thanks to type inference, the code that calls Unix doesn't need to specify the result type, which would be more verbose.

> **NOTE**   Lesson 13 demonstrates how to declare new types like time.Time and big.Int.

The time package declares and exports the Time type, which begins with an uppercase letter, just like the Unix function. By using capitalization to indicate what's exported, it's apparent that the Time type is accessible from other packages.

The Unix function accepts two parameters of the same type, documented as follows:

```
func Unix(sec int64, nsec int64) Time
```

But when parameters are listed in a function declaration, you only need to specify the type when it changes, so it could have been written like this:

```
func Unix(sec, nsec int64) Time
```

This shortcut is optional, but it's used elsewhere, such as the Contains function in the strings package, which accepts two parameters of type string:

```
func Contains(s, substr string) bool
```

> **TIP**   The documentation at golang.org/pkg sometimes has examples that can be expanded, and you'll find additional examples at gobyexample.com. If you're forging ahead on your own projects while learning Go, these examples can be invaluable.

Many programming languages have functions that accept multiple parameters, but Go functions can also return multiple results. First shown in lesson 10, the Atoi function converts a string to a number and returns two results, which are assigned to countdown and err here:

```
countdown, err := strconv.Atoi("10")
```

The documentation for the strconv package declares Atoi like this:

```
func Atoi(s string) (i int, err error)
```

Two results are specified between parentheses, much like the parameter list, with a name followed by a type for each result. In function declarations you can also list the result types without names:

```
func Atoi(s string) (int, error)
```

> **NOTE**   The error type is a built-in type for errors, which lesson 28 covers in depth.

A function you've been using since the beginning of this book is Println. It's a rather unique function in that it can accept one parameter, or two, or more. It can also accept parameters of different types, including integers and strings:

```
fmt.Println("Hello, playground")
fmt.Println(186, "seconds")
```

The function declaration in the documentation may look a bit strange, because it uses features we haven't yet covered:

```
func Println(a ...interface{}) (n int, err error)
```

The Println function accepts a single parameter, a, but you've already seen that passing it multiple arguments is possible. More specifically, you can pass the Println function a variable number of arguments, a feature indicated by the ellipsis (..). There's a special term for this: Println is said to be a *variadic* function. The parameter a is a collection of the arguments passed to the function. We'll return to variadic functions in lesson 18.

The type of the a parameter is interface{}, known as the *empty interface* type. We won't be covering interfaces until lesson 24, but now you know that this special type is what enables Println to accept an int, float64, string, time.Time, or any other type without the Go compiler reporting an error.

The combination of variadic functions and the empty interface, written together as ...interface{}, means you can pass Println any number of arguments of any type. It does a good job of displaying whatever you throw at it.

> **NOTE** So far we've been ignoring the two results that Println returns, even though ignoring errors is considered a bad practice. Good error-handling practices are covered in lesson 28.

Quick check 12.1
1. Do you call a function with arguments or parameters?
2. Does a function accept arguments or parameters?
3. How does a function with an uppercase first letter (Contains) differ from one with a lowercase first letter (contains)?
4. What does the ellipsis (...) in a function declaration indicate?

QC 12.1 answer
1. Arguments
2. Parameters
3. Lowercase indicates functions that can only be used by the package they are declared in, whereas capitalized functions are exported for use anywhere.
4. The function is variadic. You can pass it a variable number of arguments.

12.2 Writing a function

So far, the code in this book has been placed in the main function. When approaching larger applications, such as an environmental monitoring program, splitting the problem into smaller pieces becomes valuable. Organizing your code into functions makes it easier to understand, reuse, and maintain.

Temperature data from sensor readouts should be reported in units that are meaningful to Earthlings. The sensors provide data on the Kelvin scale, where 0° K is absolute zero, the lowest temperature possible. A function in the next listing converts temperatures to Celsius. Once the conversion function is written, it can be reused whenever that temperature conversion is needed.

Listing 12.1 Kelvin to Celsius: kelvin.go

```
package main

import "fmt"
                                          Declares a function that
                                          accepts one parameter
                                          and returns one result
// kelvinToCelsius converts °K to °C
func kelvinToCelsius(k float64) float64 {
    k -= 273.15
    return k                        Calls the function
                                    passing kelvin as
}                                   the first argument
func main() {
    kelvin := 294.0                        Prints 294° K is
                                           20.850000000000023° C
    celsius := kelvinToCelsius(kelvin)
    fmt.Print(kelvin, "° K is ", celsius, "° C")
}
```

The kelvinToCelsius function in listing 12.1 accepts one parameter with the name k and the type float64. Following Go conventions, the comment for kelvinToCelsius begins with the function's name, followed by what it does.

This function returns one value of type float64. The result of the calculation is delivered back to the caller with the return keyword, which is then used to initialize a new celsius variable in the main function.

Notice that functions within the same package are invoked without specifying a package name.

Isolation can be a good thing

The kelvinToCelsius function in listing 12.1 is isolated from other functions. Its only input is the parameter it accepts, and its only output is the result it returns. It makes no modifications to external state. Such functions are *side-effect-free* and are the the easiest to understand, test, and reuse.

The kelvinToCelsius function does modify the variable k, but k and kelvin are completely independent variables, so assigning a new value to k inside the function has no impact on the kelvin variable in main. This behavior is called *pass by value*, because the k parameter is initialized with the value of the kelvin argument. Pass by value facilitates the boundary between functions, helping to isolate one function from another.

We've given the variables different names, but pass by value applies even if arguments and parameters have the same names.

Additionally, the variable named k in kelvinToCelsius is completely independent from any variable named k in other functions, thanks to variable scope. Scope is covered in lesson 4, but to reiterate, the parameters in a function declaration and the variables declared within a function body have *function scope*. Variables declared in different functions are completely independent, even if they have the same name.

Quick check 12.2 What are some advantages of splitting code into functions?

 Summary

- Functions are declared with a name, a list of parameters, and a list of results.
- Capitalized function names and types are made available to other packages.
- Each parameter or result is a name followed by a type, though types may be elided when multiple named parameters or results have the same type. Results can also be listed as types without names.
- Function calls are prefixed with the name of the package where the function is declared, unless the function is declared in the same package it's called from.
- Functions are called with arguments that correspond to the parameters they accept. Results are returned to the caller with the return keyword.

QC 12.2 answer Functions are reusable, they provide isolation for variables through function scope, and they provide a name for the action they perform which makes code easier to follow and understand.

Let's see if you got this...

Experiment: functions.go

Use the Go Playground at play.golang.org to type in listing 12.1 and declare additional temperature conversion functions:

- Reuse the `kelvinToCelsius` function to convert 233° K to Celsius.
- Write and use a `celsiusToFahrenheit` temperature conversion function. Hint: the formula for converting to Fahrenheit is: (c * 9.0 / 5.0) + 32.0.
- Write a `kelvinToFahrenheit` function and verify that it converts 0° K to approximately –459.67° F.

Did you use `kelvinToCelsius` and `celsiusToFahrenheit` in your new function or write an independent function with a new formula? Both approaches are perfectly valid.

METHODS

After reading lesson 13, you'll be able to

- Declare new types
- Rewrite functions as methods

Methods are like functions that enhance types with additional behavior. Before you can declare a method, you need to declare a new type. This lesson takes the `kelvinToCelsius` function from lesson 12 and transforms it into a type with methods.

At first it may look like methods are just a different syntax for doing what functions already do, and you would be right. Methods provide another way to organize code, an arguably nicer way for the examples in this lesson. Later lessons, those in unit 5 in particular, demonstrate how methods can be combined with other language features to bring new capabilities.

> **Consider this**   When you type numbers on a calculator versus a typewriter, the expected behavior is quite different. Go has built-in functionality to operate on numbers and text (+) in unique ways, as demonstrated in lesson 10.
>
> What if you want to represent a new type of thing and bundle behaviors with it? A float64 is too generic to adequately represent a thermometer, and a dog's bark() is entirely different from the bark of a tree. Functions have a place, but types and methods provide another useful way to organize code and represent the world around you.
>
> Before you start on this lesson, look around and consider the types around you and the behaviors they each have.

13.1 Declaring new types

Go declares a number of types, many of which are covered in unit 2. Sometimes those types don't adequately describe the kind of values you want to hold.

A temperature isn't a float64, though that may be its underlying representation. Temperature is a measurement in Celsius, Fahrenheit, or Kelvin. Declaring new types not only makes code clearer, it can help prevent errors.

The type keyword declares a new type with a name and an underlying type, as shown in the following listing.

Listing 13.1 A Celsius type: celsius.go

```
type celsius float64                    The underlying type
                                        is float64.
var temperature celsius = 20

fmt.Println(temperature)         Prints 20
```

The numeric literal 20, like all numeric literals, is an *untyped* constant. It can be assigned to a variable of type int, float64, or any other numeric type. The celsius type is a new numeric type with the same behavior and representation as a float64, so the assignment in the previous listing works.

You can also add values to temperature and generally use it as though it were a float64, as shown in the next listing.

Listing 13.2 A celsius type behaves like a `float64`: celsius-addition.go

```
type celsius float64

const degrees = 20
var temperature celsius = degrees

temperature += 10
```

The `celsius` type is a unique type, not a type alias like those mentioned in lesson 9. If you try to use it with a `float64`, you'll get a mismatched types error:

```
var warmUp float64 = 10          Invalid operation:
temperature += warmUp            mismatched types
```

To add `warmUp`, it must first be converted to the `celsius` type. This version works:

```
var warmUp float64 = 10
temperature += celsius(warmUp)
```

Being able to define your own types can be incredibly useful for improving both readability and reliability. The following listing demonstrates that `celsius` and `fahrenheit` types can't accidentally be compared or combined.

Listing 13.3 Types can't be mixed

```
type celsius float64
type fahrenheit float64

var c celsius = 20
var f fahrenheit = 20

if c == f {              Invalid operation:
}                        mismatched types
                         celsius and fahrenheit
c += f
```

> **Quick check 13.1** What are some advantages of declaring new types, such as `celsius` and `fahrenheit`?

QC 13.1 answer The new type can better describe the value it contains, such as `celsius` instead of `float64`. Having unique types helps avoid silly mistakes, like adding a Fahrenheit value to a Celsius value.

13.2 Bring your own types

The previous section declared new celsius and fahrenheit types, bringing the domain of temperatures to the code, while de-emphasizing the underlying storage representation. Whether a temperature is represented as a float64 or float32 says little about the value a variable contains, whereas types like celsius, fahrenheit, and kelvin convey their purpose.

Once you declare a type, you can use it everywhere you would use a predeclared Go type (int, float64, string, and so on), including function parameters and results, as shown in the following listing.

Listing 13.4 Functions with custom types: temperature-types.go

```
package main

import "fmt"

type celsius float64
type kelvin float64

// kelvinToCelsius converts °K to °C
func kelvinToCelsius(k kelvin) celsius {
    return celsius(k - 273.15)
}
func main() {
    var k kelvin = 294.0
    c := kelvinToCelsius(k)
    fmt.Print(k, "° K is ", c, "° C")
}
```

A type conversion is necessary.

The argument must be of type kelvin.

Prints 294° K is 20.850000000000023° C

The kelvinToCelsius function will only accept an argument of the kelvin type, which can prevent silly mistakes. It won't accept an argument of the wrong type, such as fahrenheit, kilometers, or even float64. Go is a pragmatic language, so it's still possible to pass a literal value or untyped constant. Rather than write kelvinToCelsius(kelvin(294)), you can write kelvinToCelsius(294).

The result returned from kelvinToCelsius is of type celsius, not kelvin, so the type must be converted to celsius before it can be returned.

13.3 Adding behavior to types with methods

Though this be madness, yet there is method in 't.

—Shakespeare, *Hamlet*

For decades classical object-oriented languages have taught that methods belong with classes. Go is different. There are no classes or even objects, really, yet Go has methods. That may seem odd, maybe even a bit crazy, but methods in Go are actually more flexible than in languages of the past.

Functions like `kelvinToCelsius`, `celsiusToFahrenheit`, `fahrenheitToCelsius`, and `celsiusToKelvin` get the job done, but we can do better. Declaring a few methods in their place will make temperature-conversion code nice and concise.

QC 13.2 answer

```go
func celsiusToKelvin(c celsius) kelvin {
    return kelvin(c + 273.15)
}

func main() {
    var c celsius = 127.0
    k := celsiusToKelvin(c)
    fmt.Print(c, "° C is ", k, "° K")
}
```

Prints 127° C is 400.15° K

You can associate methods with any type declared in the same package, but not with predeclared types (int, float64, and so forth). You've already seen how to declare a type:

```
type kelvin float64
```

The kelvin type has the same behavior as its underlying type, a float64. You can add, multiply, and perform other operations on kelvin values, just like floating-point numbers. Declaring a method to convert kelvin to celsius is as easy as declaring a function. They both begin with the func keyword, and the function body is identical to the method body:

```
func kelvinToCelsius(k kelvin) celsius {          kelvinToCelsius
    return celsius(k - 273.15)                     function
}
func (k kelvin) celsius() celsius {          celsius method on
    return celsius(k - 273.15)                the kelvin type
}
```

The celsius method doesn't accept any parameters, but it has something like a parameter before the name. It's called a *receiver*, as shown in figure 13.1. Methods and functions can both accept multiple parameters, but methods must have exactly one receiver. Inside the celsius method body, the receiver acts like any other parameter.

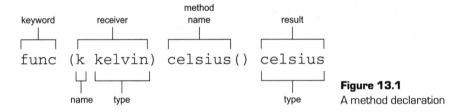

Figure 13.1
A method declaration

The syntax to use a method is different than calling a function:

```
var k kelvin = 294.0
var c celsius                          Calls the kelvinToCelsius
                                       function
c = kelvinToCelsius(k)
c = k.celsius()          Calls the celsius method
```

Methods are called with *dot notation*, which looks like calling a function in another package. But in this case a variable of the correct type is followed by a dot and the method name.

Now that temperature conversion is a method on the `kelvin` type, a name like `kelvinToCelsius` is superfluous. A package can only have a single function with a given name, and it can't be the same name as a type, so a `celsius` function that returns a `celsius` type isn't possible. But each temperature type can provide a `celsius` method, so for example, the `fahrenheit` type can be enhanced as follows:

```
type fahrenheit float64

// celsius converts °F to °C
func (f fahrenheit) celsius() celsius {
    return celsius((f - 32.0) * 5.0 / 9.0)
}
```

This creates a nice symmetry, where every type of temperature can have a `celsius` method to convert to Celsius.

> **Quick check 13.3** Identify the receiver in this method declaration: `func (f fahrenheit) celsius() celsius`

Summary

- Declaring your own types can help with readability and reliability.
- Methods are like functions associated to a type by way of a receiver specified before the method name. Methods can accept multiple parameters and return multiple results, just like functions, but they must always have exactly one receiver. Within the method body, the receiver behaves just like any other parameter.
- The calling syntax for methods uses dot notation, with a variable of the appropriate type followed by a dot, the method name, and any arguments.

Let's see if you got this...

Experiment: methods.go

Write a program with `celsius`, `fahrenheit`, and `kelvin` types and methods to convert from any temperature type to any other temperature type.

QC 13.3 answer The receiver is f of type `fahrenheit`.

FIRST-CLASS FUNCTIONS

After reading lesson 14, you'll be able to

- Assign functions to variables
- Pass functions to functions
- Write functions that create functions

In Go you can assign functions to variables, pass functions to functions, and even write functions that return functions. Functions are *first-class*—they work in all the places that integers, strings, and other types work.

This lesson explores some potential uses of first-class functions as part of a theoretical Rover Environmental Monitoring Station (REMS) program that reads from (fake) temperature sensors.

> **Consider this**   A recipe for tacos calls for salsa. You can either turn to page 93 of the cookbook to make homemade salsa or open a jar of salsa from the store.
>
> First-class functions are like tacos that call for salsa. As code, the makeTacos function needs to call a function for the salsa, whether that be makeSalsa or openSalsa. The salsa functions could be used independently as well, but the tacos won't be complete without salsa.
>
> Other than recipes and temperature sensors, what's another example of a function that can be customized with a function?

14.1 Assigning functions to variables

The weather station sensors provide an air temperature reading from 150–300° K. You have functions to convert Kelvin to other temperature units once you have the data, but unless you have a sensor attached to your computer (or Raspberry Pi), retrieving the data is a bit problematic.

For now you can use a fake sensor that returns a pseudorandom number, but then you need a way to use realSensor or fakeSensor interchangeably. The following listing does just that. By designing the program this way, different real sensors could also be plugged in, for example, to monitor both ground and air temperature.

Listing 14.1 Interchangeable sensor functions: sensor.go

```go
package main

import (
    "fmt"
    "math/rand"
)

type kelvin float64

func fakeSensor() kelvin {
    return kelvin(rand.Intn(151) + 150)
}

func realSensor() kelvin {
    return 0
}

func main() {
    sensor := fakeSensor
    fmt.Println(sensor())

    sensor = realSensor
    fmt.Println(sensor())
}
```

To-do: implement a real sensor ← (pointing to `return 0`)

Assigns a function to a variable ← (pointing to `sensor := fakeSensor`)

In the previous listing, the sensor variable is assigned to the fakeSensor function itself, not the result of calling the function. Function and method calls always have parentheses, such as fakeSensor(), which isn't the case here.

Now calling sensor() will effectively call either realSensor or fakeSensor, depending on which function sensor is assigned to.

The sensor variable is of type function, where the function accepts no parameters and returns a kelvin result. When not relying on type inference, the sensor variable would be declared like this:

```
var sensor func() kelvin
```

> **NOTE**   You can reassign sensor to realSensor in listing 14.1 because it matches the *function signature* of fakeSensor. Both functions have the same number and type of parameters and return values.

Quick check 14.1

1   How can you distinguish between assigning a function to a variable versus assigning the result of calling the function?
2   If there existed a groundSensor function that returned a celsius temperature, could it be assigned to the sensor in listing 14.1?

 ## 14.2   Passing functions to other functions

Variables can refer to functions, and variables can be passed to functions, which means Go allows you to pass functions to other functions.

To log temperature data every second, listing 14.2 declares a new measureTemperature function that accepts a sensor function as a parameter. It calls the sensor function periodically, whether it's a fakeSensor or a realSensor.

The ability to pass functions around gives you a powerful way to split up your code. If not for first-class functions, you would likely end up with measureRealTemperature and measureFakeTemperature functions containing nearly identical code.

QC 14.1 answer

1   Function and method calls always have parentheses (for example, fn()) whereas the function itself can be assigned by specifying a function name without parentheses.
2   No. The parameters and return values must be of the same type to reassign the sensor variable. The Go compiler will report an error: cannot use groundSensor in assignment.

Listing 14.2 A function as a parameter: function-parameter.go

```go
package main

import (
    "fmt"
    "math/rand"
    "time"
)

type kelvin float64

func measureTemperature(samples int, sensor func() kelvin) {
    for i := 0; i < samples; i++ {
        k := sensor()
        fmt.Printf("%v° K\n", k)
        time.Sleep(time.Second)
    }
}

func fakeSensor() kelvin {
    return kelvin(rand.Intn(151) + 150)
}

func main() {
    measureTemperature(3, fakeSensor)
}
```

measureTemperature accepts a function as the second parameter.

Passes the name of a function to a function

The measureTemperature function accepts two parameters, with the second parameter being of type func() kelvin. This declaration looks like a variable declaration of the same type:

```go
var sensor func() kelvin
```

The main function is able to pass the name of a function to measureTemperature.

Quick check 14.2   How is the ability to pass functions to other functions beneficial?

QC 14.2 answer   First-class functions provide another way to divide and reuse code.

14.3 Declaring function types

It's possible to declare a new type for a function to condense and clarify the code that refers to it. You used the kelvin type to convey a unit of temperature rather than the underlying representation. The same can be done for functions that are being passed around:

```
type sensor func() kelvin
```

Rather than a function that accepts no parameters and returns a kelvin value, the code is about sensor functions. This type can be used to condense other code, so the declaration

```
func measureTemperature(samples int, s func() kelvin)
```

can now be written like this:

```
func measureTemperature(samples int, s sensor)
```

In this example, it may not seem like an improvement, as you now need to know what sensor is when looking at this line of code. But if sensor were used in several places, or if the function type had multiple parameters, using a type would significantly reduce the clutter.

> **Quick check 14.3**   Rewrite the following function signature to use a function type:
> ```
> func drawTable(rows int, getRow func(row int) (string, string))
> ```

 ## 14.4 Closures and anonymous functions

An *anonymous function*, also called a *function literal* in Go, is a function without a name. Unlike regular functions, function literals are *closures* because they keep references to variables in the surrounding scope.

QC 14.3 answer
```
type getRowFn func(row int) (string, string)
func drawTable(rows int, getRow getRowFn)
```

You can assign an anonymous function to a variable and then use that variable like any other function, as shown in the following listing.

Listing 14.3 Anonymous function: masquerade.go

```go
package main

import "fmt"

var f = func() {           // Assigns an anonymous
    fmt.Println("Dress up for the masquerade.")   // function to a variable
}

func main() {              // Prints Dress up for
    f()                    // the masquerade.
}
```

The variable you declare can be in the scope of the package or within a function, as shown in the next listing.

Listing 14.4 Anonymous function: funcvar.go

```go
package main

import "fmt"

func main() {
    f := func(message string) {     // Assigns an anonymous
        fmt.Println(message)        // function to a variable
```

```
    }
    f("Go to the party.")          ⟵  Prints Go to the party.
}
```

You can even declare and invoke an anonymous function in one step, as shown in the following listing.

Listing 14.5 Anonymous function: anonymous.go

```
package main

import "fmt"
                            Declares an
func main() {               anonymous
    func() {           ⟵   function
        fmt.Println("Functions anonymous")
    }()              ⟵
}                           Invokes the function
```

Anonymous functions can come in handy whenever you need to create a function on the fly. One such circumstance is when returning a function from another function. Although it's possible for a function to return an existing named function, declaring and returning a new anonymous function is much more useful.

In listing 14.6 the calibrate function adjusts for errors in air temperature readings. Using first-class functions, calibrate accepts a fake or real sensor as a parameter and returns a replacement function. Whenever the new sensor function is called, the original function is invoked, and the reading is adjusted by an offset.

Listing 14.6 Sensor calibration: calibrate.go

```
package main

import "fmt"

type kelvin float64

// sensor function type
type sensor func() kelvin

func realSensor() kelvin {
    return 0       ⟵   To-do: implement
}                        a real sensor
func calibrate(s sensor, offset kelvin) sensor {
```

```
    return func() kelvin {              Declares and returns
        return s() + offset             an anonymous
    }                                   function
}
func main() {
    sensor := calibrate(realSensor, 5)
    fmt.Println(sensor())               Prints 5
}
```

The anonymous function in the preceding listing makes use of closures. It references the s and offset variables that the calibrate function accepts as parameters. Even after the calibrate function returns, the variables captured by the closure survive, so calls to sensor still have access to those variables. The anonymous function *encloses* the variables in scope, which explains the term *closure*.

Because a closure keeps a *reference* to surrounding variables rather than a copy of their values, changes to those variables are reflected in calls to the anonymous function:

```
var k kelvin = 294.0
sensor := func() kelvin {
    return k
}
fmt.Println(sensor())              Prints 294

k++
fmt.Println(sensor())              Prints 295
```

Keep this in mind, particularly when using closures inside for loops.

Quick check 14.4
1   What's another name for an anonymous function in Go?
2   What do closures provide that regular functions don't?

QC 14.4 answer
1   An anonymous function is also called a function literal in Go.
2   Closures keep references to variables in the surrounding scope.

 **Summary**

- When functions are treated as first-class, they open up new possibilities for splitting up and reusing code.
- To create functions on the fly, use anonymous functions with closures.

Let's see if you got this...

Experiment: calibrate.go

Type listing 14.6 into the Go Playground to see it in action:

- Rather than passing 5 as an argument to calibrate, declare and pass a variable. Modify the variable and you'll notice that calls to sensor() still result in 5. That's because the offset parameter is a copy of the argument (pass by value).
- Use calibrate with the fakeSensor function from listing 14.2 to create a new sensor function. Call the new sensor function multiple times and notice that the original fakeSensor is still being called each time, resulting in random values.

CAPSTONE: TEMPERATURE TABLES

Write a program that displays temperature conversion tables. The tables should use equals signs (=) and pipes (|) to draw lines, with a header section:

```
===============================
| °C      | °F      |
===============================
| -40.0   | -40.0   |
| ...     | ...     |
===============================
```

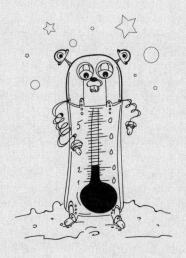

The program should draw two tables. The first table has two columns, with °C in the first column and °F in the second column. Loop from –40° C through 100° C in steps of 5° using the temperature conversion methods from lesson 13 to fill in both columns.

After completing one table, implement a second table with the columns reversed, converting from °F to °C.

Drawing lines and padding values is code you can reuse for any data that needs to be displayed in a two-column table. Use functions to separate the table drawing code from the code that calculates the temperatures for each row.

Implement a drawTable function that takes a first-class function as a parameter and calls it to get data for each row drawn. Passing a different function to drawTable should result in different data being displayed.

Collections

Collections are just groups of things. You probably have a music collection. Each album has a collection of songs, and each song has a collection of musical notes. If you want to build a music player, you'll be happy to know that programming languages have collections too.

In Go, you can use the primitive types covered in unit 2 to compose more interesting *composite types*. These composite types allow you to group values together, providing new ways to collect and access data.

ARRAYED IN SPLENDOR

After reading lesson 16, you'll be able to

- Declare and initialize arrays
- Assign and access the elements of an array
- Iterate through arrays

Arrays are ordered collections of elements with a fixed length. This lesson uses arrays to store the names of planets and dwarf planets in our solar system, but you can collect anything you like.

> **Consider this** Do you have a collection or did you in the past? Maybe stamps, coins, stickers, books, shoes, trophies, movies, or something else?
>
> Arrays are for collecting many of the same type of thing. What collections could you represent with an array?

16.1 Declaring arrays and accessing their elements

The following planets array contains exactly eight elements:

```
var planets [8]string
```

Every element of an array has the same type. In this case, planets is an array of strings.

Individual elements of an array can be accessed by using square brackets [] with an index that begins at 0, as illustrated in figure 16.1 and shown in listing 16.1.

Listing 16.1 Array of planets: array.go

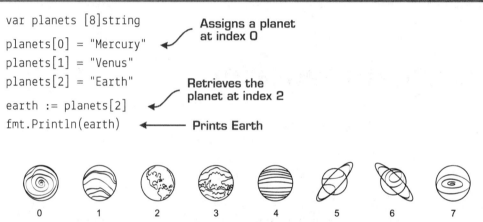

```
var planets [8]string
planets[0] = "Mercury"        Assigns a planet
planets[1] = "Venus"          at index 0
planets[2] = "Earth"
                              Retrieves the
earth := planets[2]           planet at index 2
fmt.Println(earth)        ◄────── Prints Earth
```

```
0      1      2      3      4      5      6      7
```

Figure 16.1   Planets with indices 0 through 7

Even though only three planets have been assigned, the planets array has eight elements. The length of an array can be determined with the built-in len function. The other elements contain the zero value for their type, an empty string:

```
fmt.Println(len(planets))      ◄────── Prints 8
fmt.Println(planets[3] == "")  ◄────── Prints true
```

> **NOTE** Go has a handful of built-in functions that don't require an import statement. The len function can determine the length for a variety of types. In this case it returns the size of the array.

Quick check 16.1

1 How do you access the first element of the planets array?
2 What is the default value for elements of a new array of integers?

 ## 16.2 Don't go out of bounds

An eight-element array has indices from 0 through 7. The Go compiler will report an error when it detects access to an element outside of this range:

```
var planets [8]string

planets[8] = "Pluto"
pluto := planets[8]
```

Invalid array index 8 (out of bounds for 8-element array)

If the Go compiler is unable to detect the error, your program may *panic* while it's running:

```
var planets [8]string

i := 8
planets[i] = "Pluto"
pluto := planets[i]
```

Panic: runtime error: index out of range

A panic will crash your program, which is still better than modifying memory that doesn't belong to the planets array, leading to unspecified behavior (as is the case with the C programming language).

Quick check 16.2 Will planets[11] cause an error at compile-time or a panic at runtime?

QC 16.1 answer

1 planets[0]
2 Elements of an array are initially the zero value for the array's type, which means 0 for integer arrays.

QC 16.2 answer The Go compiler will detect an invalid array index.

16.3   Initialize arrays with composite literals

A *composite literal* is a concise syntax to initialize any composite type with the values you want. Rather than declare an array and assign elements one by one, Go's composite literal syntax will declare and initialize an array in a single step, as shown in the following listing.

Listing 16.2 Array of dwarf planets: dwarfs.go

```
dwarfs := [5]string{"Ceres", "Pluto", "Haumea", "Makemake", "Eris"}
```

The curly braces {} contain five comma-separated strings to populate elements of the new array.

With larger arrays, breaking the composite literal across multiple lines can be more readable. And as a convenience, you can ask the Go compiler to count the number of elements in the composite literal by specifying the ellipsis … instead of a number. The planets array in the following listing still has a fixed length.

Listing 16.3 A full array of planets: composite.go

```
planets := [...]string{
    "Mercury",
    "Venus",
    "Earth",
    "Mars",
    "Jupiter",
    "Saturn",
    "Uranus",
    "Neptune",
}
```

The Go compiler counts the elements.

The trailing comma is required.

Quick check 16.3   How many planets are there in listing 16.3? Use the len built-in function to find out.

QC 16.3 answer   The planets array has eight elements (8).

16.4 Iterating through arrays

Iterating through each element of an array is similar to iterating over each character of a string in lesson 9, as shown in the following listing.

Listing 16.4 Looping through an array: array-loop.go

```go
dwarfs := [5]string{"Ceres", "Pluto", "Haumea", "Makemake", "Eris"}
for i := 0; i < len(dwarfs); i++ {
    dwarf := dwarfs[i]
    fmt.Println(i, dwarf)
}
```

The range keyword provides an index and value for each element of an array with less code and less chance for mistakes, as shown in the next listing.

Listing 16.5 Iterating through an array with range: array-range.go

```go
dwarfs := [5]string{"Ceres", "Pluto", "Haumea", "Makemake", "Eris"}
for i, dwarf := range dwarfs {
    fmt.Println(i, dwarf)
}
```

Both listings 16.4 and 16.5 produce the same output:

```
0 Ceres
1 Pluto
2 Haumea
3 Makemake
4 Eris
```

> **NOTE** Remember that you can use the blank identifier (underscore) if you don't need the index variable provided by range.

16.5 Arrays are copied

Assigning an array to a new variable or passing it to a function makes a complete copy of its contents, as you can see in the following listing.

Listing 16.6 Arrays are values: array-value.go

```go
planets := [...]string{
    "Mercury",
    "Venus",
    "Earth",
    "Mars",
    "Jupiter",
    "Saturn",
    "Uranus",
    "Neptune",
}
planetsMarkII := planets        Copies planets array

planets[2] = "whoops"           Makes way for an
                                interstellar bypass

fmt.Println(planets)            Prints [Mercury Venus
                                whoops Mars Jupiter Saturn
fmt.Println(planetsMarkII)      Uranus Neptune]
```

Prints [Mercury Venus
Earth Mars Jupiter
Saturn Uranus Neptune]

TIP   In the event that you escape the destruction of Earth, you will want Go installed on your own computer. See the instructions at golang.org.

Arrays are values, and functions pass by value, which means the terraform function in the following listing is completely ineffective.

Listing 16.7 Arrays pass by value: terraform.go

```go
package main

import "fmt"

// terraform accomplishes nothing
func terraform(planets [8]string) {
    for i := range planets {
        planets[i] = "New " + planets[i]
    }
}
func main() {
    planets := [...]string{
        "Mercury",
        "Venus",
        "Earth",
        "Mars",
        "Jupiter",
        "Saturn",
        "Uranus",
        "Neptune",
    }
    terraform(planets)
    fmt.Println(planets)
}
```

Prints [Mercury Venus Earth Mars Jupiter Saturn Uranus Neptune]

The terraform function is operating on a copy of the planets array, so the modifications don't affect planets in the main function.

Also, it's important to recognize that the length of an array is part of its type. The type [8]string and type [5]string are both collections of strings, but they're two different types. The Go compiler will report an error when attempting to pass an array of a different length:

```go
dwarfs := [5]string{"Ceres", "Pluto", "Haumea", "Makemake", "Eris"}
terraform(dwarfs)
```

Can't use dwarfs (type [5]string) as type [8]string in argument to terraform

For these reasons, arrays aren't used as function parameters nearly as often as *slices*, covered in the next lesson.

 ## 16.6 Arrays of arrays

You've seen arrays of strings, but you can also have arrays of integers, arrays of floating-point numbers, and even arrays of arrays. The 8 x 8 chessboard in the following listing is an array of arrays of strings.

Listing 16.8 Chessboard: chess.go

```go
var board [8][8]string          ← An array of eight
                                  arrays of eight strings
board[0][0] = "r"
board[0][7] = "r"               ← Places a rook at a
                                  [row][column] coordinate
for column := range board[1] {
    board[1][column] = "p"
}

fmt.Print(board)
```

QC 16.5 answer

   1 The planetsMarkII variable received a copy of the planets array, so modifications to either array are independent of each other.

   2 The terraform function could return the revised [8]string array, so that main could reassign planets to the new value. Lesson 17 on slices and lesson 26 on pointers present other alternatives.

Quick check 16.6   Consider the game of Sudoku. What would the declaration look like for a 9 x 9 grid of integers?

Summary

- Arrays are ordered collections of elements with a fixed length.
- Composite literals provide a convenient means to initialize arrays.
- The range keyword can iterate over arrays.
- When accessing elements of an array, you must stay inside its boundaries.
- Arrays are copied when assigned or passed to functions.

Let's see if you got this...

Experiment: chess.go

- Extend listing 16.8 to display all the chess pieces at their starting positions using the characters kqrbnp for black pieces along the top and uppercase KQRBNP for white pieces on the bottom.
- Write a function that nicely displays the board.
- Instead of strings, use [8][8]rune to represent the board. Recall that rune literals are surrounded with single quotes and can be printed with the %c format verb.

QC 16.6 answer

```
var grid [9][9]int
```

SLICES: WINDOWS INTO ARRAYS

After reading lesson 17, you'll be able to

- Use slices to view the solar system through a window
- Alphabetize slices with the standard library

The planets in our solar system are classified as terrestrial, gas giants, and ice giants, as shown in figure 17.1. You can focus on the terrestrial ones by slicing the first four elements of the `planets` array with `planets[0:4]`. *Slicing* doesn't alter the `planets` array. It just creates a window or view into the array. This view is a type called a *slice*.

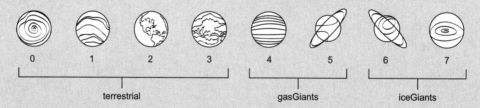

Figure 17.1   Slicing the solar system

> **Consider this** If you have a collection, is it organized in a certain way? The books on a library shelf may be ordered by the last name of the author, for example. This arrangement allows you to focus in on other books they wrote.
>
> You can use slices to zero in on part of a collection in the same way.

 ## 17.1 Slicing an array

Slicing is expressed with a *half-open range*. For example, in the following listing, planets[0:4] begins with the planet at index 0 and continues up to, but not including, the planet at index 4.

Listing 17.1 Slicing an array: slicing.go

```
planets := [...]string{
    "Mercury",
    "Venus",
    "Earth",
    "Mars",
    "Jupiter",
    "Saturn",
    "Uranus",
    "Neptune",
}
terrestrial := planets[0:4]
gasGiants := planets[4:6]
iceGiants := planets[6:8]

fmt.Println(terrestrial, gasGiants, iceGiants)
```

Prints [Mercury
Venus Earth Mars]
[Jupiter Saturn]
[Uranus Neptune]

Though terrestrial, gasGiants, and iceGiants are slices, you can still index into slices like arrays:

```
fmt.Println(gasGiants[0])
```

← Prints Jupiter

You can also slice an array, and then slice the resulting slice:

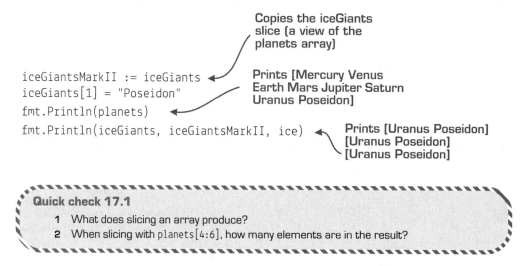

```
giants := planets[4:8]
gas := giants[0:2]
ice := giants[2:4]
fmt.Println(giants, gas, ice)
```

Prints [Jupiter Saturn
Uranus Neptune]
[Jupiter Saturn]
[Uranus Neptune]

The terrestrial, gasGiants, iceGiants, giants, gas, and ice slices are all views of the same planets array. Assigning a new value to an element of a slice modifies the underlying planets array. The change will be visible through the other slices:

Copies the iceGiants
slice (a view of the
planets array)

```
iceGiantsMarkII := iceGiants
iceGiants[1] = "Poseidon"
fmt.Println(planets)
fmt.Println(iceGiants, iceGiantsMarkII, ice)
```

Prints [Mercury Venus
Earth Mars Jupiter Saturn
Uranus Poseidon]

Prints [Uranus Poseidon]
[Uranus Poseidon]
[Uranus Poseidon]

Quick check 17.1

1 What does slicing an array produce?
2 When slicing with planets[4:6], how many elements are in the result?

17.1.1 Default indices for slicing

When slicing an array, omitting the first index defaults to the beginning of the array. Omitting the last index defaults to the length of the array. This allows the slicing from listing 17.1 to be written as shown in the following listing.

Listing 17.2 Default indices: slicing-default.go

```
terrestrial := planets[:4]
gasGiants := planets[4:6]
iceGiants := planets[6:]
```

> **NOTE** Slice indices may not be negative.

QC 17.1 answer

1 A slice.
2 Two.

You can probably guess what omitting both indices does. The `allPlanets` variable is a slice containing all eight planets:

```
allPlanets := planets[:]
```

Slicing strings

The slicing syntax for arrays also works on strings:

```
neptune := "Neptune"
tune := neptune[3:]

fmt.Println(tune)   ◄─────── Prints tune
```

The result of slicing a string is another string. However, assigning a new value to neptune won't change the value of tune or vice versa:

```
neptune = "Poseidon"
fmt.Println(tune)   ◄─────── Prints tune
```

Be aware that the indices indicate the number of bytes, not runes:

```
question := "¿Cómo estás?"
fmt.Println(question[:6])   ◄─────── Prints ¿Cóm
```

Quick check 17.2 If Earth and Mars were the only colonized planets, how could you derive the slice colonized from terrestrial?

17.2 Composite literals for slices

Many functions in Go operate on slices rather than arrays. If you need a slice that reveals every element of the underlying array, one option is to declare an array and then slice it with [:], like this:

```
dwarfArray := [...]string{"Ceres", "Pluto", "Haumea", "Makemake", "Eris"}
dwarfSlice := dwarfArray[:]
```

QC 17.2 answer

```
colonized := terrestrial[2:]
```

Slicing an array is one way to create a slice, but you can also declare a slice directly. A slice of strings has the type []string, with no value between the brackets. This differs from an array declaration, which always specifies a fixed length or ellipsis between the brackets.

In the following listing, dwarfs is a slice initialized with the familiar composite literal syntax.

Listing 17.3 Start with a slice: dwarf-slice.go

```
dwarfs := []string{"Ceres", "Pluto", "Haumea", "Makemake", "Eris"}
```

There is still an underlying array. Behind the scenes, Go declares a five-element array and then makes a slice that views all of its elements.

Quick check 17.3 Use the %T format verb to compare the types of dwarfArray and the dwarfs slice.

17.3 The power of slices

What if there were a way to fold the fabric of space-time, bringing worlds together for instantaneous travel? Using the Go standard library and some ingenuity, the hyperspace function in listing 17.4 modifies a slice of worlds, removing the (white) space between them.

QC 17.3 answer

```
fmt.Printf("array %T\n", dwarfArray)    ←——— Prints array [5]string
fmt.Printf("slice %T\n", dwarfs)        ←——— Prints slice []string
```

Listing 17.4 Bringing worlds together: hyperspace.go

```
package main

import (
    "fmt"
    "strings"
)

// hyperspace removes the space surrounding worlds
func hyperspace(worlds []string) {          ← This argument is a
    for i := range worlds {                    slice, not an array.
        worlds[i] = strings.TrimSpace(worlds[i])
    }
}
                                                              Planets
                                                              surrounded
func main() {                                                 by space
    planets := []string{" Venus   ", "Earth   ", " Mars"} ←
    hyperspace(planets)

    fmt.Println(strings.Join(planets, ""))  ←   Prints
}                                               VenusEarthMars
```

Both worlds and planets are slices, and though worlds is a copy, they both point to the same
underlying array.

If hyperspace were to change where the worlds slice points, begins, or ends, those changes
would have no impact on the planets slice. But hyperspace is able to reach into the underlying array that worlds points to and change its elements. Those changes are visible by
other slices (views) of the array.

Slices are more versatile than arrays in other ways too. Slices have a length, but unlike
arrays, the length isn't part of the type. You can pass a slice of any size to the hyperspace
function:

```
dwarfs := []string{" Ceres   ", " Pluto"}
hyperspace(dwarfs)
```

Arrays are rarely used directly. Gophers prefer slices for their versatility, especially
when passing arguments to functions.

Quick check 17.4 Look up TrimSpace and Join in the Go documentation at golang.org/pkg. What functionality do they provide?

17.4 Slices with methods

In Go you can define a type with an underlying slice or array. Once you have a type, you can attach methods to it. Go's ability to declare methods on types proves more versatile than the classes of other languages.

The sort package in the standard library declares a StringSlice type:

```
type StringSlice []string
```

Attached to StringSlice is a Sort method :

```
func (p StringSlice) Sort()
```

To alphabetize the planets, the following listing converts planets to the sort.StringSlice type and then calls the Sort method.

Listing 17.5 Sorting a slice of strings: sort.go

```
package main

import (
    "fmt"
    "sort"
)

func main() {
    planets := []string{
        "Mercury", "Venus", "Earth", "Mars",
        "Jupiter", "Saturn", "Uranus", "Neptune",
    }
    sort.StringSlice(planets).Sort()      ← Sorts planets alphabetically
    fmt.Println(planets)      ← Prints [Earth Jupiter Mars Mercury Neptune Saturn Uranus Venus]
}
```

QC 17.4 answer

1a TrimSpace returns a slice with leading and trailing white space removed.

1b Join concatenates a slice of elements with a separator placed between them.

To make it even simpler, the sort package has a Strings helper function that performs the type conversion and calls the Sort method for you:

```
sort.Strings(planets)
```

> **Quick check 17.5** What does sort.StringSlice(planets) do?

 # Summary

- Slices are windows or views into an array.
- The range keyword can iterate over slices.
- Slices share the same underlying data when assigned or passed to functions.
- Composite literals provide a convenient means to initialize slices.
- You can attach methods to slices.

Let's see if you got this...

Experiment: terraform.go

Write a program to terraform a slice of strings by prepending each planet with "New ". Use your program to terraform Mars, Uranus, and Neptune.

Your first iteration can use a terraform function, but your final implementation should introduce a Planets type with a terraform method, similar to sort.StringSlice.

QC 17.5 answer The planets variable is converted from []string to the StringSlice type, which is declared in the sort package.

A BIGGER SLICE

After reading lesson 18, you'll be able to

- Append more elements to slices
- Investigate how length and capacity work

Arrays have a fixed number of elements, and slices are just views into those fixed-length arrays. Programmers often need a variable-length array that grows as needed. By combining slices and a built-in function named append, Go provides the capabilities of variable-length arrays. This lesson delves into how it works.

Consider this Have you ever had your books outgrow your shelves, or your family outgrow your home or vehicle?

Like bookshelves, arrays have a certain capacity. A slice can focus on the portion of the array where the books are, and grow to reach the capacity of the shelf. If the shelf is full, you can replace the shelf with a larger one and move all the books over. Then point the slice at the books on the new shelf with a greater capacity.

18.1 The append function

The International Astronomical Union (IAU) recognizes five dwarf planets in our solar system, but there could be more. To add more elements to the dwarfs slice, use the built-in append function as shown in the following listing.

Listing 18.1 More dwarf planets: append.go

```
dwarfs := []string{"Ceres", "Pluto", "Haumea", "Makemake", "Eris"}
dwarfs = append(dwarfs, "Orcus")
fmt.Println(dwarfs)
```
Prints [Ceres Pluto
Haumea Makemake
Eris Orcus]

The append function is *variadic*, like Println, so you can pass multiple elements to append in one go:

```
dwarfs = append(dwarfs, "Salacia", "Quaoar", "Sedna")
fmt.Println(dwarfs)
```
Prints [Ceres Pluto Haumea
Makemake Eris Orcus
Salacia Quaoar Sedna]

The dwarfs slice began as a view into a five-element array, yet the preceding code appends four more elements. How is that possible? To investigate, you'll first need to understand *capacity* and the built-in function cap.

> **Quick check 18.1**   How many dwarf planets are in listing 18.1? What function can be used to determine this?

QC 18.1 answer   The slice contains nine dwarf planets, which can be determined with the len built-in function:

```
fmt.Println(len(dwarfs))
```
Prints 9

18.2 Length and capacity

The number of elements that are visible through a slice determines its length. If a slice has an underlying array that is larger, the slice may still have *capacity* to grow.

The following listing declares a function to print out the length and capacity of a slice.

Listing 18.2 Len and cap: **slice-dump.go**

```go
package main

import "fmt"

// dump slice length, capacity, and contents
func dump(label string, slice []string) {
    fmt.Printf("%v: length %v, capacity %v %v\n", label, len(slice),
    cap(slice), slice)
}

func main() {
    dwarfs := []string{"Ceres", "Pluto", "Haumea", "Makemake", "Eris"}
    dump("dwarfs", dwarfs)
    dump("dwarfs[1:2]", dwarfs[1:2])
}
```

Prints dwarfs: length 5, capacity 5 [Ceres Pluto Haumea Makemake Eris]

Prints dwarfs[1:2]: length 1, capacity 4 [Pluto]

The slice created by dwarfs[1:2] has a length of 1, but the capacity to hold 4 elements.

Quick check 18.2   Why does the dwarfs[1:2] slice have a capacity of 4?

QC 18.2 answer   Pluto Haumea Makemake Eris provide a capacity of 4 even though the length is 1.

18.3 Investigating the append function

Using the dump function from listing 18.2, the next listing shows how append affects capacity.

Listing 18.3 append to slice: slice-append.go

```
dwarfs1 := []string{"Ceres", "Pluto", "Haumea", "Makemake", "Eris"}
dwarfs2 := append(dwarfs1, "Orcus")
dwarfs3 := append(dwarfs2, "Salacia", "Quaoar", "Sedna")
```

Length 5, capacity 5

Length 6, capacity 10   Length 9, capacity 10

The array backing dwarfs1 doesn't have enough room (capacity) to append Orcus, so append copies the contents of dwarfs1 to a freshly allocated array with twice the capacity, as illustrated in figure 18.1. The dwarfs2 slice points at the newly allocated array. The additional capacity happens to provide enough room for the next append.

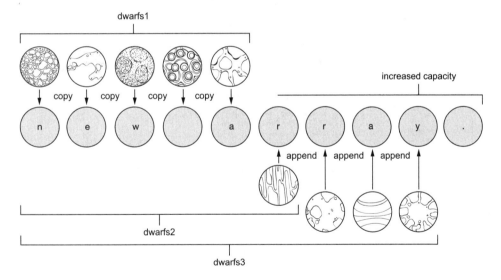

Figure 18.1 append allocates a new array with increased capacity when necessary.

To demonstrate that dwarfs2 and dwarfs3 refer to a different array than dwarfs1, simply modify an element and print out the three slices.

> **Quick check 18.3** If you modify an element of dwarfs3 in listing 18.3, will dwarfs2 or dwarfs1 change?
>
> ```
> dwarfs3[1] = "Pluto!"
> ```

 ## 18.4 Three-index slicing

Go version 1.2 introduced *three-index slicing* to limit the capacity of the resulting slice. In the next listing, terrestrial has a length and capacity of 4. Appending Ceres causes a new array to be allocated, leaving the planets array unaltered.

Listing 18.4 Capacity after slicing: three-index-slicing.go

```
planets := []string{
    "Mercury", "Venus", "Earth", "Mars",
    "Jupiter", "Saturn", "Uranus", "Neptune",
}
terrestrial := planets[0:4:4]          Length 4, capacity 4
worlds := append(terrestrial, "Ceres")

fmt.Println(planets)          Prints [Mercury Venus
                              Earth Mars Jupiter
                              Saturn Uranus Neptune]
```

If the third index isn't specified, terrestrial will have a capacity of 8. Appending Ceres doesn't allocate a new array, but instead overwrites Jupiter:

```
                              Length 4, capacity 8
terrestrial = planets[0:4]
worlds = append(terrestrial, "Ceres")

fmt.Println(planets)          Prints [Mercury Venus
                              Earth Mars Ceres Saturn
                              Uranus Neptune]
```

QC 18.3 answer dwarfs3 and dwarfs2 are changed, but dwarfs1 remains the same because it points to a different array.

Unless you want to overwrite Jupiter, you should default to three-index slicing whenever you take a slice.

> **Quick check 18.4** When should three-index slicing be used?

 ## 18.5 Preallocate slices with make

When there isn't enough capacity for append, Go must allocate a new array and copy the contents of the old array. You can avoid extra allocations and copies by *preallocating* a slice with the built-in make function.

The make function in the next listing specifies both the length (0) and capacity (10) of the dwarfs slice. Up to 10 elements can be appended before dwarfs runs out of capacity, causing append to allocate a new array.

Listing 18.5 Make a slice: slice-make.go

```
dwarfs := make([]string, 0, 10)
dwarfs = append(dwarfs, "Ceres", "Pluto", "Haumea", "Makemake", "Eris")
```

The capacity argument is optional. To start with a length and capacity of 10, you can use make([]string, 10). Each of the 10 elements will contain the zero value for their type, an empty string in this case. The append built-in function would add the 11th element.

> **Quick check 18.5** What is the benefit of making slices with make?

QC 18.4 answer When shouldn't three-index slicing be used? Unless you specifically want to overwrite the elements of the underlying array, it's far safer to set the capacity with a three-index slice.

QC 18.5 answer Preallocating with make can set an initial capacity, thereby avoiding additional allocations and copies to enlarge the underlying array.

18.6 Declaring variadic functions

Printf and append are *variadic* functions because they accept a variable number of arguments. To declare a variadic function, use the ellipsis … with the last parameter, as shown
in the following listing.

Listing 18.6 Variable arity functions: variadic.go

```go
func terraform(prefix string, worlds ...string) []string {
    newWorlds := make([]string, len(worlds))

    for i := range worlds {
        newWorlds[i] = prefix + " " + worlds[i]
    }

    return newWorlds
}
```

> Makes a new slice
> rather than modifying
> worlds directly

The worlds parameter is a slice of strings that contains zero or more arguments passed to
terraform:

```go
twoWorlds := terraform("New", "Venus", "Mars")
fmt.Println(twoWorlds)
```

> Prints [New Venus
> New Mars]

To pass a slice instead of multiple arguments, expand the slice with an ellipsis:

```go
planets := []string{"Venus", "Mars", "Jupiter"}
newPlanets := terraform("New", planets...)
fmt.Println(newPlanets)
```

> Prints [New Venus New
> Mars New Jupiter]

If terraform were to modify (or *mutate*) elements of the worlds parameter, the planets slice
would also see those changes. By using newWorlds, the terraform function avoids modifying
the passed arguments.

Quick check 18.6   What are three uses for the ellipsis …?

QC 18.6 answer

1 Have the Go compiler count the number of elements in a composite literal for an array.
2 Make the last parameter of a variadic function capture zero or more arguments as a slice.
3 Expand the elements of a slice into arguments passed to a function.

Summary

- Slices have a length and a capacity.
- When there isn't enough capacity, the built-in `append` function will allocate a new underlying array.
- You can use the `make` function to preallocate a slice.
- Variadic functions accept multiple arguments, which are placed in a slice.

Let's see if you got this...

Experiment: capacity.go

Write a program that uses a loop to continuously append an element to a slice. Print out the capacity of the slice whenever it changes. Does `append` always double the capacity when the underlying array runs out of room?

THE EVER-VERSATILE MAP

After reading lesson 19, you'll be able to

- Use maps as collections for unstructured data
- Declare, access, and iterate over maps
- Explore some uses of the versatile map type

Maps come in handy when you're searching for something, and we're not just talking about Google Maps (www.google.com/mars/). Go provides a map collection with keys that *map* to values. Whereas arrays and slices are indexed by sequential integers, *map keys* can be nearly any type.

> **NOTE** This collection goes by several different names: dictionaries in Python, hashes in Ruby, and objects in JavaScript. Associative arrays in PHP and tables in Lua serve as both maps and conventional arrays.

Maps are especially useful for unstructured data where the keys are determined while a program is running. Programs written in scripting languages tend to use maps for *structured data* as well—data where the keys are known ahead of time. Lesson 21 covers Go's structure type, which is better suited for those cases.

19.1 Declaring a map

The keys of maps can be nearly any type, unlike arrays and slices, which have sequential integers for keys. You must specify a type for the keys and values in Go. To declare a map with keys of type `string` and values of type `int`, the syntax is `map[string]int`, as shown in figure 19.1.

Figure 19.1 A map with string keys and integer values

The `temperature` map declared in listing 19.1 contains average temperatures from the Planetary Fact Sheet (nssdc.gsfc.nasa.gov/planetary/factsheet/). You can declare and initialize maps with composite literals, much like other collection types. For each element, specify a key and value of the appropriate type. Use square brackets [] to look up values by key, to assign over existing values, or to add values to the map.

Listing 19.1 Average temperature map: map.go

```go
temperature := map[string]int{
    "Earth": 15,          ← Composite literals
    "Mars":  -65,            are key-value pairs
}                           for maps.

temp := temperature["Earth"]
fmt.Printf("On average the Earth is %v° C.\n", temp)   ← Prints On average
                                                         the Earth is 15° C.

temperature["Earth"] = 16        ← A little climate
temperature["Venus"] = 464         change

fmt.Println(temperature)     ← Prints map[Venus:464
                               Earth:16 Mars:-65]
```

If you access a key that doesn't exist in the map, the result is the zero value for the type (int):

```
moon := temperature["Moon"]        Prints 0
fmt.Println(moon)
```

Go provides the *comma, ok* syntax, which you can use to distinguish between the "Moon" not existing in the map versus being present in the map with a temperature of 0° C:

```
                                    The comma,
                                    ok syntax
if moon, ok := temperature["Moon"]; ok {
    fmt.Printf("On average the moon is %v° C.\n", moon)
} else {
    fmt.Println("Where is the moon?")        Prints Where
}                                            is the moon?
```

The moon variable will contain the value found at the "Moon" key or the zero value. The additional ok variable will be true if the key is present, or false otherwise.

> **NOTE**   When using the comma, ok syntax you can use any variable names you like:
>
> ```
> temp, found := temperature["Venus"]
> ```

Quick check 19.1

1   What type would you use to declare a map with 64-bit floating-point keys and integer values?
2   If you modify listing 19.1 so that the "Moon" key is present with a value of 0, what's the result of using the comma, ok syntax?

QC 19.1 answer

1   The map type is map[float64]int.
2   The value of ok will be true:

```
temperature := map[string]int{
    "Earth": 15,
    "Mars":  -65,
    "Moon":   0,                           Prints On
}                                          average the
                                           moon is 0° C.
if moon, ok := temperature["Moon"]; ok {
    fmt.Printf("On average the moon is %v° C.\n", moon)
} else {
    fmt.Println("Where is the moon?")
}
```

19.2 Maps aren't copied

As you learned in lesson 16, arrays are copied when assigned to new variables or when passed to functions or methods. The same is true for primitive types like int and float64.

Maps behave differently. In the next listing, both planets and planetsMarkII share the same underlying data. As you can see, changes to one impact the other. That's a bit unfortunate given the circumstances.

Listing 19.2 Pointing at the same data: whoops.go

```go
planets := map[string]string{
    "Earth": "Sector ZZ9",
    "Mars":  "Sector ZZ9",
}
planetsMarkII := planets
planets["Earth"] = "whoops"       Prints map[Earth:whoops
                                   Mars:Sector ZZ9]
fmt.Println(planets)
fmt.Println(planetsMarkII)

delete(planets, "Earth")          Removes Earth
fmt.Println(planetsMarkII)        from the map

          Prints
      map[Mars:Sector ZZ9]
```

When the delete built-in function removes an element from the map, both planets and planetsMarkII are impacted by the change. If you pass a map to a function or method, it may alter the contents of the map. This behavior is similar to multiple slices that point to the same underlying array.

Quick check 19.2

1 Why are changes to planets also reflected in planetsMarkII in listing 19.2?
2 What does the delete built-in function do?

QC 19.2 answer

1 The planetsMarkII variable points at the same underlying data as planets.
2 The delete function removes an element from a map.

19.3 Preallocating maps with make

Maps are similar to slices in another way. Unless you initialize them with a composite literal, maps need to be allocated with the make built-in function.

For maps, make only accepts one or two parameters. The second one preallocates space for a number of keys, much like capacity for slices. A map's initial length will always be zero when using make:

```
temperature := make(map[float64]int, 8)
```

> **Quick check 19.3** What do you suppose is the benefit of preallocating a map with make?

 ## 19.4 Using maps to count things

The code in listing 19.3 determines the frequency of temperatures taken from the MAAS API (github.com/ingenology/mars_weather_api). If frequency were a slice, the keys would need to be integers, and the underlying array would need to reserve space to count temperatures that never actually occur. A map is clearly a better choice in this case.

QC 19.3 answer As with slices, specifying an initial size for a map can save the computer some work later when the map gets bigger.

Listing 19.3 Frequency of temperatures: frequency.go

```go
temperatures := []float64{
    -28.0, 32.0, -31.0, -29.0, -23.0, -29.0, -28.0, -33.0,
}

frequency := make(map[float64]int)        Iterates over a
                                          slice (index, value)
for _, t := range temperatures {
    frequency[t]++
}                                         Iterates over a
                                          map (key, value)
for t, num := range frequency {
    fmt.Printf("%+.2f occurs %d times\n", t, num)
}
```

Iteration with the range keyword works similarly for slices, arrays, and maps. Rather than an index and value, maps provide the key and value for each iteration. Be aware that Go doesn't guarantee the order of map keys, so the output may change from one run to another.

Quick check 19.4 When iterating over a map, what are the two variables populated with?

 ## 19.5 Grouping data with maps and slices

Instead of determining the frequency of temperatures, let's group temperatures together in divisions of 10° each. To do that, the following listing maps from a group to a slice of temperatures in that group.

Listing 19.4 A map of slices: group.go

```go
temperatures := []float64{
    -28.0, 32.0, -31.0, -29.0, -23.0, -29.0, -28.0, -33.0,
}
groups := make(map[float64][]float64)          A map with float64 keys
                                               and []float64 values
for _, t := range temperatures {
```

QC 19.4 answer The key and the value for each element in the map.

```
    g := math.Trunc(t/10) * 10
    groups[g] = append(groups[g], t)
}
```

Rounds temperatures down
to -20, -30, and so on

```
for g, temperatures := range groups {
    fmt.Printf("%v: %v\n", g, temperatures)
}
```

The previous listing produces output like this:

```
30: [32]
-30: [-31 -33]
-20: [-28 -29 -23 -29 -28]
```

Quick check 19.5   What is the type for the keys and values in the declaration `var groups`
`map[string][]int`?

 ## 19.6 Repurposing maps as sets

A *set* is a collection similar to an array, except that each element is guaranteed to occur
only once. Go doesn't provide a set collection, but you can always improvise by using a
map, as shown in the following listing. The value isn't important, but `true` is convenient
for checking *set membership*. If a temperature is present in the map and it has a value of
`true`, it's a member of the set.

Listing 19.5 A makeshift set: set.go

```
var temperatures = []float64{
    -28.0, 32.0, -31.0, -29.0, -23.0, -29.0, -28.0, -33.0,
}

set := make(map[float64]bool)
for _, t := range temperatures {
    set[t] = true
}
```

Makes a map with
Boolean values

QC 19.5 answer   The groups map has keys of type string and values that are a slice of integers.

```
if set[-28.0] {
    fmt.Println("set member")      ←——— Prints set member
}
fmt.Println(set)
```
Prints map[-31:true -29:true
-23:true -33:true -28:true 32:true]

You can see that the map only contains one key for each temperature, with any duplicates removed. But map keys have an arbitrary order in Go, so before they can be sorted, the temperatures must be converted back to a slice:

```
unique := make([]float64, 0, len(set))
for t := range set {
    unique = append(unique, t)
}
sort.Float64s(unique)

fmt.Println(unique)      ←——— Prints [-33 -31 -29 -28 -23 32]
```

Quick check 19.6 How would you check whether 32.0 is a member of set?

Summary

- Maps are versatile collections for unstructured data.
- Composite literals provide a convenient means to initialize maps.
- The range keyword can iterate over maps.
- Maps share the same underlying data when assigned or passed to functions.
- Collections become more powerful when combined with each other.

QC 19.6 answer
```
if set[32.0] {
    // set member
}
```

Let's see if you got this...

Experiment: words.go

Write a function to count the frequency of words in a string of text and return a map of words with their counts. The function should convert the text to lowercase, and punctuation should be trimmed from words. The `strings` package contains several helpful functions for this task, including `Fields`, `ToLower`, and `Trim`.

Use your function to count the frequency of words in the following passage and then display the count for any word that occurs more than once.

> As far as eye could reach he saw nothing but the stems of the great plants about him receding in the violet shade, and far overhead the multiple transparency of huge leaves filtering the sunshine to the solemn splendour of twilight in which he walked. Whenever he felt able he ran again; the ground continued soft and springy, covered with the same resilient weed which was the first thing his hands had touched in Malacandra. Once or twice a small red creature scuttled across his path, but otherwise there seemed to be no life stirring in the wood; nothing to fear—except the fact of wandering unprovisioned and alone in a forest of unknown vegetation thousands or millions of miles beyond the reach or knowledge of man.
>
> —C.S. Lewis, *Out of the Silent Planet,*
> (see mng.bz/V7nO)

CAPSTONE: A SLICE OF LIFE

For this challenge, you will build a simulation of underpopulation, overpopulation, and reproduction called Conway's Game of Life (see mng.bz/xOyY). The simulation is played out on a two-dimensional grid of cells. As such, this challenge focuses on slices.

Each cell has eight adjacent cells in the horizontal, vertical, and diagonal directions. In each generation, cells live or die based on the number of living neighbors.

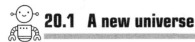 **20.1 A new universe**

For your first implementation of the Game of Life, limit the universe to a fixed size.
Decide on the dimensions of the grid and define some constants:

```
const (
    width  = 80
    height = 15
)
```

Next, define a Universe type to hold a two-dimensional field of cells. With a Boolean type,
each cell will be either dead (false) or alive (true):

```
type Universe [][]bool
```

Uses slices rather than arrays so that a universe can be shared with, and modified by,
functions or methods.

> **NOTE** Lesson 26 introduces pointers, an alternative that allows you to directly share
> arrays with functions and methods.

Write a NewUniverse function that uses make to allocate and return a Universe with height
rows and width columns per row:

```
func NewUniverse() Universe
```

Freshly allocated slices will default to the zero value, which is false, so the universe
begins empty.

20.1.1 Looking at the universe

Write a method to print a universe to the screen using the fmt package. Represent live
cells with an asterisk and dead cells with a space. Be sure to move to a new line after
printing each row:

```
func (u Universe) Show()
```

Write a main function to create a NewUniverse and Show it. Before continuing, be sure that you
can run your program, even though the universe is empty.

20.1.2 Seeding live cells

Write a Seed method that randomly sets approximately 25% of the cells to alive (true):

```
func (u Universe) Seed()
```

Remember to import math/rand to use the Intn function. When you're done, update main to populate the universe with Seed and display your handiwork with Show.

 ## 20.2 Implementing the game rules

The rules of Conway's Game of Life are as follows:

- A live cell with less than two live neighbors dies.
- A live cell with two or three live neighbors lives on to the next generation.
- A live cell with more than three live neighbors dies.
- A dead cell with exactly three live neighbors becomes a live cell.

To implement the rules, break them down into three steps, each of which can be a method:

- A way to determine whether a cell is alive
- The ability to count the number of live neighbors
- The logic to determine whether a cell should be alive or dead in the next generation

20.2.1 Dead or alive?

It should be easy to determine whether a cell is dead or alive. Just look up a cell in the Universe slice. If the Boolean is true, the cell is alive.

Write an Alive method on the Universe type with the following signature:

```
func (u Universe) Alive(x, y int) bool
```

A complication arises when the cell is outside of the universe. Is (–1,–1) dead or alive? On an 80 x 15 grid, is (80,15) dead or alive?

To address this, make the universe wrap around. The neighbor above (0,0) will be (0,14) instead of (0,–1), which can be calculated by adding height to y. If y exceeds the height of the grid, you can turn to the modulus operator (%) that we used for leap year calculations. Use % to divide y by height and keep the remainder. The same goes for x and width.

20.2.2 Counting neighbors

Write a method to count the number of live neighbors for a given cell, from 0 to 8. Rather than access the universe data directly, use the Alive method so that the universe wraps around:

```
func (u Universe) Neighbors(x, y int) int
```

Be sure to only count adjacent neighbors and not the cell in question.

20.2.3 The game logic

Now that you can determine whether a cell has two, three, or more neighbors, you can implement the rules shown at the beginning of this section. Write a `Next` method to do this:

```
func (u Universe) Next(x, y int) bool
```

Don't modify the universe directly. Instead, return whether the cell should be dead or alive in the next generation.

 ## 20.3 Parallel universe

To complete the simulation, you need to step through each cell in the universe and determine what its `Next` state should be.

There's one catch. When counting neighbors, your count should be based on the previous state of the universe. If you modify the universe directly, those changes will influence the neighbor counts for the surrounding cells.

A simple solution is to create two universes of the same size. Read through universe A while setting cells in universe B. Write a `Step` function to perform this operation:

```
func Step(a, b Universe)
```

Once universe B holds the next generation, you can swap universes and repeat:

```
a, b = b, a
```

To clear the screen before displaying a new generation, print `"\x0c"`, which is a special ANSI escape sequence. Then display the universe and use the `Sleep` function from the `time` package to slow down the animation.

> **NOTE** Outside of the Go Playground, you may need another mechanism to clear the screen, such as `"\033[H"` on macOS.

Now you should have everything you need to write a complete Game of Life simulation and run it in the Go Playground.

When you're done, share a Playground link to your solution in the Manning forums at forums.manning.com/forums/get-programming-with-go.

State and behavior

In Go, values represent *state*, such as whether a door is opened or closed. Functions and methods define *behavior*—actions on state, such as opening a door.

As programs grow larger, they become more difficult to manage and maintain, unless you have the right tools.

If there are several doors that can independently be opened or closed, it's helpful to bundle the state and behavior together. Programming languages also allow you to express abstract ideas, such as *things that can be opened*. Then on a hot summer day, you can open everything that can be opened, whether door or window.

There are a lot of big words to describe these ideas: object-orientation, encapsulation, polymorphism, and composition. The lessons in this unit aim to demystify the concepts and demonstrate Go's rather unique approach to object-oriented design.

A LITTLE STRUCTURE

After reading lesson 21, you'll be able to

- Give coordinates on Mars a little structure
- Encode structures to the popular JSON data format

A vehicle is made up of many parts, and those parts may have associated values (or state). The engine is on, the wheels are turning, the battery is fully charged. Using a separate variable for each value is akin to the vehicle sitting in the shop disassembled. Likewise, a building may have windows that are open and a door that is unlocked. To assemble the parts or construct a structure, Go provides a *structure* type.

> **Consider this** Whereas collections are of the same type, *structures* allow you to group disparate things together. Take a look around. What do you see that could be represented with a structure?

21.1 Declaring a structure

A pair of coordinates are good candidates for adopting a little structure. Latitude and longitude go everywhere together. In a world without structures, a function to calculate the distance between two locations would need two pairs of coordinates:

```
func distance(lat1, long1, lat2, long2 float64) float64
```

Though this does work, passing independent coordinates around is prone to errors and just plain tedious. Latitude and longitude are a single unit, and structures let you treat them as such.

The curiosity structure in the next listing is declared with floating-point fields for latitude and longitude. To assign a value to a field or access the value of a field, use *dot notation* with variable name *dot* field name, as shown.

Listing 21.1   Introducing a little structure: struct.go

```
var curiosity struct {
    lat  float64
    long float64
}
curiosity.lat = -4.5895        Assigns values
curiosity.long = 137.4417      to fields of the
                               structure
fmt.Println(curiosity.lat, curiosity.long)    Prints -4.5895 137.4417
fmt.Println(curiosity)    Prints {-4.5895 137.4417}
```

> **NOTE** The Print family of functions will display the contents of structures for you.

The Mars Curiosity rover began its journey at Bradbury Landing, located at 4°35'22.2" S, 137°26'30.1" E. In listing 21.1 the latitude and longitude for Bradbury Landing are expressed in *decimal degrees*, with positive latitudes to the north and positive longitudes to the east, as illustrated in figure 21.1.

Figure 21.1   Latitude and longitude in decimal degrees

21.2 Reusing structures with types

If you need multiple structures with the same fields, you can define a type, much like the celsius type in lesson 13. The location type declared in the following listing is used to place the Spirit rover at Columbia Memorial Station and the Opportunity rover at Challenger Memorial Station.

Listing 21.2 Location type: location.go

```go
type location struct {
    lat  float64
    long float64
}

var spirit location
spirit.lat = -14.5684
spirit.long = 175.472636

var opportunity location
opportunity.lat = -1.9462
opportunity.long = 354.4734

fmt.Println(spirit, opportunity)
```

Reuses the location type

Prints
{-14.5684 175.472636}
{-1.9462 354.4734}

21.3 Initialize structures with composite literals

Composite literals for initializing structures come in two different forms. In listing 21.3, the `opportunity` and `insight` variables are initialized using field-value pairs. Fields may be in any order, and fields that aren't listed will retain the zero value for their type. This form tolerates change and will continue to work correctly even if fields are added to the structure or if fields are reordered. If `location` gained an altitude field, both `opportunity` and `insight` would default to an altitude of zero.

Listing 21.3 Composite literal with field-value pairs: struct-literal.go

```go
type location struct {
    lat, long float64
}

opportunity := location{lat: -1.9462, long: 354.4734}
fmt.Println(opportunity)    ←── Prints {-1.9462 354.4734}
insight := location{lat: 4.5, long: 135.9}
fmt.Println(insight)    ←── Prints {4.5 135.9}
```

The composite literal in listing 21.4 doesn't specify field names. Instead, a value must be provided for each field in the same order in which they're listed in the structure definition. This form works best for types that are stable and only have a few fields. If the `location` type gains an altitude field, `spirit` must specify a value for altitude for the program to compile. Mixing up the order of `lat` and `long` won't cause a compiler error, but the program won't produce correct results.

Listing 21.4 Composite literal with values only: struct-literal.go

```
spirit := location{-14.5684, 175.472636}
fmt.Println(spirit)    ←——— Prints {-14.5684 175.472636}
```

No matter how you initialize a structure, you can modify the %v format verb with a plus sign + to print out the field names, as shown in the next listing. This is especially useful for inspecting large structures.

Listing 21.5 Printing keys of structures: struct-literal.go

```
curiosity := location{-4.5895, 137.4417}

fmt.Printf("%v\n", curiosity)    ←——— Prints {-4.5895 137.4417}
fmt.Printf("%+v\n", curiosity)   ←——— Prints {lat:-4.5895
                                            long:137.4417}
```

> **Quick check 21.3** In what ways is the field-value composite literal syntax preferable to the values-only form?

 ## 21.4 Structures are copied

When the Curiosity rover heads east from Bradbury Landing to Yellowknife Bay, the location of Bradbury Landing doesn't change in real life, nor in the next listing. The curiosity variable is initialized with a copy of the values contained in bradbury, so the values change independently.

Listing 21.6 Assignment makes a copy: struct-value.go

```
bradbury := location{-4.5895, 137.4417}
curiosity := bradbury

curiosity.long += 0.0106    ←——— Heads east to
                                 Yellowknife Bay
fmt.Println(bradbury, curiosity)  ←——— Prints {-4.5895 137.4417}
                                        {-4.5895 137.4523}
```

QC 21.3 answer

1 Fields may be listed in any order.
2 Fields are optional, taking on the zero value if not listed.
3 No changes are required when reordering or adding fields to the structure declaration.

> **Quick check 21.4**   If curiosity were passed to a function that manipulated lat or long, would the caller see those changes?

 ## 21.5 A slice of structures

A slice of structures, []struct is a collection of zero or more values (a slice) where each value is based on a structure instead of a primitive type like float64.

If a program needed a collection of landing sites for Mars rovers, the way *not* to do it would be two separate slices for latitudes and longitudes, as shown in the following listing.

> **Listing 21.7 Two slices of floats: slice-struct.go**

```
lats := []float64{-4.5895, -14.5684, -1.9462}
longs := []float64{137.4417, 175.472636, 354.4734}
```

This already looks bad, especially in light of the location structure introduced earlier in this lesson. Now imagine more slices being added for altitude and so on. A mistake when editing the previous listing could easily result in data misaligned across slices or even slices of different lengths.

A better solution is to create a single slice where each value is a structure. Then each location is a single unit, which you can extend with the name of the landing site or other fields as needed, as shown in the next listing.

> **Listing 21.8 A slice of locations: slice-struct.go**

```
type location struct {
    name string
    lat  float64
    long float64
}
locations := []location{
    {name: "Bradbury Landing", lat: -4.5895, long: 137.4417},
    {name: "Columbia Memorial Station", lat: -14.5684, long: 175.472636},
    {name: "Challenger Memorial Station", lat: -1.9462, long: 354.4734},
}
```

QC 21.4 answer   No, the function would receive a copy of curiosity, as is the case with arrays.

Quick check 21.5 What is the danger of using multiple interrelated slices?

 ## 21.6 Encoding structures to JSON

JavaScript Object Notation, or JSON (json.org), is a standard data format popularized by Douglas Crockford. It's based on a subset of the JavaScript language but it's widely supported in other programming languages. JSON is commonly used for web APIs (Application Programming Interfaces), including the MAAS API (github.com/ingenology/mars_weather_api) that provides weather data from the Curiosity rover.

The Marshal function from the json package is used in listing 21.9 to encode the data in location into JSON format. Marshal returns the JSON data as bytes, which can be sent over the wire or converted to a string for display. It may also return an error, a topic that's covered in lesson 28.

Listing 21.9 Marshalling location: json.go

```go
package main

import (
    "encoding/json"
    "fmt"
    "os"
)

func main() {
    type location struct {          // Fields must begin
        Lat, Long float64           // with an uppercase
    }                               // letter.

    curiosity := location{-4.5895, 137.4417}

    bytes, err := json.Marshal(curiosity)
    exitOnError(err)                // Prints
                                    // {"Lat":-4.5895,
    fmt.Println(string(bytes))      // "Long":137.4417}
}
```

QC 21.5 answer It's easy to end up with data misaligned across slices.

```
// exitOnError prints any errors and exits.
func exitOnError(err error) {
    if err != nil {
        fmt.Println(err)
        os.Exit(1)
    }
}
```

Notice that the JSON keys match the field names of the `location` structure. For this to work, the `json` package requires fields to be exported. If `Lat` and `Long` began with a lower-case letter, the output would be {}.

> **Quick check 21.6**   What does the abbreviation JSON stand for?

21.7 Customizing JSON with struct tags

Go's `json` package requires that fields have an initial uppercase letter and multiword field names use *CamelCase* by convention. You may want JSON keys in *snake_case*, particularly when interoperating with Python or Ruby. The fields of a structure can be tagged with the field names you want the `json` package to use.

The only change from listing 21.9 to listing 21.10 is the inclusion of *struct tags* that alter the output of the `Marshal` function. Notice that the `Lat` and `Long` fields must still be exported for the `json` package to see them.

> **Listing 21.10** **Customizing location fields: json-tags.go**

```
type location struct {
    Lat  float64 `json:"latitude"`      Struct tags alter
    Long float64 `json:"longitude"`     the output.
}

curiosity := location{-4.5895, 137.4417}

bytes, err := json.Marshal(curiosity)
exitOnError(err)                         Prints
                                         {"latitude":-4.5895,
fmt.Println(string(bytes))     ←         "longitude":137.4417}
```

QC 21.6 answer   JSON stands for JavaScript Object Notation.

Struct tags are ordinary strings associated with the fields of a structure. Raw string literals (` `` `) are preferable, because quotation marks don't need to be escaped with a backslash, as in the less readable `"json:\"latitude\""`.

The struct tags are formatted as `key:"value"`, where the key tends to be the name of a package. To customize the `Lat` field for both JSON and XML, the struct tag would be `` `json:"latitude" xml:"latitude"` ``.

As the name implies, struct tags are only for the fields of structures, though `json.Marshal` will encode other types.

Quick check 21.7 Why must the `Lat` and `Long` fields begin with an uppercase letter when encoding JSON?

 **Summary**

- Structures group values together into one unit.
- Structures are values that are copied when assigned or passed to functions.
- Composite literals provide a convenient means to initialize structures.
- Struct tags decorate exported fields with additional information that packages can use.
- The `json` package utilizes struct tags to control the output of field names.

Let's see if you got this...

Experiment: landing.go

Write a program that displays the JSON encoding of the three rover landing sites in listing 21.8. The JSON should include the name of each landing site and use struct tags as shown in listing 21.10.

To make the output friendlier, make use of the `MarshalIndent` function from the `json` package.

QC 21.7 answer Fields must be exported for the `json` package to see them.

GO'S GOT NO CLASS

After reading lesson 22, you'll be able to

- Write methods that provide behavior to structured data
- Apply principles of object-oriented design

Go isn't like classical languages. It has no classes and no objects, and it omits features like inheritance. Yet Go still provides what you need to apply ideas from object-oriented design. This lesson explores the combination of structures with methods.

Consider this   *Synergy* is a buzzword commonly heard in entrepreneurial circles. It means "greater than the sum of its parts." The Go language has types, methods on types, and structures. Together, these provide much of the functionality that classes do for other languages, without needing to introduce a new concept into the language.

What other aspects of Go exhibit this property of combining to create something greater?

22.1 Attaching methods to structures

In lesson 13, you attached celsius and fahrenheit methods to the kelvin type to convert temperatures. In the same way, methods can be attached to other types you declare. It works the same whether the underlying type is a float64 or a struct.

To start, you need to declare a type, such as the coordinate structure in the following listing.

Listing 22.1 The coordinate type: coordinate.go

```
// coordinate in degrees, minutes, seconds in a N/S/E/W hemisphere.
type coordinate struct {
    d, m, s float64
    h       rune
}
```

Bradbury Landing is located at 4°35'22.2" S, 137°26'30.1" E in DMS format (degrees, minutes, seconds). There are 60 seconds (") in one minute, and 60 minutes (') in one degree, but these minutes and seconds represent a location, not a time.

The decimal method in the following listing will convert a DMS coordinate to decimal degrees.

Listing 22.2 The decimal method: coordinate.go

```
// decimal converts a d/m/s coordinate to decimal degrees.
func (c coordinate) decimal() float64 {
    sign := 1.0
    switch c.h {
    case 'S', 'W', 's', 'w':
        sign = -1
    }
    return sign * (c.d + c.m/60 + c.s/3600)
}
```

Now you can provide coordinates in the friendly DMS format and convert them to decimal degrees to perform calculations:

```
// Bradbury Landing: 4°35'22.2" S, 137°26'30.1" E
lat := coordinate{4, 35, 22.2, 'S'}
```

```
long := coordinate{137, 26, 30.12, 'E'}
fmt.Println(lat.decimal(), long.decimal())
```
Prints -4.5895
137.4417

Quick check 22.1   What is the receiver for the decimal method in listing 22.2?

 ## 22.2 Constructor functions

To construct a decimal degrees location from degrees, minutes, and seconds, you can use the decimal method from listing 22.2 with a composite literal:

```
type location struct {
    lat, long float64
}

curiosity := location{lat.decimal(), long.decimal()}
```

If you need a composite literal that's anything more than a list of values, consider writing a constructor function. The following listing declares a constructor function named newLocation.

Listing 22.3 Construct a new location: construct.go

```
// newLocation from latitude, longitude d/m/s coordinates.
func newLocation(lat, long coordinate) location {
    return location{lat.decimal(), long.decimal()}
}
```

Classical languages provide constructors as a special language feature to construct objects. Python has _init_, Ruby has initialize, and PHP has __construct(). Go doesn't have a language feature for constructors. Instead newLocation is an ordinary function with a name that follows a convention.

QC 22.1 answer   The receiver is c of type coordinate.

Functions in the form `newType` or `NewType` are used to construct a value of said type. Whether you name it `newLocation` or `NewLocation` depends on whether the function is exported for other packages to use, as covered in lesson 12. You use `newLocation` like any other function:

```
curiosity := newLocation(coordinate{4, 35, 22.2, 'S'},
  coordinate{137, 26, 30.12, 'E'})
fmt.Println(curiosity)          Prints {-4.5895
                                137.4417}
```

If you want to construct locations from a variety of inputs, just declare multiple functions with suitable names—perhaps `newLocationDMS` and `newLocationDD` for degrees, minutes, and seconds and decimal degrees, respectively.

> **NOTE** Sometimes constructor functions are named `New`, as is the case with the `New` function in the `errors` package. Because function calls are prefixed with the package they belong to, naming the function `NewError` would be read as `errors.NewError` rather than the more concise and preferable `errors.New`.

Quick check 22.2 What would you name a function that constructs a variable of type `Universe`?

QC 22.2 answer By convention the function would be named `NewUniverse`, or `newUniverse` if not exported.

22.3 The class alternative

Go doesn't have the class of classical languages like Python, Ruby, and Java. Yet a structure with a few methods fulfills much of the same purpose. If you squint, they aren't that different.

To drive the point home, build a whole new world type from the ground up. It will have a field for the radius of the planet, which you'll use to calculate the distance between two locations, as shown in the following listing.

Listing 22.4 A whole new world: world.go

```
type world struct {
    radius float64
}
```

Mars has a volumetric mean radius of 3,389.5 kilometers. Rather than declare 3389.5 as a constant, use the world type to declare Mars as one of many possible worlds:

```
var mars = world{radius: 3389.5}
```

Then a distance method is attached to the world type, giving it access to the radius field. It accepts two parameters, both of type location, and will return a distance in kilometers:

```
func (w world) distance(p1, p2 location) float64 {

                    To-do: some math
}                   using w.radius
```

This is going to involve some math, so be sure to import the math package, as follows:

```
import "math"
```

The location type uses degrees for latitude and longitude, but the math functions in the standard library use radians. Given that a circle has 360° or 2π radians, the following function performs the necessary conversion:

```
// rad converts degrees to radians.
func rad(deg float64) float64 {
    return deg * math.Pi / 180
}
```

Now for the distance calculation. It uses a number of trigonometric functions including sine, cosine, and arccosine. If you're a math geek, you can look up the formulas (www.movable-type.co.uk/scripts/latlong.html) and research the Spherical Law of

Cosines to understand how this works. Mars isn't a perfect sphere, but this formula achieves a "good enough" approximation for our purposes:

```
// distance calculation using the Spherical Law of Cosines.
func (w world) distance(p1, p2 location) float64 {
    s1, c1 := math.Sincos(rad(p1.lat))
    s2, c2 := math.Sincos(rad(p2.lat))
    clong := math.Cos(rad(p1.long - p2.long))
    return w.radius * math.Acos(s1*s2+c1*c2*clong)
}
```
← Uses the world's radius field

If your eyes just glazed over, don't worry. The math is needed in a program that calculates distance, but as long as distance returns the correct results, fully understanding how all the math works is optional (though a good idea).

Speaking of results, to see distance in action, declare some locations and use the mars variable declared earlier:

```
spirit := location{-14.5684, 175.472636}
opportunity := location{-1.9462, 354.4734}

dist := mars.distance(spirit, opportunity)
fmt.Printf("%.2f km\n", dist)
```
← Uses the distance method on mars
← Prints 9669.71 km

If you get a different result, go back to ensure the code is typed exactly as shown. One missing rad will result in incorrect calculations. If all else fails, download the code from github.com/nathany/get-programming-with-go and resign yourself to copy and paste.

The distance method was adopted from formulas for Earth, but using the radius of Mars. By declaring distance as a method on the world type, you can calculate distance for other worlds, such as Earth. The radius for each planet is found in table 22.2, as provided by the Planetary Fact Sheet (nssdc.gsfc.nasa.gov/planetary/factsheet/).

Quick check 22.3 How is it beneficial to declare a distance method on the world type compared to a less object-oriented approach?

QC 22.3 answer It provides a clean way to calculate distance for different worlds, and there's no need to pass the volumetric mean radius into the distance method, because it already has access to w.radius.

 **Summary**

- Combining methods and structures provides much of what classical languages provide without introducing a new language feature.
- Constructor functions are ordinary functions.

Let's see if you got this...

Experiment: landing.go

Use the code from listings 22.1, 22.2, and 22.3 to write a program that declares a `location` for each location in table 22.1. Print out each of the locations in decimal degrees.

Experiment: distance.go

Use the `distance` method from listing 22.4 to write a program that determines the distance between each pair of landing sites in table 22.1.

Which two landing sites are the closest?

Which two are farthest apart?

To determine the distance between the following locations, you'll need to declare other worlds based on table 22.2:

- Find the distance from London, England (51°30′N 0°08′W) to Paris, France (48°51′N 2°21′E).
- Find the distance from your city to the capital of your country.
- Find the distance between Mount Sharp (5°4′ 48″S, 137°51′E) and Olympus Mons (18°39′N, 226°12′E) on Mars.

Table 22.1   Landing sites on Mars

Rover or lander	Landing site	Latitude	Longitude
Spirit	Columbia Memorial Station	14°34′6.2″ S	175°28′21.5″ E
Opportunity	Challenger Memorial Station	1°56′46.3″ S	354°28′24.2″ E
Curiosity	Bradbury Landing	4°35′22.2″ S	137°26′30.1″ E
InSight	Elysium Planitia	4°30′0.0″ N	135°54′0″ E

Table 22.2   The volumetric mean radius of various planets

Planet	Radius (km)	Planet	Radius (km)
Mercury	2439.7	Jupiter	69911
Venus	6051.8	Saturn	58232
Earth	6371.0	Uranus	25362
Mars	3389.5	Neptune	24622

COMPOSITION AND FORWARDING

After reading lesson 23, you'll be able to

- Compose structures with composition
- Forward methods to other methods
- Forget about classical inheritance

When you look around the world, everything you see is made up of smaller parts. People tend to have bodies with limbs, which in turn have fingers or toes. Flowers have petals and stems. Mars Rovers have wheels and treads and entire subsystems, like the Rover Environmental Monitoring Station (REMS). Each part plays its role.

In the world of object-oriented programming, objects are *composed of* smaller objects in the same way. Computer scientists call this *object composition* or simply *composition*.

Gophers use composition with structures, and Go provides a special language feature called *embedding* to forward methods. This lesson demonstrates composition and embedding with a fictional weather report from REMS.

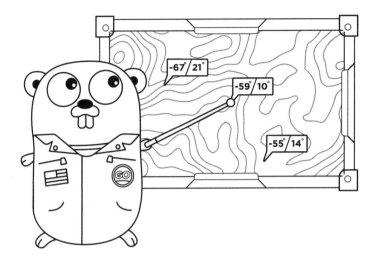

Consider this Designing hierarchies can be difficult. A hierarchy of the animal kingdom would attempt to group animals with the same behaviors. Some mammals walk on land while others swim, yet blue whales also nurse their young. How would you organize them? It can be difficult to change hierarchies too, as even a small change can have a wide impact.

Composition is a far simpler and more flexible approach: implement walking, swimming, nursing, and other behaviors and associate the appropriate ones with each animal.

As a bonus, if you design a robot, the walking behavior can be reused.

 ## 23.1 Composing structures

A weather report includes a variety of data, such as the high and low temperatures, current day (sol), and location. A naive solution is to define all the necessary fields in a single report structure like the following listing.

Listing 23.1 Without composition: unorganized.go

```go
type report struct {
    sol       int
    high, low float64
    lat, long float64
}
```

Looking at listing 23.1, report is a mix of disparate data. It gets unwieldy when the report grows to include even more data, such as wind speed and direction, pressure, humidity, season, sunrise, and sunset.

Fortunately you can group related fields together with structures and composition. The following listing defines a report structure composed of structures for temperature and location.

Listing 23.2 Structs inside of structs: compose.go

```go
type report struct {
    sol         int
    temperature temperature
    location    location
}

type temperature struct {
    high, low celsius
}

type location struct {
    lat, long float64
}

type celsius float64
```

The temperature field is a structure of type temperature.

With these types defined, a weather report is built up from location and temperature data as follows:

```go
bradbury := location{-4.5895, 137.4417}
t := temperature{high: -1.0, low: -78.0}
report := report{sol: 15, temperature: t,
    location: bradbury}

fmt.Printf("%+v\n", report)
fmt.Printf("a balmy %v° C\n", report.temperature.high)
```

Prints {sol:15
temperature:{high:-1 low:-78}
location:{lat:-4.5895
long:137.4417}}

Prints a balmy -1° C

Take another look at listing 23.2. Notice that high and low clearly refer to temperatures, whereas the same fields in listing 23.1 are ambiguous.

By building a weather report out of smaller types, you can further organize your code by hanging methods from each type. For example, to calculate the average temperature, you can write a method like the one shown in the next listing.

Listing 23.3 An average method: average.go

```
func (t temperature) average() celsius {
    return (t.high + t.low) / 2
}
```

The temperature type and average method can be used independently of the weather report as follows:

```
t := temperature{high: -1.0, low: -78.0}
fmt.Printf("average %v° C\n", t.average())
```
Prints average
-39.5° C

When you create a weather report, the average method is accessible by chaining off the temperature field:

Prints average
-39.5° C

```
report := report{sol: 15, temperature: t}
fmt.Printf("average %v° C\n", report.temperature.average())
```

If you want to expose the average temperature directly through the report type, there's no need to duplicate the logic in listing 23.3. Write a method that forwards to the real implementation instead:

```
func (r report) average() celsius {
    return r.temperature.average()
}
```

With a method to forward from report to temperature, you gain convenient access to report.average() while still structuring your code around smaller types. The remainder of this lesson examines a Go feature that promises to make method forwarding effortless.

Quick check 23.1   Compare listings 23.1 to 23.2. Which code do you prefer and why?

QC 23.1 answer   The structures in listing 23.2 are more organized, by splitting out temperatures and locations into separate reusable structures.

23.2 Forwarding methods

Method forwarding can make it more convenient to use the methods. Imagine asking Curiosity the weather on Mars. It could *forward* your request to the REMS system, which in turn would forward your request to a thermometer to determine the air temperature. With forwarding, you don't need to know the path to the method—you just ask Curiosity.

What isn't so convenient is manually writing methods to forward from one type to another like in listing 23.3. Such repetitive code, called *boilerplate*, adds nothing but clutter.

Fortunately, Go will do method forwarding for you with *struct embedding*. To embed a type in a structure, specify the type without a field name, as shown in the following listing.

Listing 23.4 Struct embedding: embed.go

```go
type report struct {
    sol         int
    temperature
    location
}
```
A temperature type
embedded into report

All the methods on the `temperature` type are automatically made accessible through the `report` type:

```go
report := report{
    sol:         15,
    location:    location{-4.5895, 137.4417},
    temperature: temperature{high: -1.0, low: -78.0},
}
fmt.Printf("average %v° C\n", report.average())
```
Prints average
-39.5° C

Though no field name was specified, a field still exists with the same name as the embedded type. You can access the `temperature` field as follows:

```go
fmt.Printf("average %v° C\n", report.temperature.average())
```
Prints average
-39.5° C

Embedding doesn't only forward methods. Fields of an inner structure are accessible from the outer structure. In addition to `report.temperature.high`, you can access the high temperature with `report.high` as follows:

```
fmt.Printf("%v° C\n", report.high)        ◄──────── Prints -1° C
report.high = 32
fmt.Printf("%v° C\n", report.temperature.high)  ◄──────── Prints 32° C
```

As you can see, changes to the report.high field are reflected in report.temperature.high. It's just another way to access the same data.

You can embed any type in a structure, not just structures. In the following listing, the sol type has an underlying type of int, yet it's embedded just like the location and temperature structures.

Listing 23.5 Embedding other types: sol.go

```
type sol int

type report struct {
    sol
    location
    temperature
}
```

Any methods declared on the sol type can be accessed through the sol field or through the report type:

```
func (s sol) days(s2 sol) int {
    days := int(s2 - s)
    if days < 0 {
        days = -days
    }
    return days
}

func main() {
    report := report{sol: 15}
    fmt.Println(report.sol.days(1446))      Prints 1431
    fmt.Println(report.days(1446))
}
```

23.3 Name collisions

The weather report works fine. Then someone wants to know the number of days it takes for a rover to travel between two locations. The Curiosity rover drives approximately 200 meters per day, so you add a days method to the location type to do the math, as shown in the next listing.

Listing 23.6 Another method with the same name: collision.go

```
func (l location) days(l2 location) int {
    // To-do: complicated distance calculation
    return 5                                          ←── See lesson 22.
}
```

The report structure embeds both sol and location, two types with a method named days.

The good news is that if none of your code is using the days method on a report, everything continues to work fine. The Go compiler is smart enough to only point out a name collision if it's a problem.

If the days method on the report type is being used, the Go compiler doesn't know if it should forward the call to the method on sol or the method on location, so it reports an error:

```
d := report.days(1446)    ←── Ambiguous selector
                              report.days
```

Resolving an *ambiguous selector* error is straightforward. If you implement the days method on the report type, it will take precedence over the days methods from the embedded types. You can manually forward to the embedded type of your choosing or perform some other behavior:

```
func (r report) days(s2 sol) int {
    return r.sol.days(s2)
}
```

This isn't the inheritance you were looking for

Classical languages like C++, Python, Java, PHP, Ruby, and Swift can use composition, but they also supply a language feature called inheritance.

Inheritance is a different way of thinking about designing software. With *inheritance*, a rover is a type of vehicle and thereby *inherits* the functionality that all vehicles share.

With composition, a rover has an engine and wheels and various other parts that provide the functionality a rover needs. A truck may reuse several of those parts, but there is no vehicle type or hierarchy descending from it.

Composition is generally considered more flexible, allowing greater reuse and easier changes than software built with inheritance. This isn't a new revelation, either—this wisdom was published in 1994:

> *Favor object composition over class inheritance.*
>
> —Gang of Four,
> *Design Patterns: Elements of Reusable*
> *Object-Oriented Software*

When people first see embedding, some initially think that it's the same as inheritance, but it's not. Not only is it a different way of thinking about software design, there's a subtle technical difference.

The receiver of `average()` in listing 23.3 is always of type `temperature`, even when forwarded through `report`. With *delegation* or inheritance, the receiver could be of type `report`, but Go has neither delegation nor inheritance. That's okay, though, because inheritance isn't needed:

> *Use of classical inheritance is always optional; every problem that it solves can be solved another way.*
>
> —Sandi Metz, *Practical Object-Oriented Design in Ruby*

Go is an independent new language that's able to shed the weight of antiquated paradigms, and so it does.

Quick check 23.3   If multiple embedded types implement a method of the same name, does the Go compiler report an error?

QC 23.3 answer   The Go compiler only reports an error if the method is being used.

Summary

- Composition is a technique of breaking large structures down into small structures and putting them together.
- Embedding gives access to the fields of inner structures in the outer structure.
- Methods are automatically forwarded when you embed types in a structure.
- Go will inform you of name collisions caused by embedding, but only if those methods are being used.

Let's see if you got this...

Experiment: gps.go

Write a program with a gps structure for a Global Positioning System (GPS). This struct should be composed of a current location, destination location, and a world.

Implement a description method for the location type that returns a string containing the name, latitude, and longitude. The world type should implement a distance method using the math from lesson 22.

Attach two methods to the gps type. First, attach a distance method that finds the distance between the current and destination locations. Then implement a message method that returns a string describing how many kilometers remain to the destination.

As a final step, create a rover structure that embeds the gps and write a main function to test everything out. Initialize a GPS for Mars with a current location of Bradbury Landing (-4.5895, 137.4417) and a destination of Elysium Planitia (4.5, 135.9). Then create a curiosity rover and print out its message (which forwards to the gps).

LESSON

INTERFACES

After reading lesson 24, you'll be able to

- Get your types talking
- Discover interfaces as you go
- Explore interfaces in the standard library
- Save humanity from a Martian invasion

Pen and paper aren't the only tools you could use to jot down your latest insight. A nearby crayon and napkin can serve the purpose. Crayons, permanent markers, and mechanical pencils can all satisfy your need to write a reminder in a notepad, a slogan on construction paper, or an entry in a journal. Writing is very flexible.

The Go standard library has an *interface* for writing. It goes by the name of Writer, and with it you can write text, images, comma-separated values (CSV), compressed archives, and more. You can write to the screen, a file on disk, or a response to a web request. With the help of a single interface, Go can write any number of things to any number of places. Writer is very flexible.

A 0.5 mm ballpoint pen with blue ink is a *concrete* thing, whereas a writing instrument is a fuzzier idea. With interfaces, code can express *abstract* concepts such as *a thing that writes*. Think of what something can do, rather than what it is. This way of thinking, as expressed through interfaces, will help your code to adapt to change.

Consider this   What are some *concrete* things around you? What can you do with them? Can you do the same thing with something else? What is the common behavior or interface that they have?

 ## 24.1 The interface type

The majority of types focus on the values they store: integers for whole numbers, strings for text, and so on. The interface type is different. Interfaces are concerned with what a type can do, not the value it holds.

Methods express the behavior a type provides, so interfaces are declared with a set of methods that a type must satisfy. The following listing declares a variable with an interface type.

Listing 24.1 A set of methods: talk.go

```
var t interface {
    talk() string
}
```

The variable t can hold any value of any type that *satisfies* the interface. More specifically, a type will satisfy the interface if it declares a method named talk that accepts no arguments and returns a string.

The following listing declares two types that meet these requirements.

Listing 24.2 Satisfying an interface: talk.go

```
type martian struct{}
func (m martian) talk() string {
    return "nack nack"
}

type laser int
func (l laser) talk() string {
    return strings.Repeat("pew ", int(l))
}
```

Though `martian` is a structure with no fields and `laser` is an integer, both types provide a `talk` method and therefore can be assigned to t, as in the following listing.

Listing 24.3 Polymorphism: talk.go

```
var t interface {
    talk() string
}
t = martian{}
fmt.Println(t.talk())        ← Prints nack nack

t = laser(3)
fmt.Println(t.talk())        ← Prints pew pew pew
```

The shape-shifting variable t is able to take the form of a `martian` or `laser`. Computer scientists say that interfaces provide *polymorphism*, which means "many shapes."

NOTE Unlike Java, in Go `martian` and `laser` don't explicitly declare that they implement an interface. The benefit of this is covered later in the lesson.

Typically interfaces are declared as named types that can be reused. There's a convention of naming interface types with an *-er* suffix: a *talker* is anything that talks, as shown in the following listing.

Listing 24.4 A `talker` type: shout.go

```
type talker interface {
    talk() string
}
```

An interface type can be used anywhere other types are used. For example, the following shout function has a parameter of type talker.

Listing 24.5 Shout what was spoken: shout.go

```go
func shout(t talker) {
    louder := strings.ToUpper(t.talk())
    fmt.Println(louder)
}
```

You can use the shout function with any value that satisfies the talker interface, whether martians or lasers, as shown in the next listing.

Listing 24.6 Shouting: shout.go

```go
shout(martian{})    ←——— Prints NACK NACK
shout(laser(2))     ←——— Prints PEW PEW
```

The argument you pass to the shout function must satisfy the talker interface. For example, the crater type doesn't satisfy the talker interface, so if you expect a crater to shout, Go refuses to compile your program:

```go
type crater struct{}        crater does not
                            implement talker
shout(crater{})   ←————     (missing talk method)
```

Interfaces exhibit their flexibility when you need to change or extend code. When you declare a new type with a talk method, the shout function will work with it. Any code that only depends on the interface can remain the same, even as implementations are added and modified.

It's worth noting that interfaces can be used with struct embedding, the language feature covered in lesson 23. For example, the following listing embeds laser in a starship.

Listing 24.7 Embedding satisfies interfaces: starship.go

```go
type starship struct {
    laser
}
s := starship{laser(3)}
                              Prints pew pew pew
fmt.Println(s.talk())   ←———
shout(s)   ←——— Prints PEW PEW PEW
```

When a starship talks, the laser does the talking. Embedding `laser` gives the `starship` a `talk` method that forwards to the `laser`. Now the starship also satisfies the `talker` interface, allowing it to be used with `shout`.

> *Used together, composition and interfaces make a very powerful design tool.*
>
> —Bill Venners, *JavaWorld*
> (see mng.bz/B5eg)

Quick check 24.1

1. Modify the laser's `talk` method in listing 24.4 to prevent the Martian guns from firing, thus saving humanity from the invasion.
2. Expand listing 24.4 by declaring a new `rover` type with a `talk` method that returns "whir whir". Use the `shout` function with your new type.

 ## 24.2 Discovering the interface

With Go you can begin implementing your code and discover the interfaces as you go. Any code can implement an interface, even code that already exists. This section walks you through an example.

QC 24.1 answer

1.
```go
func (l laser) talk() string {
    return strings.Repeat("toot ", int(l))
}
```

2.
```go
type rover string

func (r rover) talk() string {
    return string(r)
}

func main() {
    r := rover("whir whir")
    shout(r)   ⟵——— Prints WHIR WHIR
}
```

The following listing derives a fictional stardate from the day of the year and hour of the day.

Listing 24.8 Stardate calculation: stardate.go

```go
package main

import (
    "fmt"
    "time"
)

// stardate returns a fictional measure of time for a given date.
func stardate(t time.Time) float64 {
    doy := float64(t.YearDay())
    h := float64(t.Hour()) / 24.0
    return 1000 + doy + h
}

func main() {
    day := time.Date(2012, 8, 6, 5, 17, 0, 0, time.UTC)
    fmt.Printf("%.1f Curiosity has landed\n", stardate(day))
}
```

Prints 1219.2
Curiosity has
landed

The stardate function in listing 24.8 is limited to Earth dates. To remedy this, the following listing declares an interface for stardate to use.

Listing 24.9 Stardate interface: stardater.go

```go
type stardater interface {
    YearDay() int
    Hour() int
}

// stardate returns a fictional measure of time.
func stardate(t stardater) float64 {
    doy := float64(t.YearDay())
    h := float64(t.Hour()) / 24.0
    return 1000 + doy + h
}
```

The new stardate function in listing 24.9 continues to operate on Earth dates because the time.Time type in the standard library satisfies the stardater interface. Interfaces in Go are satisfied implicitly, which is especially helpful when working with code you didn't write.

> **NOTE** This wouldn't be possible in a language like Java because java.time would need to explicitly say that it implements stardater.

With the stardater interface in place, listing 24.9 can be expanded with a sol type that satisfies the interface with methods for YearDay and Hour, as shown in the following listing.

Listing 24.10 Sol implementation: stardater.go

```
type sol int
func (s sol) YearDay() int {
    return int(s % 668)         ← There are 668 sols in
}                                 a Martian year.
func (s sol) Hour() int {
    return 0      ←——— The hour is unknown.
}
```

Now the stardate function operates on both Earth dates and Martian sols, as shown in the next listing.

Listing 24.11 In use: stardater.go

```
day := time.Date(2012, 8, 6, 5, 17, 0, 0, time.UTC)
fmt.Printf("%.1f Curiosity has landed\n", stardate(day))    ← Prints
                                                              1219.2
s := sol(1422)                                                Curiosity
fmt.Printf("%.1f Happy birthday\n", stardate(s))    ←        has landed

                                        Prints 1086.0
                                        Happy birthday
```

> **Quick check 24.2** How is implicitly satisfying interfaces advantageous?

QC 24.2 answer You can declare an interface that's satisfied by code you didn't write, providing more flexibility.

24.3   Satisfying interfaces

The standard library exports a number of single-method interfaces that you can implement in your code.

> *Go encourages composition over inheritance, using simple, often one-method interfaces …*
> *that serve as clean, comprehensible boundaries between components.*
>
> —Rob Pike,
> "Go at Google: Language Design in the
> Service of Software Engineering"
> (see talks.golang.org/ 2012/splash.article)

As an example, the fmt package declares a Stringer interface as follows:

```
type Stringer interface {
    String() string
}
```

If a type provides a String method, Println, Sprintf, and friends will use it. The following listing provides a String method to control how the fmt package displays a location.

Listing 24.12   Satisfying stringer: stringer.go

```
package main

import "fmt"

// location with a latitude, longitude in decimal degrees.
type location struct {
    lat, long float64
}

// String formats a location with latitude, longitude.
func (l location) String() string {
    return fmt.Sprintf("%v, %v", l.lat, l.long)
}

func main() {
    curiosity := location{-4.5895, 137.4417}      Prints -4.5895,
    fmt.Println(curiosity)  ←                      137.4417
}
```

In addition to fmt.Stringer, popular interfaces in the standard library include io.Reader, io.Writer, and json.Marshaler.

TIP   The io.ReadWriter interface provides an example of interface embedding that looks similar to struct embedding from lesson 23. Unlike structures, interfaces don't have fields or attached methods, so interface embedding saves some typing and little else.

Quick check 24.3   Write a String method on the coordinate type and use it to display coordinates in a more readable format.

```
type coordinate struct {
    d, m, s float64
    h       rune
}
```

Your program should output Elysium Planitia is at 4°30'0.0" N, 135°54'0.0" E.

QC 24.3 answer

```go
// String formats a DMS coordinate.
func (c coordinate) String() string {
    return fmt.Sprintf("%v°%v'%.1f\" %c", c.d, c.m, c.s, c.h)
}
// location with a latitude, longitude in decimal degrees.
type location struct {
    lat, long coordinate
}
// String formats a location with latitude, longitude.
func (l location) String() string {
    return fmt.Sprintf("%v, %v", l.lat, l.long)
}
func main() {
    elysium := location{
        lat:  coordinate{4, 30, 0.0, 'N'},
        long: coordinate{135, 54, 0.0, 'E'},
    }
    fmt.Println("Elysium Planitia is at", elysium)
}
```

Prints Elysium Planitia is at 4°30'0.0" N, 135°54'0.0" E

24.4 Summary

- Interface types specify required behaviors with a set of methods.
- Interfaces are satisfied implicitly by new or existing code in any package.
- A structure will satisfy the interfaces that embedded types satisfy.
- Follow the example set by the standard library and strive to keep interfaces small.

Let's see if you got this...

Experiment: marshal.go

Write a program that outputs coordinates in JSON format, expanding on work done for the preceding quick check. The JSON output should provide each coordinate in decimal degrees (DD) as well as the degrees, minutes, seconds format:

```
{
    "decimal": 135.9,
    "dms": "135°54'0.0\" E",
    "degrees": 135,
    "minutes": 54,
    "seconds": 0,
    "hemisphere": "E"
}
```

This can be achieved without modifying the coordinate structure by satisfying the json.Marshaler interface to customize the JSON. The MarshalJSON method you write may make use of json.Marshal.

> **NOTE** To calculate decimal degrees, you'll need the decimal method introduced in lesson 22.

CAPSTONE: MARTIAN ANIMAL SANCTUARY

In the distant future, humankind may be able to comfortably live on what is currently a dusty red planet. Mars is farther from the Sun and therefore much colder. Warming up the planet could be the first step in *terraforming* the climate and surface of Mars. Once water begins to flow and plants begin to grow, organisms can be introduced.

> *Tropical trees can be planted; insects and some small animals can be introduced. Humans will still need gas masks to provide oxygen and prevent high levels of carbon dioxide in the lungs.*
>
> —Leonard David,
> *Mars: Our Future on the Red Planet*

Right now the Martian atmosphere is approximately 96% carbon dioxide (see en.wikipedia.org/wiki/Atmosphere_of_Mars). It could take a very, very long time to change that. Mars will remain a different world.

Now it's time to use your imagination. What do you think would happen if an ark full of Earth animals were introduced to a terraformed Mars? What lifeforms might spring forth as the climate adjusts to support life?

Your task is to create a simulation of the first animal sanctuary on Mars. Make a few types of animals. Each animal should have a name and adhere to the Stringer interface to return their name.

Every animal should have methods to move and eat. The move method should return a description of the movement. The eat method should return the name of a random food that the animal likes.

Implement a day/night cycle and run the simulation for three 24-hour sols (72 hours). All the animals should sleep from sunset until sunrise. For every hour of the day, pick an animal at random to perform a random action (move or eat). For every action, print out a description of what the animal did.

Your implementation should make use of structures and interfaces.

Down the gopher hole

It's time to get your hands dirty, delving deeper into programming with Go.

You'll need to consider how memory is organized and shared, bringing new levels of control and responsibility. You'll learn how `nil` can be beneficial, while avoiding the dreaded *nil pointer dereference*. And you'll see how exercising diligence in error handing can make your programs more reliable.

A FEW POINTERS

After reading lesson 26, you'll be able to

- Declare and use pointers
- Understand the relationship between pointers and random access memory (RAM)
- Know when to use—and not use—pointers

Walk around any neighborhood and you'll likely encounter homes with individual addresses and street signs to guide you on your way. You may happen upon a closed-down shop with an apologetic sign: "Sorry, we've moved!" Pointers are a bit like the sign in the store window that directs you to a different address.

SORRY, WE'VE MOVED!

A *pointer* is a variable that points to the address of another variable. In computer science, pointers are a form of *indirection*, and indirection can be a powerful tool.

> *All problems in computer science can be solved by another level of indirection...*
>
> —David Wheeler

Pointers are quite useful, but over the years they've been associated with a great deal of angst. Languages in the past—C in particular—had little emphasis on safety. Many crashes and security vulnerabilities can be tied back to the misuse of pointers. This gave rise to several languages that don't expose pointers to programmers.

Go does have pointers, but with an emphasis on memory safety. Go isn't plagued with issues like *dangling pointers*. This would be like heading to the address for your favorite shop, only to find it was accidentally replaced with the parking lot for a new casino.

If you've encountered pointers before, take a deep breath. This isn't going to be so bad. If this is your first encounter, relax. Go is a safe place to learn pointers.

> **Consider this**   Like the shop sign directing visitors to a new address, pointers direct a computer where to look for a value. What's another situation where you're directed to look somewhere else?

 ## 26.1 The ampersand and the asterisk

Pointers in Go adopt the well-established syntax used by C. There are two symbols to be aware of, the ampersand (&) and the asterisk (*), though the asterisk serves a dual purpose, as you'll soon see.

The *address operator*, represented by an ampersand, determines the address of a variable in memory. Variables store their values in a computer's RAM, and the location where a value is stored is known as its *memory address*. The following listing prints a memory address as a hexadecimal number, though the address on your computer will differ.

Listing 26.1 Address operator: memory.go

```
answer := 42
fmt.Println(&answer)        ◀────── Prints 0x1040c108
```

This is the location in memory where the computer stored 42. Thankfully, you can use the variable name answer to retrieve the value, rather than the memory address your computer uses.

> **NOTE** You can't take the address of a literal string, number, or Boolean. The Go compiler will report an error for &42 or &"another level of indirection".

The address operator (&) provides the memory address of a value. The reverse operation is known as *dereferencing*, which provides the value that a memory address refers to. The following listing dereferences the address variable by prefixing it with an asterisk (*).

Listing 26.2 Dereference operator: memory.go

```
answer := 42
fmt.Println(&answer)      ◄─────── Prints 0x1040c108

address := &answer
fmt.Println(*address)    ◄─────── Prints 42
```

In the preceding listing and in figure 26.1, the address variable holds the memory address of answer. It doesn't hold the answer (42), but it knows where to find it.

> **NOTE** Memory addresses in C can be manipulated with pointer arithmetic (for example address++), but Go disallows unsafe operations.

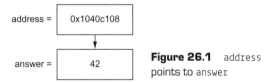

Figure 26.1 address points to answer

> **Quick check 26.1**
> 1 What does fmt.Println(*&answer) display for listing 26.2?
> 2 How might the Go compiler know the difference between dereferencing and multiplication?

QC 26.1 answer
1 It prints 42 because the memory address (&) is dereferenced (*) back to the value.
2 Multiplication is an *infix* operator requiring two values, whereas dereferencing prefixes a single variable.

26.1.1 Pointer types

Pointers store memory addresses.

The `address` variable in listing 26.2 is a pointer of type `*int`, as the `%T` format verb reveals in the following listing.

Listing 26.3 **A pointer type: type.go**

```
answer := 42
address := &answer

fmt.Printf("address is a %T\n", address)
```
← Prints address is a *int

The asterisk in `*int` denotes that the type is a pointer. In this case, it can point to other variables of type `int`.

Pointer types can appear anywhere types are used, including in variable declarations, function parameters, return types, structure field types, and so on. In the following listing, the asterisk (*) in the declaration of `home` indicates that it's a pointer type.

Listing 26.4 **Declaring a pointer: home.go**

```
canada := "Canada"

var home *string
fmt.Printf("home is a %T\n", home)
```
← Prints home is a *string

```
home = &canada
fmt.Println(*home)
```
← Prints Canada

> **TIP** An asterisk prefixing a type denotes a pointer type, whereas an asterisk prefixing a variable name is used to dereference the value that variable points to.

The `home` variable in the previous listing can point at any variable of type `string`. However, the Go compiler won't allow `home` to point to a variable of any other type, such as `int`.

> **NOTE** The C type system is easily convinced that a memory address holds a different type. That can be useful at times but, once again, Go avoids potentially unsafe operations.

26.2 Pointers are for pointing

Charles Bolden became the administrator of NASA on July 17, 2009. He was preceded
by Christopher Scolese. By representing the administrator role with a pointer, the following listing can point administrator at whoever fills the role (see figure 26.2).

Listing 26.5 Administrator for NASA: nasa.go

```
var administrator *string

scolese := "Christopher J. Scolese"
administrator = &scolese
fmt.Println(*administrator)          ◄——— Prints Christopher J. Scolese

bolden := "Charles F. Bolden"
administrator = &bolden
fmt.Println(*administrator)          ◄——— Prints Charles F. Bolden
```

```
scolese =   | Christopher J.
            |   Scolese

administrator = | 0xc42000e280
                        |
                        ▼
bolden =    | Charles F.         Figure 26.2  administrator
            |   Bolden           points to bolden
```

Changes to the value of bolden can be made in one place, because the administrator variable points to bolden rather than storing a copy:

```
bolden = "Charles Frank Bolden Jr."
fmt.Println(*administrator)
```
Prints Charles Frank Bolden Jr.

It's also possible to dereference administrator to change the value of bolden indirectly:

```
*administrator = "Maj. Gen. Charles Frank Bolden Jr."
fmt.Println(bolden)
```
Prints Maj. Gen. Charles Frank Bolden Jr.

Assigning major to administrator results in a new pointer that's also pointing at the bolden string (see figure 26.3):

```
major := administrator
*major = "Major General Charles Frank Bolden Jr."
fmt.Println(bolden)
```
Prints Major General Charles Frank Bolden Jr.

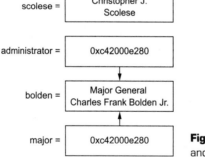

scolese = | Christopher J. Scolese

administrator = | 0xc42000e280

bolden = | Major General Charles Frank Bolden Jr.

major = | 0xc42000e280

Figure 26.3   administrator and major point to bolden

The major and administrator pointers both hold the same memory address and therefore are equal:

```
fmt.Println(administrator == major)
```
Prints true

Charles Bolden was succeeded by Robert M. Lightfoot Jr. on January 20, 2017. After this change, administrator and major no longer point to the same memory address (see figure 26.4):

```
lightfoot := "Robert M. Lightfoot Jr."
administrator = &lightfoot
fmt.Println(administrator == major)
```
Prints false

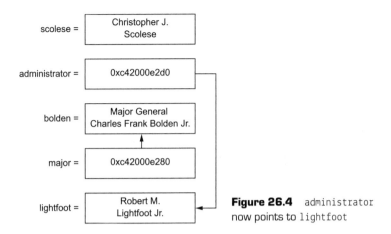

Figure 26.4 administrator
now points to lightfoot

Assigning the dereferenced value of major to another variable makes a copy of the string. After the clone is made, direct and indirect modifications to bolden have no effect on the value of charles, or vice versa:

```
charles := *major
*major = "Charles Bolden"
fmt.Println(charles)
fmt.Println(bolden)
```

Prints Major General Charles Frank Bolden Jr.

Prints Charles Bolden

If two variables contain the same string, they're considered equal, as with charles and bolden in the following code. This is the case even though they have different memory addresses:

```
charles = "Charles Bolden"
fmt.Println(charles == bolden)
fmt.Println(&charles == &bolden)
```

Prints true

Prints false

In this section, the value of bolden was modified indirectly by dereferencing the administrator and major pointers. This demonstrates what pointers can do, though it would be straightforward to assign values directly to bolden in this instance.

26.2.1 Pointing to structures

Pointers are frequently used with structures. As such, the Go language designers chose to provide a few ergonomic amenities for pointers to structures.

Unlike strings and numbers, composite literals can be prefixed with an address operator. In the following listing, the `timmy` variable holds a memory address pointing to a `person` structure.

Listing 26.6 Person structure: struct.go

```
type person struct {
    name, superpower string
    age              int
}

timmy := &person{
    name: "Timothy",
    age:  10,
}
```

Furthermore, it isn't necessary to dereference structures to access their fields. The following listing is preferable to writing `(*timmy).superpower`.

Listing 26.7 Composite literals: struct.go

```
timmy.superpower = "flying"
fmt.Printf("%+v\n", timmy)
```
Prints &{name:Timothy superpower:flying age:10}

Quick check 26.4

1 What are valid uses of the address operator?
  a Literal strings: &"Timothy"
  b Literal integers: &10
  c Composite literals: &person{name: "Timothy"}
  d All of the above
2 What's the difference between `timmy.superpower` and `(*timmy).superpower`?

26.2.2 Pointing to arrays

As with structures, composite literals for arrays can be prefixed with the address operator (&) to create a new pointer to an array. Arrays also provide automatic dereferencing,
as shown in the following listing.

Listing 26.8 Pointer to an array: superpowers.go

```
superpowers := &[3]string{"flight", "invisibility", "super strength"}

fmt.Println(superpowers[0])      ⟵  Prints flight
fmt.Println(superpowers[1:2])    ⟵  Prints [invisibility]
```

The array in the previous listing is dereferenced automatically when indexing or slicing
it. There's no need to write the more cumbersome `(*superpowers)[0]`.

> **NOTE** Unlike the C language, arrays and pointers in Go are completely independent types.

Composite literals for slices and maps can also be prefixed with the address operator (&),
but there's no automatic dereferencing.

QC 26.4 answer

1 The address operator is valid with variable names and composite literals, but not literal strings
  or numbers.
2 There's no functional difference because Go automatically dereferences pointers for fields, but
  `timmy.superpower` is easier to read and is therefore preferable.

Quick check 26.5   What's another way to write `(*superpowers)[2:]` where `superpowers` is a pointer to an array?

 ## 26.3 Enabling mutation

Pointers are used to enable mutation across function and method boundaries.

26.3.1 Pointers as parameters

Function and method parameters are passed by value in Go. That means functions always operate on a copy of passed arguments. When a pointer is passed to a function, the function receives a copy of the memory address. By dereferencing the memory address, a function can mutate the value a pointer points to.

In listing 26.9 a `birthday` function is declared with one parameter of type `*person`. This allows the function body to dereference the pointer and modify the value it points to. As with listing 26.7, it isn't necessary to explicitly dereference the `p` variable to access the `age` field. The syntax in the following listing is preferable to `(*p).age++`.

Listing 26.9 Function parameters: birthday.go

```
type person struct {
    name, superpower string
    age              int
}
func birthday(p *person) {
    p.age++
}
```

The `birthday` function requires the caller to pass a pointer to a person, as shown in the following listing.

QC 26.5 answer   Writing `superpowers[2:]` is the same, thanks to automatic dereferencing for arrays.

Listing 26.10 Function arguments: birthday.go

```
rebecca := person{
    name:       "Rebecca",
    superpower: "imagination",
    age:        14,
}

birthday(&rebecca)

fmt.Printf("%+v\n", rebecca)
```

Prints {name:Rebecca
superpower:imagination
age:15}

Quick check 26.6

1 What code would return Timothy 11? Refer to listing 26.6.
  a birthday(&timmy)
  b birthday(timmy)
  c birthday(*timmy)
2 What age would Rebecca be if the birthday(p person) function didn't use a pointer?

26.3.2 Pointer receivers

Method receivers are similar to parameters. The birthday method in the next listing uses a pointer for the receiver, which allows the method to mutate a person's attributes. This behavior is just like the birthday function in listing 26.9.

Listing 26.11 Pointer receiver: method.go

```
type person struct {
    name string
    age  int
}
func (p *person) birthday() {
    p.age++
}
```

QC 26.6 answer

1 The timmy variable is a pointer already, so the correct answer is b. birthday(timmy).
2 Rebecca would forever remain 14 if birthday didn't utilize a pointer.

In the following listing, declaring a pointer and calling the `birthday` method increments Terry's age.

Listing 26.12   Method call with a pointer: method.go

```
terry := &person{
    name: "Terry",
    age:  15,
}
terry.birthday()
fmt.Printf("%+v\n", terry)        Prints &{name:Terry
                                  age:16}
```

Alternatively, the method call in the next listing doesn't use a pointer, yet it still works. Go will automatically determine the address of (&) a variable when calling methods with dot notation, so you don't need to write `(&nathan).birthday()`.

Listing 26.13   Method call without a pointer: method.go

```
nathan := person{
    name: "Nathan",
    age:  17,
}
nathan.birthday()
fmt.Printf("%+v\n", nathan)       Prints {name:Nathan
                                  age:18}
```

Whether called with a pointer or not, the `birthday` method declared in listing 26.11 must specify a pointer receiver—otherwise, `age` wouldn't increment.

Structures are frequently passed around with pointers. It makes sense for the `birthday` method to mutate a person's attributes rather than create a whole new person. That said, not every structure should be mutated. The standard library provides a great example in the `time` package. The methods of the `time.Time` type never use a pointer receiver, preferring to return a new time instead, as shown in the next listing. After all, tomorrow is a new day.

Listing 26.14   Tomorrow is a new day: day.go

```
const layout = "Mon, Jan 2, 2006"

day := time.Now()
tomorrow := day.Add(24 * time.Hour)
fmt.Println(day.Format(layout))          Prints Tue, Nov 10, 2009
fmt.Println(tomorrow.Format(layout))     Prints Wed, Nov 11, 2009
```

TIP You should use pointer receivers consistently. If some methods need pointer receivers, use pointer receivers for all methods of the type (see golang.org/doc/faq#methods_on_values_or_pointers).

Quick check 26.7 How do you know that `time.Time` never uses a pointer receiver?

26.3.3 Interior pointers

Go provides a handy feature called *interior pointers,* used to determine the memory address of a field inside of a structure. The `levelUp` function in the following listing mutates a `stats` structure and therefore requires a pointer.

Listing 26.15 The `levelUp` function: interior.go

```
type stats struct {
    level              int
    endurance, health int
}
func levelUp(s *stats) {
    s.level++
    s.endurance = 42 + (14 * s.level)
    s.health = 5 * s.endurance
}
```

The address operator in Go can be used to point to a field within a structure, as shown in the next listing.

Listing 26.16 Interior pointers: interior.go

```
type character struct {
    name  string
    stats stats
}
player := character{name: "Matthias"}
```

QC 26.7 answer The code in listing 26.14 doesn't reveal whether or not the Add method uses a pointer receiver because dot notation is the same either way. It's best to look at the documentation for the methods of `time.Time` (see golang.org/pkg/time/#Time).

```
levelUp(&player.stats)
fmt.Printf("%+v\n", player.stats)
```

Prints {level:1
endurance:56
health:280}

The `character` type doesn't have any pointers in the structure definition, yet you can take the memory address of any field when the need arises. The code `&player.stats` provides a pointer to the interior of the structure.

> **Quick check 26.8**   What's an interior pointer?

26.3.4 Mutating arrays

Though slices tend to be preferred over arrays, using arrays can be appropriate when there's no need to change their length. The chessboard from lesson 16 is such an example. The following listing demonstrates how pointers allow functions to mutate elements of the array.

Listing 26.17 Resetting the chessboard: array.go

```
func reset(board *[8][8]rune) {
    board[0][0] = 'r'
    // ...
}
func main() {
    var board [8][8]rune
    reset(&board)
    fmt.Printf("%c", board[0][0])            ←——— Prints r
}
```

In lesson 20, the suggested implementation for Conway's Game of Life makes use of slices even though the world is a fixed size. Armed with pointers, you could rewrite the Game of Life to use arrays.

QC 26.8 answer   A pointer that points at a field inside a structure. This is achieved by using the address operator on a field of a structure, such as &player.stats.

Quick check 26.9   When is it appropriate to use a pointer to an array?

 ## 26.4 Pointers in disguise

Not all mutations require explicit use of a pointer. Go uses pointers behind the scenes for some of the built-in collections.

26.4.1 Maps are pointers

Lesson 19 states that maps aren't copied when assigned or passed as arguments. Maps are pointers in disguise, so pointing to a map is redundant. Don't do this:

```
func demolish(planets *map[string]string)         ◄─────── Unnecessary pointer
```

It's perfectly fine for the key or value of a map to be a pointer type, but there's rarely a reason to point to a map.

Quick check 26.10   Is a map a pointer?

26.4.2 Slices point at arrays

Lesson 17 describes a slice as a window into an array. To point at an element of the array, slices use a pointer.

A slice is represented internally as a structure with three elements: a pointer to an array, the capacity of the slice, and the length. The internal pointer allows the underlying data to be mutated when a slice is passed directly to a function or method.

QC 26.9 answer   Arrays are appropriate for data with fixed dimensions, such as a chess-board. Arrays are copied when passed to functions or methods unless a pointer is used, which enables mutation.

QC 26.10 answer   Yes, even though maps don't resemble pointers syntactically, they are in fact pointers. There's no way to use a map that isn't a pointer.

An explicit pointer to a slice is only useful when modifying the slice itself: the length, capacity, or starting offset. In the following listing, the `reclassify` function modifies the length of the `planets` slice. The calling function (`main`) wouldn't see this change if `reclassify` didn't utilize a pointer.

Listing 26.18 Modifying a slice: slice.go

```
func reclassify(planets *[]string) {
    *planets = (*planets)[0:8]
}
func main() {
    planets := []string{
        "Mercury", "Venus", "Earth", "Mars",
        "Jupiter", "Saturn", "Uranus", "Neptune",
        "Pluto",
    }
    reclassify(&planets)            Prints [Mercury Venus
                                    Earth Mars Jupiter
    fmt.Println(planets)  ◄───      Saturn Uranus Neptune]
}
```

Instead of mutating the passed slice as in listing 26.18, an arguably cleaner approach is to write the `reclassify` function to return a new slice.

> **Quick check 26.11** Functions and methods wanting to mutate the data they receive will require a pointer for which two data types?

 ## 26.5 Pointers and interfaces

The following listing demonstrates that both `martian` and a pointer to `martian` satisfy the `talker` interface.

QC 26.11 answer   Structures and arrays.

Listing 26.19 **Pointers and interfaces: martian.go**

```go
type talker interface {
    talk() string
}
func shout(t talker) {
    louder := strings.ToUpper(t.talk())
    fmt.Println(louder)
}
type martian struct{}
func (m martian) talk() string {
    return "nack nack"
}
func main() {
    shout(martian{})        |  Prints
    shout(&martian{})       |  NACK NACK
}
```

It's different when methods use pointer receivers, as shown in the following listing.

Listing 26.20 **Pointers and interfaces: interface.go**

```go
type laser int
func (l *laser) talk() string {
    return strings.Repeat("pew ", int(*l))
}
func main() {
    pew := laser(2)        Prints PEW PEW
    shout(&pew)    ◄──
}
```

In the preceding listing, &pew is of type *laser, which satisfies the talker interface that shout requires. But shout(pew) doesn't work because laser doesn't satisfy the interface in this case.

> **Quick check 26.12**   When does a pointer satisfy an interface?

 ## 26.6   Use pointers wisely

Pointers can be useful, but they also add complexity. It can be more difficult to follow code when values could be changed from multiple places.

Use pointers when it makes sense, but don't overuse them. Programming languages that don't expose pointers often use them behind the scenes, such as when composing a class of several objects. With Go you decide when to use pointers and when to *not* use them.

> **Quick check 26.13**   Why shouldn't pointers be overused?

 ## Summary

- Pointers store memory addresses.
- The address operator (&) provides the memory address of a variable.
- A pointer can be dereferenced (*) to access or modify the value it points to.
- Pointers are types declared with a preceding asterisk, such as `*int`.
- Use pointers to mutate values across function and method boundaries.
- Pointers are most useful with structures and arrays.
- Maps and slices use pointers behind the scenes.
- Interior pointers can point at fields inside structures without declaring those fields as pointers.
- Use pointers when it makes sense but don't overuse them.

QC 26.12 answer   A pointer to a value satisfies all the interfaces that the non-pointer version of the type satisfies.

QC 26.13 answer   Code that doesn't use pointers may be simpler to understand.

Let's see if you got this...

Experiment: turtle.go

Write a program with a turtle that can move up, down, left, or right. The turtle should store an (x, y) location where positive values go down and to the right. Use methods to increment/decrement the appropriate variable. A `main` function should exercise the methods you've written and print the final location.

> **TIP** Method receivers will need to use pointers in order to manipulate the x and y values.

MUCH ADO ABOUT NIL

After reading lesson 27, you'll be able to

- Do something with nothing
- Understand the trouble with nil
- See how Go improves on nil's story

The word *nil* is a noun that means nothing or zero. In the Go programming language, nil is a zero value. Recall from unit 2 that an integer declared without a value will default to 0. An empty string is the zero value for strings, and so on. A pointer with nowhere to point has the value nil. And the nil identifier is the zero value for slices, maps, and interfaces too.

Many programming languages incorporate the concept of nil, though they may call it NULL, null, or None. In 2009, prior to the release of Go, language designer Tony Hoare gave a presentation titled "Null References: The Billion Dollar Mistake." In his talk (see mng.bz/dNzX), Hoare claims responsibility for inventing the null reference in 1965 and suggests that pointers to nowhere weren't one of his brightest ideas.

> **NOTE** Tony Hoare went on to invent communicating sequential processes (CSP) in 1978. His ideas are the basis for concurrency in Go, the topic of unit 7.

Nil is somewhat friendlier in Go, and less prevalent than in past languages, but there are still caveats to be aware of. Nil has some unexpected uses too, which Francesc Campoy talked about in his presentation at GopherCon 2016 (see www.youtube.com/ watch?v= ynoY2xz-F8s), providing inspiration for this lesson.

> **Consider this** Consider representing a constellation, where each star contains a pointer to its nearest neighboring star. After the math is done, every star will point somewhere, and finding the nearest star becomes a quick pointer dereference away.
>
> But until all the calculations are done, where should the pointers point? This is one situation where nil comes in handy. Nil can stand in for the nearest star until it's known.
>
> What is another situation where a pointer to nowhere could be useful?

 ## 27.1 Nil leads to panic

If a pointer isn't pointing anywhere, attempting to dereference the pointer won't work, as listing 27.1 demonstrates. Dereference a nil pointer, and the program will crash. As a rule, people tend to dislike apps that crash.

I call it my billion-dollar mistake.

—Tony Hoare

Listing 27.1 Nil leads to panic: panic.go

```
var nowhere *int
fmt.Println(nowhere)        Prints <nil>
                            Panic: nil pointer
fmt.Println(*nowhere)       dereference
```

Avoiding panic is fairly straightforward. It's a matter of guarding against a nil pointer dereference with an `if` statement, as shown in the following listing.

Listing 27.2 Guard against panic: nopanic.go

```
var nowhere *int

if nowhere != nil {
    fmt.Println(*nowhere)
}
```

To be fair, programs can crash for many reasons, not only because of nil pointer dereferences. For example, divide by zero also causes a panic, and the remedy is similar. Even so, considering all the software written in the past 50 years, the number of accidental nil pointer dereferences could be fairly costly for users and programmers alike. The existence of nil does burden the programmer with more decisions. Should the code check for nil, and if so, where should the check be? What should the code do if a value is nil? Does all this make *nil* a bad word?

"We shall say nil to you ... if you do not appease us."—The Knights Who Say nil

There's no need to cover your ears or avoid nil altogether. In truth, nil can be quite useful, as the remainder of this lesson demonstrates. Additionally, nil pointers in Go are less prevalent than null pointers are in some other languages, and there are ways to avoid their use when appropriate.

Quick check 27.1   What's the zero value for the type *string?

QC 27.1 answer   The zero value for a pointer is nil.

27.2 Guarding your methods

Methods frequently receive a pointer to a structure, which means the receiver could be nil, as shown in the following listing. Whether a pointer is dereferenced explicitly (`*p`) or implicitly by accessing a field of the struct (`p.age`), a nil value will panic.

Listing 27.3 Nil receivers: method.go

```go
type person struct {
    age int
}
func (p *person) birthday() {
    p.age++          ←———  nil pointer
}                                dereference
func main() {
    var nobody *person
    fmt.Println(nobody)   ←———
    nobody.birthday()            Prints <nil>
}
```

A key observation is that the panic is caused when the `p.age++` line executes. Remove that line, and the program will run.

> **NOTE** Contrast this to the equivalent program in Java, where a null receiver will crash the program immediately when a method is called.

Go will happily call methods even when the receiver has a nil value. A nil receiver behaves no differently than a nil parameter. This means methods can guard against nil values, as shown in the following listing.

Listing 27.4 Guard clause: guard.go

```go
func (p *person) birthday() {
    if p == nil {
        return
    }
    p.age++
}
```

Rather than check for `nil` before every call to the `birthday` method, the preceding listing guards against nil receivers inside the method.

> **NOTE** In Objective-C, invoking a method on nil doesn't crash, but rather than call the method, it returns a zero value.

You decide how to handle `nil` in Go. Your methods can return zero values, or return an error, or let it crash.

> **Quick check 27.2**   What does accessing a field (`p.age`) do if p is nil?

 ## 27.3 Nil function values

When a variable is declared as a function type, its value is `nil` by default. In the following listing, `fn` has the type of a function, but it isn't assigned to any specific function.

Listing 27.5 Function types that are nil: fn.go

```
var fn func(a, b int) int
fmt.Println(fn == nil)        ← Prints true
```

If the preceding listing were to call `fn(1, 2)`, the program would panic with a nil pointer dereference, because there's no function assigned to `fn`.

It's possible to check whether a function value is `nil` and provide default behavior. In the next listing, `sort.Slice` is used to sort a slice of strings with a first-class `less` function. If `nil` is passed for the `less` argument, it defaults to a function that sorts alphabetically.

Listing 27.6 A default function: sort.go

```
package main

import (
    "fmt"
    "sort"
)
```

QC 27.2 answer   It panics, crashing the program, unless the code checks for nil before the field access.

```
func sortStrings(s []string, less func(i, j int) bool) {
    if less == nil {
        less = func(i, j int) bool { return s[i] < s[j] }
    }
    sort.Slice(s, less)
}

func main() {
    food := []string{"onion", "carrot", "celery"}
    sortStrings(food, nil)
    fmt.Println(food)
}
```

Prints [carrot celery onion]

Quick check 27.3 Write a line of code to sort food from the shortest to longest string in listing 27.6.

27.4 Nil slices

A slice that's declared without a composite literal or the make built-in will have a value of nil. Fortunately, the range keyword, len built-in, and append built-in all work with nil slices, as shown in the following listing.

Listing 27.7 Growing a slice: slice.go

```
var soup []string
fmt.Println(soup == nil)
```
Prints true

```
for _, ingredient := range soup {
    fmt.Println(ingredient)
}
fmt.Println(len(soup))
```
Prints 0

```
soup = append(soup, "onion", "carrot", "celery")
fmt.Println(soup)
```
Prints [onion carrot celery]

QC 27.3 answer

```
sortStrings(food, func(i, j int) bool { return len(food[i]) < len(food[j]) })
```

An empty slice and a nil slice aren't equivalent, but they can often be used interchangeably. The following listing passes `nil` to a function that accepts a slice, skipping the step of making an empty slice.

Listing 27.8 Start with nil: mirepoix.go

```go
func main() {
    soup := mirepoix(nil)         Prints [onion
    fmt.Println(soup)             carrot celery]
}

func mirepoix(ingredients []string) []string {
    return append(ingredients, "onion", "carrot", "celery")
}
```

Whenever you write a function that accepts a slice, ensure that a nil slice has the same behavior as an empty slice.

> **Quick check 27.4**   Which actions are safe to perform on a nil slice?

27.5 Nil maps

As with slices, a map declared without a composite literal or the `make` built-in has a value of `nil`. Maps can be read even when nil, as shown in the following listing, though writing to a nil map will panic.

Listing 27.9 Reading a map: map.go

```go
var soup map[string]int           Prints true
fmt.Println(soup == nil)

measurement, ok := soup["onion"]
if ok {
    fmt.Println(measurement)
}
```

QC 27.4 answer   The built-ins `len`, `cap`, and `append` are safe to use with a nil slice, as is the `range` keyword. As with an empty slice, directly accessing an element of a nil slice (`soup[0]`) will panic with index out of range.

```
for ingredient, measurement := range soup {
    fmt.Println(ingredient, measurement)
}
```

If a function only reads from a map, it's fine to pass the function `nil` instead of making an empty map.

Quick check 27.5 What action on a nil map will cause a panic?

 ## 27.6 Nil interfaces

When a variable is declared to be an interface type without an assignment, the zero value is `nil`. The following listing demonstrates that the interface type and value are both `nil`, and the variable compares as equal to `nil`.

Listing 27.10 Interfaces can be nil: interface.go

```
var v interface{}
fmt.Printf("%T %v %v\n", v, v, v == nil)        ⟵ Prints <nil> <nil> true
```

When a variable with an interface type is assigned a value, the interface internally points to the type and value of that variable. This leads to the rather surprising behavior of a nil value that doesn't compare as equal to `nil`. Both the interface type and value need to be `nil` for the variable to equal `nil`, as shown in the following listing.

Listing 27.11 Wat?: interface.go

```
var p *int
v = p
fmt.Printf("%T %v %v\n", v, v, v == nil)        ⟵ Prints *int <nil> false
```

The `%#v` format verb is shorthand to see both type and value, also revealing that the variable contains `(*int)(nil)` rather than just `<nil>`, as shown in listing 27.12.

QC 27.5 answer Writing to a nil map (`soup["onion"] = 1`) will panic with: assignment to entry in nil map.

Listing 27.12 Inspecting the Go representation: interface.go

```
fmt.Printf("%#v\n", v)            ←———— Prints (*int)(nil)
```

To avoid surprises when comparing interfaces to nil, it's best to use the `nil` identifier explicitly, rather than pointing to a variable that contains a nil.

Quick check 27.6   What's the value of s when declared as `var s fmt.Stringer`?

 ## 27.7 An alternative to nil

It can be tempting to adopt nil whenever a value can be nothing. For example, a pointer to an integer (`*int`) can represent both zero and nil. Pointers are intended for pointing, so using a pointer just to provide a `nil` value isn't necessarily the best option.

Instead of using a pointer, one alternative is to declare a small structure with a few methods. It requires a little more code, but it doesn't require a pointer or nil, as shown in the following listing.

Listing 27.13 Number is set: valid.go

```
type number struct {
    value int
    valid bool
}
func newNumber(v int) number {
    return number{value: v, valid: true}
}
func (n number) String() string {
    if !n.valid {
        return "not set"
    }
    return fmt.Sprintf("%d", n.value)
}
```

QC 27.6 answer   The value is `nil` because `fmt.Stringer` is an interface and the zero value for interfaces is `nil`.

```
func main() {
    n := newNumber(42)
    fmt.Println(n)          ◄──────── Prints 42

    e := number{}
    fmt.Println(e)          ◄──────── Prints not set
}
```

Quick check 27.7 What are some advantages to the approach taken in listing 27.13?

Summary

- Nil pointer dereferences will crash your program.
- Methods can guard against receiving `nil` values.
- Default behavior can be provided for functions passed as arguments.
- A nil slice is often interchangeable with an empty slice.
- A nil map can be read from but not written to.
- If an interface looks like it's nil, be sure both the type and value are `nil`.
- Nil isn't the only way to represent nothing.

Let's see if you got this...

Experiment: knights.go

A knight blocks Arthur's path. Our hero is empty-handed, represented by a `nil` value for `leftHand *item`. Implement a `character` struct with methods such as `pickup(i *item)` and `give(to *character)`. Then use what you've learned in this lesson to write a script that has Arthur pick up an item and give it to the knight, displaying an appropriate description for each action.

QC 27.7 answer It completely avoids nil pointer dereferences by not having pointers or `nil` values. The `valid` Boolean has a clear intention, whereas the meaning of `nil` is less clear.

TO ERR IS HUMAN

After reading lesson 28, you'll be able to

- Write files and handle failure
- Handle errors with a flair of creativity
- Make and identify specific errors
- Keep calm and carry on

The sirens sound. Students and teachers shuffle out of classrooms to the nearest exit and congregate at the muster point. There's no danger in sight and nothing is on fire. It's another routine fire drill. Everyone is better prepared in the event of a real emergency.

File not found, invalid format, the server is unreachable. What does software do when something goes wrong? Maybe the problem can be extinguished, allowing operations to carry on as usual. Perhaps the best course of action is to exit safely, closing doors on the way out—or crash through a fourth story window as a last resort.

It's important to have a plan. Consider the errors that could occur, how to communicate those errors, and the steps to handle them. Go keeps error handling front and center, encouraging you to think about failure and how to handle it. Like the tenth fire drill, error handling can feel mundane at times, but it ultimately leads to reliable software.

This lesson explores a few ways to handle errors and delves into how errors are made. It closes by contrasting Go's style of error handling with that of other programming languages.

> **Consider this** In the early 18th century, Alexander Pope penned a poem containing a now well-known phrase: *to err is human.* Take a moment to consider this phrase and how it might relate to computer programming.
>
> > *To err is human; to forgive, divine.*
> > —Alexander Pope, "An Essay on Criticism: Part 2"
>
> Here's our take: everyone makes mistakes. Systems fail. Errors happen all the time. Errors aren't exceptional, so you should expect that things could go wrong. What's important is how you choose to respond. Acknowledge errors, don't ignore them. Work to resolve issues and move on.

 ## 28.1 Handling errors

In programming languages of the past, the limitation of a single return value made error handling somewhat obscure. Functions would overload the same return value to indicate both an error or a successful value, or require a side channel to communicate the error, such as a global errno variable. Worse still, the mechanism to communicate errors was inconsistent from function to function.

Go has multiple return values, as mentioned in lesson 12. Though not specific to error handling, multiple return values provide a simple and consistent mechanism to return errors to calling functions. If a function can return an error, the convention is to use the last return value for errors. The caller should check if an error occurred *immediately* after calling a function. If no errors occurred, the error value will be nil.

To demonstrate error handling, listing 28.1 calls the ReadDir function. If an error occurs, the err variable won't be nil, causing the program to print the error and exit immediately. The nonzero value passed to os.Exit informs the operating system that an error occurred.

If ReadDir is successful, files will be assigned to a slice of os.FileInfo, providing information on the files and directories at the specified path. In this case, a dot is specified for the path, indicating the current directory.

Listing 28.1 Files: files.go

```go
files, err := ioutil.ReadDir(".")
if err != nil {
    fmt.Println(err)
    os.Exit(1)
}

for _, file := range files {
    fmt.Println(file.Name())
}
```

> **NOTE** When an error occurs, the other return values generally shouldn't be relied on. They may be set to the zero values for their type, but some functions may return partial data or something else entirely.

If you run listing 28.1 in the Go Playground, it will output a list of directories:

```
dev
etc
tmp
usr
```

To list the contents of a different directory, replace the current directory (".") in listing 28.1 with the name of another directory, such as "etc". The list may contain both files and directories. You can use file.IsDir() to distinguish between the two.

> **Quick check 28.1**
>
> 1 Revise listing 28.1 to read a make-believe directory, such as "unicorns". What error message is displayed?
> 2 What error message is displayed if you use ReadDir on a file, such as "/etc/hosts", rather than a directory?

QC 28.1 answer

1 open unicorns: No such file or directory
2 readdirent: Invalid argument

28.2 Elegant error handling

Gophers are encouraged to consider and handle any errors that functions return. The amount of code dedicated to handling errors can quickly add up. Fortunately, there are several ways to reduce the amount of error-handling code without sacrificing reliability.

Some functions perform equations, data transformations, and other logic without ever needing to return an error. Then there are functions that communicate with files, databases, and servers. Communication is messy and can fail. One strategy to reduce error-handling code is to isolate an error-free subset of a program from the inherently error-prone code.

But what about code that does return errors? We can't remove the errors, but we can work to simplify the error-handling code. To demonstrate, we'll make a small program that writes the following Go Proverbs to a file and then improve the error handling until the code becomes palatable.

> Errors are values.
> Don't just check errors, handle them gracefully.
> Don't panic.
> Make the zero value useful.
> The bigger the interface, the weaker the abstraction.
> `interface{}` says nothing.
> Gofmt's style is no one's favorite, yet `gofmt` is everyone's favorite.
> Documentation is for users.
> A little copying is better than a little dependency.
> Clear is better than clever.
> Concurrency is not parallelism.
> Don't communicate by sharing memory, share memory by communicating.
> Channels orchestrate; mutexes serialize.
>
> —Rob Pike, Go Proverbs
> (see go-proverbs.github.io)

28.2.1 Writing a file

Any number of things can go wrong when writing a file. If the path is invalid or there's an issue with permissions, creating the file may fail before we even start writing. Once writing, the device could run out of disk space or be unplugged. In addition, a file must be closed when done, both to ensure it is successfully flushed to disk, and to avoid *leaking* resources.

NOTE Operating systems can only have so many files open at once, so every open file cuts into that limit. When a file is unintentionally left open, the waste of that resource is an example of a leak.

The main function in listing 28.2 calls proverbs to create a file and handles any error by displaying it and exiting. A different implementation could handle errors differently, perhaps prompting the user for a different path and filename. Though the proverbs function could have been written to exit on errors, it's useful to let the caller decide how to handle errors.

Listing 28.2 Calling proverbs: proverbs.go

```
err := proverbs("proverbs.txt")
if err != nil {
    fmt.Println(err)
    os.Exit(1)
}
```

The proverbs function may return an error, which is a special built-in type for errors. The function attempts to create a file. If an error occurs at this point, there's no need to close the file, so it aborts immediately. The remainder of the function writes lines out to the file and ensures that the file is closed whether it succeeds or fails, as shown in the following listing.

Listing 28.3 Writing Go Proverbs: proverbs.go

```
func proverbs(name string) error {
    f, err := os.Create(name)
    if err != nil {
        return err
    }
    _, err = fmt.Fprintln(f, "Errors are values.")
    if err != nil {
        f.Close()
        return err
    }
    _, err = fmt.Fprintln(f, "Don't just check errors, handle them gracefully.")
    f.Close()
    return err
}
```

There's a fair amount of error-handling code in the previous listing—so much so, that writing out all the Go Proverbs could become quite tedious.

On the positive side, the code that handles errors is consistently indented, which makes it easier to scan through the code without reading all the repetitive error handling. Indenting errors in this way is a common pattern in the Go community, but we can improve on this implementation.

Quick check 28.2   Why should functions return an error instead of exiting the program?

28.2.2 The defer keyword

To ensure that that the file is closed correctly, you can make use of the defer keyword. Go ensures that all deferred actions take place before the containing function returns. In the following listing, every return statement that follows defer will result in the f.Close() method being called.

Listing 28.4 defer cleanup: defer.go

```
func proverbs(name string) error {
    f, err := os.Create(name)
    if err != nil {
        return err
    }
    defer f.Close()
    _, err = fmt.Fprintln(f, "Errors are values.")
    if err != nil {
        return err
    }

    _, err = fmt.Fprintln(f, "Don't just check errors, handle them gracefully.")
    return err
}
```

NOTE   The behavior of the preceding listing is identical to that of listing 28.3. Changing the code without changing its behavior is called *refactoring*. Much like polishing the first draft of an essay, refactoring is an important skill for writing better code.

QC 28.2 answer   Returning an error gives the caller a chance to decide how to handle the error. For example, the program may decide to retry rather than exit.

You can defer any function or method, and like multiple return values, defer isn't specifically for error handling. It does improve error handling by removing the burden of always having to remember to clean up. Thanks to defer, the code that handles errors can focus on the error at hand, and nothing more.

The defer keyword has made things a little better, but checking for errors after writing each line is still a pain. It's time to get creative!

Quick check 28.3   When will the deferred action be called?

28.2.3 Creative error handling

In January 2015, a marvelous article on error handling was published on the Go blog (blog.golang.org/errors-are-values). The article describes a simple way to write to a file without repeating the same error-handling code after every line.

To apply this technique, you need to declare a new type, which we call safeWriter in listing 28.5. If an error occurs while safeWriter is writing to a file, it stores the error instead of returning it. Subsequent attempts to write to the same file will be skipped if writeln sees that an error occurred previously.

Listing 28.5 Storing error values: writer.go

```
type safeWriter struct {
    w    io.Writer
    err error          A place to store the
}                      first error

func (sw *safeWriter) writeln(s string) {
    if sw.err != nil {
        return          Skips the write if an error
    }                   occurred previously
    _, sw.err = fmt.Fprintln(sw.w, s)       Writes a line and
}                                           store any error
```

Using safeWriter, the following listing writes several lines without repetitive error handling, yet still returns any errors that occur.

Listing 28.6 The road to proverbs: writer.go

```go
func proverbs(name string) error {
    f, err := os.Create(name)
    if err != nil {
        return err
    }
    defer f.Close()

    sw := safeWriter{w: f}
    sw.writeln("Errors are values.")
    sw.writeln("Don't just check errors, handle them gracefully.")
    sw.writeln("Don't panic.")
    sw.writeln("Make the zero value useful.")
    sw.writeln("The bigger the interface, the weaker the abstraction.")
    sw.writeln("interface{} says nothing.")
    sw.writeln("Gofmt's style is no one's favorite, yet gofmt is everyone's
favorite.")
    sw.writeln("Documentation is for users.")
    sw.writeln("A little copying is better than a little dependency.")
    sw.writeln("Clear is better than clever.")
    sw.writeln("Concurrency is not parallelism.")
    sw.writeln("Don't communicate by sharing memory, share memory by
communicating.")
    sw.writeln("Channels orchestrate; mutexes serialize.")

    return sw.err          ◄─── Returns an error,
}                                if one occurred
```

This is a far cleaner way to write a text file, but that isn't the point. The same technique can be applied to creating zip files or to completely different tasks, and the big idea is even greater than a single technique:

> ...errors are values, and the full power of the Go programming language is available for processing them.
> —Rob Pike, "Errors are values"
> (see blog.golang.org/errors-are-values)

Elegant error handling is within your grasp.

Quick check 28.4 If an error occurred while listing 28.6 was writing "Clear is better than clever." to a file, what sequence of events would follow?

 ## 28.3 New errors

If a function receives parameters that are incorrect, or if something else goes wrong, you can create and return new error values to inform the caller of the problem.

To demonstrate new errors, listing 28.7 builds the foundation for a Sudoku logic puzzle, which takes place on a 9 x 9 grid. Each square on the grid may contain a digit from 1 to 9. This implementation will use a fixed-size array, and the number zero will indicate an empty square.

Listing 28.7 Sudoku grid: sudoku1.go

```
const rows, columns = 9, 9

// Grid is a Sudoku grid
type Grid [rows][columns]int8
```

The errors package (see golang.org/pkg/errors/) contains a constructor function that accepts a string for an error message. Using it, the Set method in listing 28.8 may create and return an "out of bounds" error.

> **TIP** Validating parameters at the beginning of a method guards the remainder of the method from worrying about bad input.

Listing 28.8 Validate parameters: sudoku1.go

```
func (g *Grid) Set(row, column int, digit int8) error {
    if !inBounds(row, column) {
        return errors.New("out of bounds")
    }
```

QC 28.4 answer
1 The error is stored in the sw structure.
2 The writeln function will be called three more times, but it will see the stored error and not attempt to write to the file.
3 The stored error will be returned, and defer will try to close the file.

```
    g[row][column] = digit
    return nil
}
```

The inBounds function in the next listing ensures that row and column are inside the grid boundaries. It keeps the Set method from becoming weighed down in details.

Listing 28.9 Helper function: sudoku1.go

```
func inBounds(row, column int) bool {
    if row < 0 || row >= rows {
        return false
    }
    if column < 0 || column >= columns {
        return false
    }
    return true
}
```

Finally, the main function in the next listing creates a grid and displays any error resulting from an invalid placement.

Listing 28.10 Set a digit: sudoku1.go

```
func main() {
    var g Grid
    err := g.Set(10, 0, 5)
    if err != nil {
        fmt.Printf("An error occurred: %v.\n", err)
        os.Exit(1)
    }
}
```

> **TIP** It's common to use partial sentences for error messages so that the message can be augmented with additional text before it's displayed.

Always take the time to write informative error messages. Think of error messages as part of the user interface for your program, whether for end users or other software developers. The phrase "out of bounds" is okay, but "outside of grid boundaries" may be better. A message like "error 37" isn't very helpful at all.

> **Quick check 28.5** How is it beneficial to guard against bad input at the beginning of a function?

28.3.1 Which error is which

Many Go packages declare and export variables for the errors that they could return. To apply this to the Sudoku grid, the next listing declares the two error variables at the package level.

Listing 28.11 Declare error variables: sudoku2.go

```go
var (
    ErrBounds = errors.New("out of bounds")
    ErrDigit  = errors.New("invalid digit")
)
```

> **NOTE** By convention, error messages are assigned to variables that begin with the word Err.

With ErrBounds declared, you can revise the Set method to return it instead of creating a new error, as shown in the following listing.

Listing 28.12 Return the error: sudoku2.go

```go
if !inBounds(row, column) {
    return ErrBounds
}
```

If the Set method returns an error, the caller can distinguish between possible errors and handle specific errors differently, as shown in the following listing. You can compare the error returned with error variables using == or a switch statement.

Listing 28.13 Which error in main: sudoku2.go

```go
var g Grid
err := g.Set(0, 0, 15)
if err != nil {
```

QC 28.5 answer The remainder of the function doesn't need to consider bad input because it has already been checked. Instead of letting it fail (for example, "runtime error: index out of range") a friendly message can be returned.

```
switch err {
case ErrBounds, ErrDigit:
    fmt.Println("Les erreurs de paramètres hors limites.")
default:
    fmt.Println(err)
}
os.Exit(1)
}
```

NOTE The errors.New constructor is implemented using a pointer, so the switch statement in preceding listing is comparing memory addresses, not the text contained in the error message.

Quick check 28.6 Write a validDigit function and use it to ensure that the Set method only accepts digits between 1 and 9.

28.3.2 Custom error types

As helpful as errors.New is, there are times when it's desirable to represent errors with more than a simple message. Go gives you the freedom to do this.

The error type is a built-in interface, as shown in the following listing. Any type that implements an Error() method that returns a string will implicitly satisfy the error interface. As an interface, it's possible to create new error types.

Listing 28.14 The error interface

```
type error interface {
    Error() string
}
```

QC 28.6 answer

```
func validDigit(digit int8) bool {
    return digit >= 1 && digit <= 9
}
```

The Set method should contain this additional check:

```
if !validDigit(digit) {
    return ErrDigit
}
```

Multiple errors

There could be several reasons why a digit can't be placed at a particular location in
Sudoku. The preceding section established two rules: that the row and column are
within the grid, and that the digit is between 1 and 9. What if the caller passes multiple
invalid arguments?

Rather than return one error at a time, the Set method could perform multiple valida-
tions and return all the errors at once. The SudokuError type in listing 28.15 is a slice of
error. It satisfies the error interface with a method that joins multiple errors together into
one string.

> **NOTE**   By convention, custom error types like SudokuError end with the word Error. Some-
> times they're just the word Error, such as url.Error from the url package.

Listing 28.15 Custom error type: sudoku3.go

```go
type SudokuError []error

// Error returns one or more errors separated by commas.
func (se SudokuError) Error() string {
    var s []string
    for _, err := range se {
        s = append(s, err.Error())          // Converts the errors
    }                                        // to strings
    return strings.Join(s, ", ")
}
```

To make use of SudokuError, the Set method can be modified to validate both the boundaries and digit, returning both errors at once, as shown in the following listing.

Listing 28.16 Appending errors: sudoku3.go

```go
func (g *Grid) Set(row, column int, digit int8) error {     // Returns type
    var errs SudokuError                                     // is error
    if !inBounds(row, column) {
        errs = append(errs, ErrBounds)
    }
    if !validDigit(digit) {
        errs = append(errs, ErrDigit)
    }
    if len(errs) > 0 {
```

```
        return errs
    }
    g[row][column] = digit
    return nil      ◄──────── Returns nil
}
```

If no errors occur, the Set method returns nil. This hasn't changed from listing 28.8, but it's important to highlight that it doesn't return an empty errs slice. Review nil interfaces in the preceding lesson if you're not sure why.

The method signature for Set also hasn't changed from listing 28.8. Always use the error interface type when returning errors, not concrete types like SudokuError.

> **Quick check 28.7** What happens if the Set method returns an empty errs slice on success?

Type assertions

Because listing 28.16 converts SudokuError to an error interface type before it's returned, you may wonder how to access the individual errors. The answer is with *type assertions*. Using a type assertion, you can convert an interface to the underlying concrete type.

The type assertion in listing 28.17 asserts that err is of type SudokuError with the code err.(SudokuError). If it is, ok will be true, and errs will be a SudokuError, giving access to the slice of errors in this case. Remember that the individual errors appended to SudokuError are the variables ErrBounds and ErrDigit, which allow comparisons if desired.

Listing 28.17 Type assertion: sudoku3.go

```
var g Grid
err := g.Set(10, 0, 15)
if err != nil {
    if errs, ok := err.(SudokuError); ok {
        fmt.Printf("%d error(s) occurred:\n", len(errs))
        for _, e := range errs {
            fmt.Printf("- %v\n", e)
        }
    }
}
```

QC 28.7 answer The error interface that's returned won't be nil. Even though the slice of errors is empty, the caller will think there was an error.

```
    os.Exit(1)
}
```

The preceding listing will output the following errors:

```
2 error(s) occurred:
- out of bounds
- invalid digit
```

> **NOTE**   If a type satisfies multiple interfaces, type assertions can also convert from one
> interface to another.

> **Quick check 28.8**   What does the type assertion err.(SudokuError) do?

 ## 28.4 Don't panic

Several languages rely heavily on *exceptions* for communicating and handling errors. Go
doesn't have exceptions, but it does have a similar mechanism called panic. When a *panic*
occurs, the program will crash, as is the case with unhandled exceptions in other languages.

QC 28.8 answer   It attempts to convert the err value from the error interface type to the concrete
SudokuError type.

28.4.1 Exceptions in other languages

Exceptions differ significantly from Go's error values in both behavior and implementation.

If a function throws an exception and no one is around to catch it, the exception will bubble up to the calling function, and the caller of that function, and so on, until it reaches the top of the *call stack* (for example, the `main` function).

Exceptions are a style of error handling that can be considered opt-in. It often takes no code to opt out of handling exceptions, whereas opting in to exception handling may involve a fair amount of specialized code. This is because instead of using existing language features, exceptions tend to have special keywords, such as `try`, `catch`, `throw`, `finally`, `raise`, `rescue`, `except`, and so on.

Error values in Go provide a simple, flexible alternative to exceptions that can help you build reliable software. Ignoring error values in Go is a conscious decision that is plainly evident to anyone reading the resulting code.

> **Quick check 28.9** What are two benefits of Go's error values as compared to exceptions?

28.4.2 How to panic

As mentioned, Go does have a mechanism similar to exceptions: `panic`. Whereas an invalid digit in Sudoku may be cause for an exception in another language, `panic` in Go is rare.

If the world is about to end, and you forgot your trusty towel back on Earth, then perhaps panic is warranted. The argument passed to `panic` can be any type, not only strings as shown here:

```
panic("I forgot my towel")
```

> **NOTE** Though error values are generally preferable to `panic`, `panic` is often better than `os.Exit` in that `panic` will run any deferred functions, whereas `os.Exit` does not.

There are some situations where Go will panic instead of providing an error value, such as when dividing by zero:

> **QC 28.9 answer** Go pushes developers to consider errors, which can result in more reliable software, whereas exceptions tend to be ignored by default. Error values don't require specialized keywords, making them simpler, while also being more flexible.

```
var zero int
_ = 42 / zero
```
Runtime error: integer divide by zero

28.4.3 Keep calm and carry on

To keep panic from crashing your program, Go provides a recover function, shown in listing 28.18.

Deferred functions are executed before a function returns, even in the case of panic. If a deferred function calls recover, the panic will stop, and the program will continue running. As such, recover serves a similar purpose to catch, except, and rescue in other languages.

Listing 28.18 Keep calm and carry on: panic.go

```
defer func() {
    if e := recover(); e != nil {
        fmt.Println(e)
    }
}()
panic("I forgot my towel")
```
Recovers from panic

Prints I forgot my towel

Causes panic

NOTE The preceding listing uses an anonymous function, a topic covered in lesson 14.

QC 28.10 answer Panic should be rare.

QC 28.11 answer Only deferred functions can make use of recover.

Summary

- Errors are values that interoperate with multiple return values and the rest of the Go language.
- There is a great deal of flexibility in handling errors if you're willing to get creative.
- Custom error types are possible by satisfying the error interface.
- The defer keyword helps clean up before a function returns.
- Type assertions can convert an interface to a concrete type or another interface.
- Don't panic—return an error instead.

Let's see if you got this...

Experiment: url.go

In the Go standard library, there's a function to parse web addresses (see golang.org/pkg/net/url/#Parse). Display the error that occurs when url.Parse is used with an invalid web address, such as one containing a space: https://a b.com/.

Use the %#v format verb with Printf to learn more about the error. Then perform a *url.Error type assertion to access and print the fields of the underlying structure.

> **NOTE** A URL, or Uniform Resource Locator, is the address of a page on the World Wide Web.

CAPSTONE: SUDOKU RULES

Sudoku is a logic puzzle that takes place on a 9 x 9 grid (see en.wikipedia.org/wiki/Sudoku). Each square can contain a digit from 1 through 9. The number zero indicates an empty square.

The grid is divided into nine subregions that are 3 x 3 each. When placing a digit, it must adhere to certain constraints. The digit being placed may not already appear in any of the following:

- The horizontal row it's placed in
- The vertical column it's placed in
- The 3 x 3 subregion it's placed in

Use a fixed-size (9 x 9) array to hold the Sudoku grid. If a function or method needs to modify the array, remember that you need to pass the array with a pointer.

Implement a method to set a digit at a specific location. This method should return an error if placing the digit breaks one of the rules.

Also implement a method to clear a digit from a square. This method need not adhere to these constraints, as several squares may be empty (zero).

Sudoku puzzles begin with some digits already set. Write a constructor function to prepare the Sudoku puzzle, and use a composite literal to specify the initial values. Here's an example:

```
s := NewSudoku([rows][columns]int8{
    {5, 3, 0, 0, 7, 0, 0, 0, 0},
    {6, 0, 0, 1, 9, 5, 0, 0, 0},
    {0, 9, 8, 0, 0, 0, 0, 6, 0},
    {8, 0, 0, 0, 6, 0, 0, 0, 3},
    {4, 0, 0, 8, 0, 3, 0, 0, 1},
    {7, 0, 0, 0, 2, 0, 0, 0, 6},
    {0, 6, 0, 0, 0, 0, 2, 8, 0},
    {0, 0, 0, 4, 1, 9, 0, 0, 5},
    {0, 0, 0, 0, 8, 0, 0, 7, 9},
})
```

The starting digits are fixed in place and may not be overwritten or cleared. Modify your program so that it can identify which digits are fixed and which are penciled in. Add a validation that causes set and clear to return an error for any of the fixed digits. The digits that are initially zero may be set, overwritten, and cleared.

You don't need to write a Sudoku solver for this exercise, but be sure to test that all the rules are implemented correctly.

7

Concurrent programming

Computers are excellent at doing many things at the same time. You might want the computer to speed up a calculation, download many web pages simultaneously, or control different parts of a robot independently. This ability to deal with several things at once is called *concurrency*.

Go has a different approach to concurrency than most other programming languages. Any Go code can be made concurrent by starting it in a *goroutine*. Goroutines use *channels* for communication and coordination, making it straightforward to have multiple concurrent tasks working toward the same end.

30

GOROUTINES AND CONCURRENCY

After reading lesson 30, you'll be able to

- Start a goroutine
- Use channels to communicate
- Understand channel pipelines

Look, it's a gopher factory! All the gophers are busy building things. Well, almost all. Over in the corner is a sleeping gopher—or maybe he's deep in thought. Here's an important gopher: she's giving orders to other gophers. They run around and do her bidding, tell others what to do, and eventually report back their findings to her. Some gophers are sending things from the factory. Others are receiving things sent from outside.

Until now, all the Go we've written has been like a single gopher in this factory,

busy with her own tasks and not bothering with anyone else's. Go programs are more often like a whole factory, with many independent tasks all doing their own thing, but communicating with each other towards some common goal. These *concurrent* tasks might include fetching data from a web server, computing millions of digits of pi, or controlling a robot arm.

In Go, an independently running task is known as a *goroutine*. In this lesson, you'll learn how to start as many goroutines as you like and communicate between them with *channels*. Goroutines are similar to *coroutines, fibers, processes,* or *threads* in other languages, although they're not quite the same as any of those. They're very efficient to create, and Go makes it straightforward to coordinate many concurrent operations.

> **Consider this**   Consider writing a program that performs a sequence of actions. Each action might take a long time and could involve waiting for something to happen before it's done. It could be written as straightforward, sequential code. But what if you want to do two or more of those sequences at the same time?
>
> For example, you might want one part of your program to go through a list of email addresses and send an email for each one, while another task waits for incoming email and stores them in a database. How would you write that?
>
> In some languages, you would need to change the code quite a bit. But in Go, you can use exactly the same kind of code for each independent task. Goroutines enable you to run any number of actions at the same time.

 ## 30.1 Starting a goroutine

Starting a goroutine is as easy as calling a function. All you need is the `go` keyword in front of the call.

The goroutine in listing 30.1 is similar to our sleepy gopher in the corner of the factory. He doesn't do much, though where that `Sleep` statement is, he could be doing some serious thought (computation) instead. When the `main` function returns, all the goroutines in the program are immediately stopped, so we need to wait long enough to see the sleepy gopher print his "… snore …" message. We'll wait for a little bit longer than necessary just to make sure.

Listing 30.1 Sleepy gopher: sleepygopher.go

```go
package main

import (
    "fmt"
    "time"
)
func main() {
    go sleepyGopher()
    time.Sleep(4 * time.Second)
}
func sleepyGopher() {
    time.Sleep(3 * time.Second)
    fmt.Println("... snore ...")
}
```

The goroutine is started.

Waiting for the gopher to snore

When we get here, all the goroutines are stopped.

The gopher sleeps.

Quick check 30.1

1 What would you use in Go if you wanted to do more than one thing at the same time?
2 What keyword is used to start a new independently running task?

QC 30.1 answer

1 A goroutine.
2 go.

30.2 More than one goroutine

Each time we use the go keyword, a new goroutine is started. All goroutines appear to run at the same time. They might not *technically* run at the same time, though, because computers only have a limited number of processing units.

In fact, these processors usually spend some time on one goroutine before proceeding to another, using a technique known as *time sharing*. Exactly how this happens is a dark secret known only to the Go runtime and the operating system and processor you're using. It's best always to assume that the operations in different goroutines may run in any order.

The main function in listing 30.2 starts five sleepyGopher goroutines. They all sleep for three seconds and then print the same thing.

Listing 30.2 Five sleepy gophers: sleepygophers.go

```go
package main

import (
    "fmt"
    "time"
)

func main() {
    for i := 0; i < 5; i++ {
        go sleepyGopher()
    }
    time.Sleep(4 * time.Second)
}

func sleepyGopher() {
    time.Sleep(3 * time.Second)
    fmt.Println("... snore ...")
}
```

We can find out which ones finish first by passing an argument to each goroutine. Passing an argument to a goroutine is like passing an argument to any function: the value is copied and passed as a parameter.

When you run the next listing, you should see that even though we started all the goroutines in order from zero to nine, they all finished at different times. If you run this outside the Go playground, you'll see a different order every time.

Listing 30.3 Identified gophers: identifiedgophers.go

```go
func main() {
    for i := 0; i < 5; i++ {
        go sleepyGopher(i)
    }
    time.Sleep(4 * time.Second)
}
func sleepyGopher(id int) {
    time.Sleep(3 * time.Second)
    fmt.Println("... ", id, " snore ...")
}
```

There's a problem with this code. It's waiting for four seconds when it only needs to wait for just over three seconds. More importantly, if the goroutines are doing more than just sleeping, we won't know how long they're going to take to do their work. We need some way for the code to know when all the goroutines have finished. Fortunately Go provides us with exactly what we need: channels.

Quick check 30.2   What order do different goroutines run in?

30.3 Channels

A channel can be used to send values safely from one goroutine to another. Think of a channel as one of those pneumatic tube systems in old offices that passed around mail. If you put an object into it, it zips to the other end of the tube and can be taken out by someone else.

Like any other Go type, channels can be used as variables, passed to functions, stored in a structure, and do almost anything else you want them to do.

QC 30.2 answer   Any order.

To create a channel, use make, the same built-in function used to make maps and slices. Channels have a type that's specified when you make them. The following channel can only send and receive integer values:

```
c := make(chan int)
```

Once you have a channel, you can send values to it and receive the values sent to it. You send or receive values on a channel with the *left arrow* operator (<-).

To send a value, point the arrow toward the channel expression, as if the arrow were telling the value on the right to flow into the channel. The send operation will wait until something (in another goroutine) tries to receive on the same channel. While it's waiting, the sender can't do anything else, although all other goroutines will continue running freely (assuming they're not waiting on channel operations too). The following sends the value 99:

```
c <- 99
```

To receive a value from a channel, the arrow points away from the channel (it's to the left of the channel). In the following code, we receive a value from channel c and assign it to variable r. Similarly to sending on a channel, the receiver will wait until another goroutine tries to send on the same channel:

```
r := <-c
```

> **NOTE** Although it's common to use a channel receive operation on its own line, that's not required. The channel receive operation can be used anywhere any other expression can be used.

The code in listing 30.4 makes a channel and passes it to five sleepy gopher goroutines. Then it waits to receive five messages, one for each goroutine that's been started. Each goroutine sleeps and then sends a value identifying itself. When execution reaches the end of the main function, we know for sure that all the gophers will have finished sleeping, and it can return without disturbing any gopher's sleep. For example, say we have a program that saves the results of some number-crunching computation to online storage. It might save several things at the same time, and we don't want to quit before all the results have been successfully saved.

Listing 30.4 Channeled sleeping gophers: simplechan.go

```
func main() {
    c := make(chan int)          ← Makes the channel to
    for i := 0; i < 5; i++ {        communicate over
        go sleepyGopher(i, c)
```

```
    }
    for i := 0; i < 5; i++ {          Receives a value from
        gopherID := <-c                a channel
        fmt.Println("gopher ", gopherID, " has finished sleeping")
    }
}
func sleepyGopher(id int, c chan int) {          Declares the channel
    time.Sleep(3 * time.Second)                   as an argument
    fmt.Println("... ", id, " snore ...")
    c <- id          Sends a value
}                     back to main
```

The square boxes in figure 30.1 represent goroutines, and the circle represents a channel. A link from a goroutine to a channel is labeled with the name of the variable that refers to the channel; the arrow direction represents the way the goroutine is using the channel. When an arrow points towards a goroutine, the goroutine is reading from the channel.

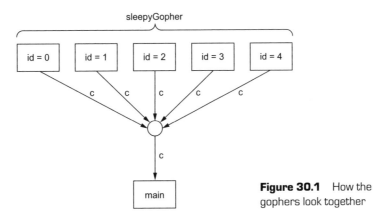

Figure 30.1 How the gophers look together

30.4 Channel surfing with select

In the preceding example, we used a single channel to wait for many goroutines. That works well when all the goroutines are producing the same type of value, but that's not always the case. Often we'll want to wait for two or more different kinds of values.

One example of this is when we're waiting for some values over a channel but we want to avoid waiting too long. Perhaps we're a little impatient with our sleepy gophers, and our patience runs out after a time. Or we may want to time out a network request after a few seconds rather than several minutes.

Fortunately, the Go standard library provides a nice function, time.After, to help. It returns a channel that receives a value after some time has passed (the goroutine that sends the value is part of the Go runtime).

We want to continue receiving values from the sleepy gophers until either they've all finished sleeping or our patience runs out. That means we need to wait on both the timer channel and the other channel at the same time. The select statement allows us to do this.

The select statement looks like the switch statement covered in lesson 3. Each case inside a select holds a channel receive or send. select waits until one case is ready and then runs it and its associated case statement. It's as if select is looking at both channels at once and takes action when it sees something happen on either of them.

The following listing uses time.After to make a timeout channel and then uses select to wait for the channel from the sleepy gophers and the timeout channel.

Listing 30.5 Impatiently waiting for sleepy gophers: select1.go

```go
timeout := time.After(2 * time.Second)
for i := 0; i < 5; i++ {
    select {                              The select statement
    case gopherID := <-c:                 Waits for a gopher to wake up
        fmt.Println("gopher ", gopherID, " has finished sleeping")
    case <-timeout:                        Waits for time
        fmt.Println("my patience ran out")   to run out
        return                             Gives up and returns
    }
}
```

TIP When there are no cases in the select statement, it will wait forever. That might be useful to stop the main function returning when you've started some goroutines that you want to leave running indefinitely.

This isn't very interesting when all the gophers are sleeping for exactly three seconds, because our patience always runs out before any gophers wake up. The gophers in the next listing sleep for a random amount of time. When you run this, you'll find that some gophers wake up in time, but others don't.

Listing 30.6 A randomly sleeping gopher: select2.go

```
func sleepyGopher(id int, c chan int) {
    time.Sleep(time.Duration(rand.Intn(4000)) * time.Millisecond)
    c <- id
}
```

TIP This pattern is useful whenever you want to limit the amount of time spent doing something. By putting the action inside a goroutine and sending on a channel when it completes, anything in Go can be timed out.

NOTE Although we've stopped waiting for the goroutines, if we haven't returned from the main function, they'll still be sitting around using up memory. It's good practice to tell them to finish, if possible.

Nil channels do nothing

Because you need to create channels explicitly with make, you may wonder what happens if you use channel values that haven't been "made." As with maps, slices, and pointers, channels can be nil. In fact, nil is their default zero value.

If you try to use a nil channel, it won't panic—instead, the operation (send or receive) will block forever, like a channel that nothing ever receives from or sends to. The exception to this is close (covered later in this lesson). If you try to close a nil channel, it will panic.

At first glance, that may not seem very useful, but it can be surprisingly helpful. Consider a loop containing a select statement. We may not want to wait for all the channels mentioned in the select every time through the loop. For example, we might only try to send on a channel when we have a value ready to send. We can do that by using a channel variable that's only non-nil when we want to send a value.

So far, all has been well. When our main function received on the channel, it found a gopher sending a value on the channel. But what would happen if we accidentally tried to read when there were no goroutines left to send? Or if we tried to send on a channel instead of receive?

30.5 Blocking and deadlock

When a goroutine is waiting to send or receive on a channel, we say that it's *blocked*. This might sound the same as if we'd written some code with a loop that spins around forever doing nothing, and on the face of it they look exactly the same. But if you run an infinite loop in a program on your laptop, you may find that the fan starts to whir and the computer gets hot because it's doing a lot of work. By contrast, a blocked goroutine takes no resources (other than a small amount of memory used by the goroutine itself). It's parked itself quietly, waiting for whatever is blocking it to stop blocking it.

When one or more goroutines end up blocked for something that can never happen, it's called *deadlock*, and your program will generally crash or hang up. Deadlocks can be caused by something as simple as this:

```
func main() {
    c := make(chan int)
    <-c
}
```

In large programs, deadlocks can involve an intricate series of dependencies between goroutines.

Although theoretically hard to guard against, in practice, by sticking to a few simple guidelines (covered soon), it's not hard to make deadlock-free programs. When you *do* find a deadlock, Go can show you the state of all the goroutines, so it's often easy to find out what's going on.

30.6 A gopher assembly line

So far, our gophers have been pretty sleepy. They just sleep for a while and then wake up and send a single value on their channel. But not all gophers in this factory are like that. Some are industriously working on an assembly line, receiving an item from a gopher earlier in the line, doing some work on it, then sending it on to the next gopher in the line. Although the work done by each gopher is simple, the assembly line can produce surprisingly sophisticated results.

This technique, known as a *pipeline*, is useful for processing large streams of data without using large quantities of memory. Although each goroutine might hold only a single value at a time, it may process millions of values over time. A pipeline is also useful because you can use it as a "thought tool" to help solve some kinds of problems more easily.

We already have all the tools we need to assemble goroutines into a pipeline. Go values flow down the pipeline, handed from one goroutine to the next. A worker in the pipeline repeatedly receives a value from its *upstream* neighbor, does something with it, and sends the result *downstream*.

Let's build an assembly line of workers that process string values. The gopher at the start of the assembly line is shown in listing 30.7—the source of the stream. This gopher doesn't read values, but only sends them. In another program, this might involve reading data from a file, a database, or the network, but here we'll just send a few arbitrary values. To tell the downstream gophers that there are no more values, the source sends a *sentinel value*, the empty string, to indicate when it's done.

Listing 30.7 Source gopher: pipeline1.go

```
func sourceGopher(downstream chan string) {
    for _, v := range []string{"hello world", "a bad apple", "goodbye all"} {
        downstream <- v
    }
    downstream <- ""
}
```

The gopher in listing 30.8 filters out anything bad from the assembly line. It reads an item from its upstream channel and only sends it on the downstream channel if the value doesn't have the string "bad" in it. When it sees the final empty string, the filter gopher quits, making sure to send the empty string to the next gopher down the line too.

Listing 30.8   Filter gopher: pipeline1.go

```go
func filterGopher(upstream, downstream chan string) {
    for {
        item := <-upstream
        if item == "" {
            downstream <- ""
            return
        }
        if !strings.Contains(item, "bad") {
            downstream <- item
        }
    }
}
```

The gopher that sits at the end of the assembly line—the print gopher—is shown in listing 30.9. This gopher doesn't have anything downstream. In another program, it might save the results to a file or a database, or print a summary of the values it's seen. Here the print gopher prints all the values it sees.

Listing 30.9   Print gopher: pipeline1.go

```go
func printGopher(upstream chan string) {
    for {
        v := <-upstream
        if v == "" {
            return
        }
        fmt.Println(v)
    }
}
```

Let's put our gopher workers together. We've got three stages in the pipeline (source, filter, print) but only two channels. We don't need to start a new goroutine for the last gopher because we want to wait for it to finish before exiting the whole program. When the printGopher function returns, we know that the two other goroutines have done their work, and we can return from `main`, finishing the whole program, as shown in the following listing and illustrated in figure 30.2.

Listing 30.10 Assembly: pipeline1.go

```
func main() {
    c0 := make(chan string)
    c1 := make(chan string)
    go sourceGopher(c0)
    go filterGopher(c0, c1)
    printGopher(c1)
}
```

Figure 30.2 Gopher pipeline

There's an issue with the pipeline code we have so far. We're using the empty string a way to signify that there aren't any more values to process, but what if we want to process an empty string as if it were any other value? Instead of strings, we *could* send a struct value containing both the string we want and a Boolean field saying whether it's the last value.

But there's a better way. Go lets us *close* a channel to signify that no more values will be sent, like so:

```
close(c)
```

When a channel is closed, you can't write any more values to it (you'll get a panic if you try), and any read will return immediately with the zero value for the type (the empty string in this case).

> **NOTE** Be careful! If you read from a closed channel in a loop without checking whether it's closed, the loop will spin forever, burning lots of CPU time. Make sure you know which channels may be closed and check accordingly.

How do we tell whether the channel has been closed? Like this:

```
v, ok := <-c
```

When we assign the result to two variables, the second variable will tell us whether we've successfully read from the channel. It's false when the channel has been closed.

With these new tools, we can easily close down the whole pipeline. The following listing shows the source goroutine at the head of the pipeline.

Listing 30.11   Assembly: pipeline2.go

```go
func sourceGopher(downstream chan string) {
    for _, v := range []string{"hello world", "a bad apple", "goodbye all"}
    {
        downstream <- v
    }
    close(downstream)
}
```

The next listing shows how the filter goroutine now looks.

Listing 30.12   Assembly: pipeline2.go

```go
func filterGopher(upstream, downstream chan string) {
    for {
        item, ok := <-upstream
        if !ok {
            close(downstream)
            return
        }
        if !strings.Contains(item, "bad") {
            downstream <- item
        }
    }
}
```

This pattern of reading from a channel until it's closed is common enough that Go provides a shortcut. If we use a channel in a range statement, it will read values from the channel until the channel is closed.

This means our code can be rewritten more simply with a range loop. The following listing accomplishes the same thing as before.

Listing 30.13   Assembly: pipeline2.go

```go
func filterGopher(upstream, downstream chan string) {
    for item := range upstream {
        if !strings.Contains(item, "bad") {
```

```
            downstream <- item
        }
    }
    close(downstream)
}
```

The final gopher on the assembly line reads all the messages and prints one after another, as shown in the next listing.

Listing 30.14 Assembly: pipeline2.go

```
func printGopher(upstream chan string) {
    for v := range upstream {
        fmt.Println(v)
    }
}
```

Quick check 30.6

1 What value do you see when you read from a closed channel?
2 How do you check whether a channel has been closed?

 Summary

- The go statement starts a new goroutine, running concurrently.
- Channels are used to send values between goroutines.
- A channel is created with make(chan string).
- The <- operator receives from a channel (when used before a channel value).
- The <- operator sends to a channel (when placed between the channel value and the value to be sent).
- The close function closes a channel.
- The range statement reads all the values from a channel until it's closed.

QC 30.6 answer

1 The zero value for the channel's type.
2 Use a two-valued assignment statement:
```
v, ok := <-c
```

Let's see if you got this...

Experiment: remove-identical.go

It's boring to see the same line repeated over and over again. Write a pipeline element (a goroutine) that remembers the previous value and only sends the value to the next stage of the pipeline if it's different from the one that came before. To make things a little simpler, you may assume that the first value is never the empty string.

Experiment: split-words.go

Sometimes it's easier to operate on words than on sentences. Write a pipeline element that takes strings, splits them up into words (you can use the `Fields` function from the `strings` package), and sends all the words, one by one, to the next pipeline stage.

CONCURRENT STATE

After reading lesson 31, you'll be able to

- Keep state safe
- Use mutexes and reply channels
- Employ service loops

Here we are back in the gopher factory. The busy gophers are still building things, but several of the production lines are running low on stock, so they need to order more.

Unfortunately, this is an old-fashioned factory that only has a single shared phone land-line to the outside world. All the production lines have their own handset, though. A gopher picks up the phone to place an order, but as she starts speaking, another gopher picks up another handset and starts dialing, interfering with the first gopher. Then another does the same thing and they all get very confused and none of them manage to place any order at all. If only they could agree to use the phone one at time!

Shared values in a Go programs are a bit like this shared phone. If two or more gorou-tines try to use a shared value at the same time, things can go wrong. It *might* turn out okay. Perhaps no two gophers will ever try to use the phone at the same time. But things can go wrong in all kinds of ways.

Perhaps two gophers talking at the same time confuse the seller at the other end of the line, and they end up ordering the wrong things, or the wrong quantity of things, or something else about the order goes wrong. There's no way to know—all bets are off.

That's the problem with shared Go values. Unless we explicitly know that it's okay to use the specific kind of value in question concurrently, we must assume that it's not okay. This kind of situation is known as a *race condition* because it's as if the goroutines are racing to use the value.

> **NOTE**   The Go compiler includes functionality that tries to find race conditions in your code. It's well worth using, and it's always worth fixing your code if it reports a race. See golang.org/doc/articles/race_detector.html.

> **NOTE**   It's okay if two goroutines read from the same thing at the same time, but if you read or write at the same time as another write, you'll get undefined behavior.

Consider this   Say we have a bunch of goroutines working away, crawling the web and *scraping* web pages. We might want to keep track of which web pages have already been visited. Let's say we want to keep track of the number of web links to each page (Google does something similar to this in order to rank web pages in its search results).

It seems like we could use a map shared between the goroutines that holds the link count for each web page. When a goroutine processes a web page, it would increment the entry in the map for that page.

However, doing that is a mistake because all the goroutines are updating the map at the same time, and that produces race conditions. We need some way of getting around that. Enter mutexes.

31.1 Mutexes

Back in the gopher factory, one clever gopher has a bright idea. She puts a glass jar in the middle of the factory floor that holds a single metal token. When a gopher needs to use the phone, they take the token out of the jar and keep it until the phone call has finished. Then they return the token to the jar. If there's no token in the jar when a gopher wants to make a call, they have to wait until the token is returned.

Note that there's nothing that physically stops a gopher from using the phone without taking the token. But if they do, there may be unintended consequences from two gophers talking over one another on the phone. Also, consider what happens if the gopher with the token forgets to return it: no other gopher will be able to use the phone until they remember to return it.

In a Go program, the equivalent of that glass jar is called a *mutex*. The word *mutex* is short for *mutual exclusion*. Goroutines can use a mutex to exclude each other from doing something at the same time. The *something* in question is up to the programmer to decide. Like the jar in the factory, the only "mutual exclusion" properties of a mutex come from the fact that we're careful to use it whenever we access the thing we're guarding with it.

Mutexes have two methods: Lock and Unlock. Calling Lock is like taking the token from the jar. We put the token back in the jar by calling Unlock. If any goroutine calls Lock while the mutex is locked, it'll wait until it's unlocked before locking it again.

To use the mutex properly, we need to make sure that any code accessing the shared values locks the mutex first, does whatever it needs to, then unlocks the mutex. If any code doesn't follow this pattern, we can end up with a race condition. Because of this, mutexes are almost always kept internal to a package. The package knows what things the mutex guards, but the Lock and Unlock calls are nicely hidden behind methods or functions.

Unlike channels, Go mutexes aren't built into the language itself. Rather, they're available in the sync package. Listing 31.1 is a complete program that locks and unlocks a global mutex value. We don't need to initialize the mutex before using it—the zero value is an unlocked mutex.

The defer keyword introduced in lesson 28 can help with mutexes too. Even if there are many lines of code in a function, the Unlock call stays next to the Lock call.

Listing 31.1 Locking and unlocking a mutex: mutex.go

```
package main
                        Imports the
import "sync"           sync package

var mu sync.Mutex       ←──────  Declares the mutex

func main() {           ╭─ Locks the mutex
    mu.Lock()
    defer mu.Unlock()   ← Unlocks the mutex
                          before returning
    // The lock is held until we return from the function.
}
```

> **NOTE** The defer statement is particularly useful when there are multiple return state-
> ments. Without defer, we'd need a call to Unlock just before every return statement, and it
> would be very easy to forget one of those.

Let's implement a type that a web crawler can use to keep track of link counts to visited
web pages. We'll store a map holding the URL of the web page and guard it with a
mutex. The sync.Mutex in listing 31.2 is a member of a struct type, a very common pattern.

> **TIP** It's good practice to keep a mutex definition immediately above the variables that it's
> guarding, and include a comment so the association is clear.

Listing 31.2 Page reference map: scrape.go

```
// Visited tracks whether web pages have been visited.
// Its methods may be used concurrently from multiple goroutines.
type Visited struct {
    // mu guards the visited map.   ╭─ Declare a mutex
    mu        sync.Mutex           ←
    visited map[string]int  ←─────  Declare a map from
}                                    URL (string) keys to
                                     integer values
```

> **NOTE** In Go, you should assume that no method is safe to use concurrently unless it's
> explicitly documented, as we've done here.

The code in the next listing defines a VisitLink method to be called when a link has been
encountered; it returns the number of times that link has been encountered before.

Listing 31.3 Visit link: scrape.go

```
// VisitLink tracks that the page with the given URL has
// been visited, and returns the updated link count.
```

```
func (v *Visited) VisitLink(url string) int {
    v.mu.Lock()          ◄──────── Locks the mutex
    defer v.mu.Unlock()  ◄──── Ensures that the
    count := v.visited[url]      mutex is unlocked
    count++
    v.visited[url] = count  ◄──
    return count                └── Updates the map
}
```

The Go playground isn't a good place to experiment with race conditions because it's kept deliberately deterministic and race-free. But you can experiment by inserting calls to time.Sleep between statements.

Try modifying listing 31.3 to use the techniques introduced at the beginning of lesson 30 to start several goroutines that all call VisitLink with different values and experiment with inserting Sleep statements in different places. Also try deleting the Lock and Unlock calls to see what happens.

With a small and well-defined piece of state to guard, a mutex is quite straightforward to use and is an essential tool when writing methods that you want to be usable from multiple goroutines at once.

Quick check 31.1
1 What might happen if two goroutines try to change the same value at the same time?
2 What happens if you try to lock the mutex again before unlocking it?
3 What happens if you unlock it without locking it?
4 Is it safe to call methods on the same type from different goroutines at the same time?

31.1.1 Mutex pitfalls

In listing 31.2, when the mutex is locked, we only do a very simple thing: we update a map. The more we do while the lock is held, the more we need to be careful. If we block to wait for something when we've locked the mutex, we may be locking others out for a

QC 31.1 answer
1 It's undefined. The program may crash or anything else may happen.
2 It will block forever.
3 It will panic: unlock of unlocked mutex.
4 No, not unless specifically documented as such.

long time. Worse, if we somehow try to lock the *same* mutex, we'll *deadlock*—the Lock call will block forever because we're never going to give up the lock while we're waiting to acquire it!

To keep on the safe side, follow these guidelines:

- Try to keep the code within the mutex simple.
- Only have one mutex for a given piece of shared state.

A mutex is good to use for simple shared state, but it's not uncommon to want something more. In the gopher factory of lesson 30, we might want gophers that act independently, responding to requests from other gophers but also doing their own thing over time. Unlike the gophers on the assembly line, gophers like this don't respond entirely to messages from other gophers, but can decide to do things on their own behalf.

> **Quick check 31.2** What are two potential problems with locking a mutex?

 ## 31.2 Long-lived workers

Consider the task of driving a rover around the surface of Mars. The software on the Curiosity Mars rover is structured as a set of independent modules that communicate by passing each other messages (see mng.bz/Z7Xa), much like Go's goroutines.

The rover's modules are responsible for different aspects of the rover's behavior. Let's try to write some Go code that drives a (highly simplified) rover around a virtual Mars. Because we don't have a real engine to drive, we'll make do by updating a variable that holds the coordinates of the rover. We want the rover to be controllable from Earth, so it needs to be responsive to external commands.

> **NOTE** The code structure we're building here can be used for any kind of long-lived task that does things independently, such as a website poller or a hardware device controller.

To drive the rover, we'll start a goroutine that will be responsible for controlling its position. The goroutine is started when the rover software starts and stays around until it's

QC 31.2 answer   It might block other goroutines that are also trying to lock the mutex; it could lead to deadlock.

shut down. Because it stays around and operates independently, we'll call this gorou-tine a *worker*.

A worker is often written as a `for` loop containing a `select` statement. The loop runs for as long as the worker is alive; the `select` waits for something of interest to happen. In this case, the "something of interest" might be a command from outside. Remember, although the worker is operating independently, we still want to be able to control it. Or it could be a timer event telling the worker that it's time to move the rover.

Here's a skeleton worker function that does nothing:

```
func worker() {
    for {
        select {
        // Wait for channels here.
        }
    }
}
```

We can start such a worker exactly as we've started goroutines in previous examples:

```
go worker()
```

> ### Event loops and goroutines
> Some other programming languages use an *event loop* —a central loop that waits for events and calls registered functions when they occur. By providing goroutines as a core concept, Go avoids the need for a central event loop. Any worker goroutine can be con-sidered an event loop in its own right.

We want our Mars rover to update its position periodically. For this, we want the worker goroutine that's driving it to wake up every so often to do the update. We can use `time.After` for this (discussed in lesson 30), which provides a channel that will receive a value after a given duration.

The worker in listing 31.4 prints a value every second. For the time being, instead of updating a position, we just increment a number. When we receive a timer event, we call `After` again so that the next time around the loop, we'll be waiting on a fresh timer channel.

Listing 31.4 Number printing worker: printworker.go

```go
func worker() {
    n := 0
    next := time.After(time.Second)      // Makes initial timer channel
    for {
        select {                          // Waits for the timer to fire
        case <-next:
            n++
            fmt.Println(n)                // Prints the number
            next = time.After(time.Second) // Makes another timer channel for another event
        }
    }
}
```

NOTE We don't need to use a select statement in this example. A select with only one case is the same as using the channel operation on its own. But we're using select here because later in this lesson, we'll change the code to wait for more than just a timer. Otherwise, we could avoid the After call entirely and use time.Sleep.

Now that we've got a worker that can act of its own accord, let's make it a little more rover-like by updating a position instead of a number. Conveniently, Go's image package provides a Point type that we can use to represent the rover's current position and direction. A Point is a structure holding X and Y coordinates with appropriate methods. For example, the Add method adds one point to another.

Let's use the X axis to represent east-west and the Y axis to represent north-south. To use Point, we must first import the image package:

```go
import "image"
```

Every time we receive a value on the timer channel, we add the point representing the current direction to the current position, as shown in the next listing. Right now, the rover will always start at the same place [10, 10] and proceed East, but we'll address that shortly.

Listing 31.5 Position updating worker: positionworker.go

```go
func worker() {
    pos := image.Point{X: 10, Y: 10}       // The current position (initially [10, 10])
    direction := image.Point{X: 1, Y: 0}   // The current direction (initially [1, 0], traveling east)
    next := time.After(time.Second)
    for {
```

```
    select {
    case <-next:
        pos = pos.Add(direction)
        fmt.Println("current position is ", pos)
        next = time.After(time.Second)
    }
  }
}
```

⟵ Prints the current position

It's not much good if a Mars rover can only move in a straight line. We'd like to be able to control the rover to make it go in different directions, or stop it, or make it go faster. We'll need another channel we can use to send commands to the worker. When the worker receives a value on the command channel, it can act on the command. In Go, it's usual to hide channels like this behind methods because channels are considered an implementation detail.

The RoverDriver type in the following listing holds the channel that we'll use to send commands to the worker. We'll use a command type that will hold the commands sent.

Listing 31.6 RoverDriver type: rover.go

```
// RoverDriver drives a rover around the surface of Mars.
type RoverDriver struct {
    commandc chan command
}
```

We can wrap the logic that creates the channel and starts the worker inside a NewRoverDriver function, shown in the next listing. We're going to define a drive method to implement our worker logic. Although it's a method, it will function the same as the worker functions from earlier in this chapter. As a method, it has access to any values in the RoverDriver structure.

Listing 31.7 Create: rover.go

```
func NewRoverDriver() *RoverDriver {
    r := &RoverDriver{
        commandc: make(chan command),
    }
    go r.drive()
    return r
}
```

Now we need to decide which commands we'd like to be able to send the rover. To keep things simple, let's only allow two commands: "turn 90° left" and "turn 90° right," as shown in the following listing.

Listing 31.8 Command type: rover.go

```
type command int

const (
    right = command(0)
    left  = command(1)
)
```

> **NOTE** A channel can be any Go type; the command type could be a struct type holding arbitrarily complex commands.

Now that we've defined the RoverDriver type and a function to create an instance of it, we need the drive method (the worker that will control the rover), which listing 31.9 provides. It's almost the the same as the position updater worker we saw earlier except that it waits on the command channel too. When it receives a command, it decides what to do by switching on the command value. To see what's going on, we log changes as they happen.

Listing 31.9 RoverDriver worker: rover.go

```
// drive is responsible for driving the rover. It
// is expected to be started in a goroutine.
func (r *RoverDriver) drive() {
    pos := image.Point{X: 0, Y: 0}
    direction := image.Point{X: 1, Y: 0}
    updateInterval := 250 * time.Millisecond
    nextMove := time.After(updateInterval)
    for {
        select {
        case c := <-r.commandc:          // Waits for commands on the command channel
            switch c {
            case right:                  // Turns right
                direction = image.Point{
                    X: -direction.Y,
                    Y: direction.X,
                }
```

```
            case left:          ◄─────── Turns left
                direction = image.Point{
                        X: direction.Y,
                        Y: -direction.X,
                }
            }
            log.Printf("new direction %v", direction)
        case <-nextMove:
            pos = pos.Add(direction)
            log.Printf("moved to %v", pos)
            nextMove = time.After(updateInterval)
        }
    }
}
```

Now we can complete the `RoverDriver` type by adding methods to control the rover, as shown in listing 31.10. We'll declare two methods, one for each command. Each method sends the correct command on the `commandc` channel. For example, if we call the `Left` method, it will send a `left` command value, which the worker will receive and change the direction of the worker.

> **NOTE** Although these methods are controlling the direction of the rover, they don't have direct access to the direction value, so there's no danger that they can change it concurrently and risk a race condition. This means we don't need a mutex, because channels allow communication with the rover's goroutine without changing any of its values directly.

Listing 31.10 `RoverDriver` **methods: rover.go**

```
// Left turns the rover left (90° counterclockwise).
func (r *RoverDriver) Left() {
    r.commandc <- left
}
// Right turns the rover right (90° clockwise).
func (r *RoverDriver) Right() {
    r.commandc <- right
}
```

Now that we have a fully functional `RoverDriver` type, listing 31.11 creates a rover and sends it some commands. It's now free to rove!

Listing 31.11 Let it go!: rover.go

```go
func main() {
    r := NewRoverDriver()
    time.Sleep(3 * time.Second)
    r.Left()
    time.Sleep(3 * time.Second)
    r.Right()
    time.Sleep(3 * time.Second)
}
```

Try experimenting with the `RoverDriver` type by using different timings and sending different commands to it.

Although we've focused on one specific example here, this worker pattern can be useful in many different situations where you need to have some long-lived goroutine controlling something while remaining responsive to external control itself.

Quick check 31.3

1 What is used instead of an event loop in Go?
2 What Go standard library package provides a `Point` data type?
3 What Go statements might you use to implement a long-lived worker goroutine?
4 How are internal details of channel use hidden?
5 What Go values can be sent down a channel?

QC 31.3 answer

1 A loop in a goroutine.
2 The `image` package.
3 The `for` statement and the `select` statement.
4 Behind method calls.
5 Any value can be sent down a channel.

Summary

- Never access state from more than one goroutine at the same time unless it's explicitly marked as okay to do so.
- Use a mutex to make sure only one goroutine is accessing something at a time.
- Use a mutex to guard one piece of state only.
- Do as little as possible with the mutex held.
- You can write a long-lived goroutine as a worker with a `select` loop.
- Hide worker details behind methods.

Let's see if you got this...

Experiment: positionworker.go

Using listing 31.5 as a starting point, change the code so that the delay time gets a half a second longer with each move.

Experiment: rover.go

Using the `RoverDriver` type as a starting point, define `Start` and `Stop` methods and associated commands and make the rover obey them.

CAPSTONE: LIFE ON MARS

 ## 32.1 A grid to rove on

Make a grid that the rover can drive around on by implementing a `MarsGrid` type. You'll need to use a mutex to make it safe for use by multiple goroutines at once. It should look something like the following:

```
// MarsGrid represents a grid of some of the surface
// of Mars. It may be used concurrently by different
// goroutines.
type MarsGrid struct {
    // To be done.
}

// Occupy occupies a cell at the given point in the grid. It
// returns nil if the point is already occupied or the point is
// outside the grid. Otherwise it returns a value that can be
// used to move to different places on the grid.
func (g *MarsGrid) Occupy(p image.Point) *Occupier

// Occupier represents an occupied cell in the grid.
// It may be used concurrently by different goroutines.
type Occupier struct {
```

```
    // To be done.
}
// Move moves the occupier to a different cell in the grid.
// It reports whether the move was successful
// It might fail because it was trying to move outside
// the grid or because the cell it's trying to move into
// is occupied. If it fails, the occupier remains in the same place.
func (g *Occupier) Move(p image.Point) bool
```

Now change the rover example from lesson 31 so that instead of only updating its coordinates locally, the rover uses a MarsGrid object passed into the NewRoverDriver function. If it hits the edge of the grid or an obstacle, it should turn and go in another random direction.

Now you can start several rovers by calling NewRoverDriver and see them drive around together on the grid.

32.2 Reporting discoveries

We want to find life on Mars, so we'll send several rovers down to search for it, but we need to know when life is found. In every cell in the grid, assign some likelihood of life, a random number between 0 and 1000. If a rover finds a cell with a life value above 900, it may have found life and it must send a radio message back to Earth.

Unfortunately, it's not always possible to send a message immediately because the relay satellite is not always above the horizon. Implement a buffer goroutine that receives messages sent from the rover and buffers them into a slice until they can be sent back to Earth.

Implement Earth as a goroutine that receives messages only occasionally (in reality for a couple of hours every day, but you might want to make the interval a little shorter than that). Each message should contain the coordinates of the cell where the life might have been found, and the life value itself.

You may also want to give a name to each of your rovers and include that in the message so you can see which rover sent it. It's also helpful to include the name in the log messages printed by the rovers so you can track the progress of each one.

Set your rovers free to search and see what they come up with!

Conclusion

WHERE TO GO FROM HERE

This concludes *Get Programming with Go*, but it's not the end of your journey. We hope your mind is full of ideas and a desire to keep learning and building. Thanks for joining us.

Under the radar

Go is a relatively small language, and you've already learned most of it. There are a few edges that *Get Programming with Go* doesn't cover in this edition:

- It doesn't cover declaring sequential constants with the handy `iota` identifier.
- It doesn't mention bit shifting (`<<` and `>>`) and bitwise operators (`&` and `|`).
- Lesson 3 covers loops but skips the `continue` keyword and jumps over the `goto` keyword and labels.
- Lesson 4 covers scope but not shadow variables—those shadowy characters.
- Lessons 6 through 8 crunch floating-point, integer, and big numbers but not complex or imaginary numbers.
- Lesson 12 shows the `return` keyword, but not bare returns—modesty is a virtue.
- Lesson 12 mentions the empty `interface{}`, but only briefly.
- Lesson 13 introduces methods but not method values.

- Lesson 28 mentions type assertions but not type switches.
- Lesson 30 doesn't mention directional channels.
- It doesn't explain initialization with `init`, a special function like `main`.
- It doesn't detail every built-in function, such as `new` for pointers and `copy` for slices (see golang.org/pkg/builtin/).
- It doesn't demonstrate writing new packages to organize code or to share with others.

Beyond the playground

If you're new to computer programming, you may have appreciated the web-based Go Playground, but the playground has some limitations.

To break free of the Playground constraints and build the next cool thing, you'll need to install Go on your computer (see golang.org/dl/). Launching the terminal or command prompt is a bit like hopping into a time machine. Learn to navigate your computer and run programs like it's 1995!

You'll also need a text editor. The authors of this book use Sublime Text and Acme, but there are many editors with good support for Go (see golang.org/doc/editors.html). Sooner or later, you'll want a version control tool like `git`—which *is* a time machine, though only for code and other files.

And much more

Go is much more than a programming language. There's a rich ecosystem of tools and libraries to be discovered.

Everything you need for automated testing, debugging, benchmarking, and much more is available. The standard library has many more packages to explore, and if you run out, the community of gophers has been busy making a huge assortment of third-party packages for any need (see godoc.org).

There are many online resources (see golang.org/wiki) to help you continue your journey, and dozens of gopher-friendly books, including *Go in Practice*, *Go Web Programming*, and *Go in Action* (see golang.org/wiki/Books).

There's always more to learn, so join in the fun! The Go community welcomes you.

Appendix

SOLUTIONS

This appendix provides our solutions for the end-of-lesson exercises and capstone projects. Please keep in mind that there is more than one solution for any problem.

> **NOTE** You can download these solutions and the rest of the source code from the Manning website at www.manning.com/books/get-programming-with-go or browse the source code online at github.com/nathany/get-programming-with-go.

Unit 0

Lesson 1

Experiment: playground.go

```go
package main

import (
    "fmt"
)

func main() {
    fmt.Println("Hello, Nathan")
```

```
        fmt.Println("你好 こんにちは Здравствуйте hola")
    }
```

Unit 1

Lesson 2

Experiment: malacandra.go

```
package main

import "fmt"

func main() {
    const hoursPerDay = 24

    var days = 28
    var distance = 56000000 // km

    fmt.Println(distance/(days*hoursPerDay), "km/h")
}
```

Lesson 3

Experiment: guess.go

```
package main

import (
    "fmt"
    "math/rand"
)

func main() {
    var number = 42

    for {
        var n = rand.Intn(100) + 1
        if n < number {
            fmt.Printf("%v is too small.\n", n)
        } else if n > number {
            fmt.Printf("%v is too big.\n", n)
```

```
        } else {
            fmt.Printf("You got it! %v\n", n)
            break
        }
    }
}
```

Lesson 4

Experiment: random-dates.go

```
package main

import (
    "fmt"
    "math/rand"
)

var era = "AD"

func main() {
    for count := 0; count < 10; count++ {
        year := 2018 + rand.Intn(10)
        leap := year%400 == 0 || (year%4 == 0 && year%100 != 0)
        month := rand.Intn(12) + 1

        daysInMonth := 31
        switch month {
        case 2:
            daysInMonth = 28
            if leap {
                daysInMonth = 29
            }
        case 4, 6, 9, 11:
            daysInMonth = 30
        }

        day := rand.Intn(daysInMonth) + 1
        fmt.Println(era, year, month, day)
    }
}
```

Capstone 5

```go
package main

import (
    "fmt"
    "math/rand"
)

const secondsPerDay = 86400

func main() {
    distance := 62100000
    company := ""
    trip := ""

    fmt.Println("Spaceline        Days Trip type  Price")
    fmt.Println("=====================================")

    for count := 0; count < 10; count++ {
        switch rand.Intn(3) {
        case 0:
            company = "Space Adventures"
        case 1:
            company = "SpaceX"
        case 2:
            company = "Virgin Galactic"
        }

        speed := rand.Intn(15) + 16               // 16-30 km/s
        duration := distance / speed / secondsPerDay // days
        price := 20.0 + speed                     // millions

        if rand.Intn(2) == 1 {
            trip = "Round-trip"
            price = price * 2
        } else {
            trip = "One-way"
        }
```

```
        fmt.Printf("%-16v %4v %-10v $%4v\n", company, duration, trip, price)
    }
}
```

Unit 2

Lesson 6

Experiment: piggy.go

```go
package main

import (
    "fmt"
    "math/rand"
)

func main() {
    piggyBank := 0.0

    for piggyBank < 20.00 {
        switch rand.Intn(3) {
        case 0:
            piggyBank += 0.05
        case 1:
            piggyBank += 0.10
        case 2:
            piggyBank += 0.25
        }
        fmt.Printf("$%5.2f\n", piggyBank)
    }
}
```

Lesson 7

Experiment: piggy.go

```go
package main

import (
    "fmt"
```

```
        "math/rand"
    )

    func main() {
        piggyBank := 0

        for piggyBank < 2000 {
            switch rand.Intn(3) {
            case 0:
                piggyBank += 5
            case 1:
                piggyBank += 10
            case 2:
                piggyBank += 25
            }

            dollars := piggyBank / 100
            cents := piggyBank % 100
            fmt.Printf("$%d.%02d\n", dollars, cents)
        }
    }
```

Lesson 8

Experiment: canis.go

```
package main

import (
    "fmt"
)

func main() {
    const distance = 236000000000000000
    const lightSpeed = 299792
    const secondsPerDay = 86400
    const daysPerYear = 365

    const years = distance / lightSpeed / secondsPerDay / daysPerYear

    fmt.Println("Canis Major Dwarf Galaxy is", years, "light years away.")
}
```

Prints Canis Major Dwarf Galaxy is 24962 light years away.

Lesson 9

Experiment: caesar.go

```go
message := "L fdph, L vdz, L frqtxhuhg."

for i := 0; i < len(message); i++ {
    c := message[i]
    if c >= 'a' && c <= 'z' {
        c -= 3
        if c < 'a' {
            c += 26
        }
    } else if c >= 'A' && c <= 'Z' {
        c -= 3
        if c < 'A' {
            c += 26
        }
    }
    fmt.Printf("%c", c)
}
```

Experiment: international.go

```go
message := "Hola Estación Espacial Internacional"

for _, c := range message {
    if c >= 'a' && c <= 'z' {
        c = c + 13
        if c > 'z' {
            c = c - 26
        }
    } else if c >= 'A' && c <= 'Z' {
        c = c + 13
        if c > 'Z' {
            c = c - 26
        }
    }
```

```
        fmt.Printf("%c", c)
}
```

Lesson 10

Experiment: input.go

```
yesNo := "1"

var launch bool

switch yesNo {
case "true", "yes", "1":
    launch = true
case "false", "no", "0":
    launch = false
default:
    fmt.Println(yesNo, "is not valid")
}

fmt.Println("Ready for launch:", launch)
```

Prints Ready for
launch: true

Capstone 11

Experiment: decipher.go

```
cipherText := "CSOITEUIWUIZNSROCNKFD"
keyword := "GOLANG"
message := ""
keyIndex := 0

for i := 0; i < len(cipherText); i++ {
    // A=0, B=1, ... Z=25
    c := cipherText[i] - 'A'
    k := keyword[keyIndex] - 'A'

    // cipher letter - key letter
    c = (c-k+26)%26 + 'A'
    message += string(c)

    // increment keyIndex
    keyIndex++
```

```
        keyIndex %= len(keyword)
}

fmt.Println(message)
```

```
message := "your message goes here"
keyword := "golang"
keyIndex := 0
cipherText := ""

message = strings.ToUpper(strings.Replace(message, " ", "", -1))
keyword = strings.ToUpper(strings.Replace(keyword, " ", "", -1))

for i := 0; i < len(message); i++ {
    c := message[i]
    if c >= 'A' && c <= 'Z' {
        // A=0, B=1, ... Z=25
        c -= 'A'
        k := keyword[keyIndex] - 'A'

        // cipher letter + key letter
        c = (c+k)%26 + 'A'

        // increment keyIndex
        keyIndex++
        keyIndex %= len(keyword)
    }
    cipherText += string(c)
}
fmt.Println(cipherText)
```

Unit 3

Lesson 12

Experiment: functions.go

```go
package main

import "fmt"

func kelvinToCelsius(k float64) float64 {
    return k - 273.15
}

func celsiusToFahrenheit(c float64) float64 {
    return (c * 9.0 / 5.0) + 32.0
}

func kelvinToFahrenheit(k float64) float64 {
    return celsiusToFahrenheit(kelvinToCelsius(k))
}

func main() {
    fmt.Printf("233° K is %.2f° C\n", kelvinToCelsius(233))
    fmt.Printf("0° K is %.2f° F\n", kelvinToFahrenheit(0))
}
```

Lesson 13

Experiment: methods.go

```go
package main

import "fmt"

type celsius float64

func (c celsius) fahrenheit() fahrenheit {
    return fahrenheit((c * 9.0 / 5.0) + 32.0)
}

func (c celsius) kelvin() kelvin {
    return kelvin(c + 273.15)
}
```

```go
type fahrenheit float64

func (f fahrenheit) celsius() celsius {
    return celsius((f - 32.0) * 5.0 / 9.0)
}

func (f fahrenheit) kelvin() kelvin {
    return f.celsius().kelvin()
}

type kelvin float64

func (k kelvin) celsius() celsius {
    return celsius(k - 273.15)
}

func (k kelvin) fahrenheit() fahrenheit {
    return k.celsius().fahrenheit()
}

func main() {
    var k kelvin = 294.0
    c := k.celsius()
    fmt.Print(k, "° K is ", c, "° C")
}
```

Lesson 14

Experiment: calibrate.go

```go
package main

import (
    "fmt"
    "math/rand"
)

type kelvin float64
type sensor func() kelvin

func fakeSensor() kelvin {
    return kelvin(rand.Intn(151) + 150)
}
```

```go
func calibrate(s sensor, offset kelvin) sensor {
    return func() kelvin {
        return s() + offset
    }
}

func main() {
    var offset kelvin = 5
    sensor := calibrate(fakeSensor, offset)

    for count := 0; count < 10; count++ {
        fmt.Println(sensor())
    }
}
```

Capstone 15

Experiment: tables.go

```go
package main

import (
    "fmt"
)

type celsius float64

func (c celsius) fahrenheit() fahrenheit {
    return fahrenheit((c * 9.0 / 5.0) + 32.0)
}

type fahrenheit float64

func (f fahrenheit) celsius() celsius {
    return celsius((f - 32.0) * 5.0 / 9.0)
}

const (
    line         = "========================="
    rowFormat    = "| %8s | %8s |\n"
    numberFormat = "%.1f"
)
```

```go
type getRowFn func(row int) (string, string)

// drawTable draws a two column table.
func drawTable(hdr1, hdr2 string, rows int, getRow getRowFn) {
    fmt.Println(line)
    fmt.Printf(rowFormat, hdr1, hdr2)
    fmt.Println(line)
    for row := 0; row < rows; row++ {
        cell1, cell2 := getRow(row)
        fmt.Printf(rowFormat, cell1, cell2)
    }
    fmt.Println(line)
}

func ctof(row int) (string, string) {
    c := celsius(row*5 - 40)
    f := c.fahrenheit()
    cell1 := fmt.Sprintf(numberFormat, c)
    cell2 := fmt.Sprintf(numberFormat, f)
    return cell1, cell2
}

func ftoc(row int) (string, string) {
    f := fahrenheit(row*5 - 40)
    c := f.celsius()
    cell1 := fmt.Sprintf(numberFormat, f)
    cell2 := fmt.Sprintf(numberFormat, c)
    return cell1, cell2
}

func main() {
    drawTable("°C", "°F", 29, ctof)
    fmt.Println()
    drawTable("°F", "°C", 29, ftoc)
}
```

Unit 4

Lesson 16

Experiment: chess.go

```go
package main

import "fmt"

func display(board [8][8]rune) {
    for _, row := range board {
        for _, column := range row {
            if column == 0 {
                fmt.Print("  ")
            } else {
                fmt.Printf("%c ", column)
            }
        }
        fmt.Println()
    }
}

func main() {
    var board [8][8]rune

    // black pieces
    board[0][0] = 'r'
    board[0][1] = 'n'
    board[0][2] = 'b'
    board[0][3] = 'q'
    board[0][4] = 'k'
    board[0][5] = 'b'
    board[0][6] = 'n'
    board[0][7] = 'r'

    // pawns
    for column := range board[1] {
        board[1][column] = 'p'
        board[6][column] = 'P'
    }
```

```
    // white pieces
    board[7][0] = 'R'
    board[7][1] = 'N'
    board[7][2] = 'B'
    board[7][3] = 'Q'
    board[7][4] = 'K'
    board[7][5] = 'B'
    board[7][6] = 'N'
    board[7][7] = 'R'

    display(board)
}
```

Lesson 17

Experiment: terraform.go

```
package main

import "fmt"

// Planets attaches methods to []string.
type Planets []string

func (planets Planets) terraform() {
    for i := range planets {
        planets[i] = "New " + planets[i]
    }
}

func main() {
    planets := []string{
        "Mercury", "Venus", "Earth", "Mars",
        "Jupiter", "Saturn", "Uranus", "Neptune",
    }
    Planets(planets[3:4]).terraform()
    Planets(planets[6:]).terraform()
    fmt.Println(planets)
}
```

Prints [Mercury Venus
Earth New Mars
Jupiter Saturn New
Uranus New Neptune]

Lesson 18

Experiment: capacity.go

```
s := []string{}
lastCap := cap(s)

for i := 0; i < 10000; i++ {
    s = append(s, "An element")
    if cap(s) != lastCap {
        fmt.Println(cap(s))
        lastCap = cap(s)
    }
}
```

Lesson 19

Experiment: words.go

```
package main

import (
    "fmt"
    "strings"
)

func countWords(text string) map[string]int {
    words := strings.Fields(strings.ToLower(text))
    frequency := make(map[string]int, len(words))
    for _, word := range words {
        word = strings.Trim(word, `.,"-`)
        frequency[word]++
    }
    return frequency
}

func main() {
    text := `As far as eye could reach he saw nothing but the stems of the
        great plants about him receding in the violet shade, and far overhead
        the multiple transparency of huge leaves filtering the sunshine to the
        solemn splendour of twilight in which he walked. Whenever he felt able
```

he ran again; the ground continued soft and springy, covered with the
same resilient weed which was the first thing his hands had touched in
Malacandra. Once or twice a small red creature scuttled across his
path, but otherwise there seemed to be no life stirring in the wood;
nothing to fear -- except the fact of wandering unprovisioned and alone
in a forest of unknown vegetation thousands or millions of miles
beyond the reach or knowledge of man.`

```go
    frequency := countWords(text)
    for word, count := range frequency {
        if count > 1 {
            fmt.Printf("%d %v\n", count, word)
        }
    }
}
```

Capstone 20

Experiment: life.go

```go
package main

import (
    "fmt"
    "math/rand"
    "time"
)

const (
    width  = 80
    height = 15
)

// Universe is a two-dimensional field of cells.
type Universe [][]bool

// NewUniverse returns an empty universe.
func NewUniverse() Universe {
    u := make(Universe, height)
    for i := range u {
        u[i] = make([]bool, width)
```

```
        }
        return u
}

// Seed random live cells into the universe.
func (u Universe) Seed() {
    for i := 0; i < (width * height / 4); i++ {
        u.Set(rand.Intn(width), rand.Intn(height), true)
    }
}

// Set the state of the specified cell.
func (u Universe) Set(x, y int, b bool) {
    u[y][x] = b
}

// Alive reports whether the specified cell is alive.
// If the coordinates are outside of the universe, they wrap around.
func (u Universe) Alive(x, y int) bool {
    x = (x + width) % width
    y = (y + height) % height
    return u[y][x]
}

// Neighbors counts the adjacent cells that are alive.
func (u Universe) Neighbors(x, y int) int {
    n := 0
    for v := -1; v <= 1; v++ {
        for h := -1; h <= 1; h++ {
            if !(v == 0 && h == 0) && u.Alive(x+h, y+v) {
                n++
            }
        }
    }
    return n
}

// Next returns the state of the specified cell at the next step.
func (u Universe) Next(x, y int) bool {
    n := u.Neighbors(x, y)
```

```go
    return n == 3 || n == 2 && u.Alive(x, y)
}

// String returns the universe as a string.
func (u Universe) String() string {
    var b byte
    buf := make([]byte, 0, (width+1)*height)

    for y := 0; y < height; y++ {
        for x := 0; x < width; x++ {
            b = ' '
            if u[y][x] {
                b = '*'
            }
            buf = append(buf, b)
        }
        buf = append(buf, '\n')
    }

    return string(buf)
}

// Show clears the screen and displays the universe.
func (u Universe) Show() {
    fmt.Print("\x0c", u.String())
}

// Step updates the state of the next universe (b) from
// the current universe (a).
func Step(a, b Universe) {
    for y := 0; y < height; y++ {
        for x := 0; x < width; x++ {
            b.Set(x, y, a.Next(x, y))
        }
    }
}

func main() {
    a, b := NewUniverse(), NewUniverse()
    a.Seed()
```

```go
    for i := 0; i < 300; i++ {
        Step(a, b)
        a.Show()
        time.Sleep(time.Second / 30)
        a, b = b, a // Swap universes
    }
}
```

Unit 5

Lesson 21

Experiment: landing.go

```go
type location struct {
    Name string `json:"name"`
    Lat  float64 `json:"latitude"`
    Long float64 `json:"longitude"`
}
locations := []location{
    {Name: "Bradbury Landing", Lat: -4.5895, Long: 137.4417},
    {Name: "Columbia Memorial Station", Lat: -14.5684, Long: 175.472636},
    {Name: "Challenger Memorial Station", Lat: -1.9462, Long: 354.4734},
}
bytes, err := json.MarshalIndent(locations, "", "  ")
if err != nil {
    fmt.Println(err)
    os.Exit(1)
}

fmt.Println(string(bytes))
```

Lesson 22

Experiment: landing.go

```go
package main

import "fmt"
```

```go
// location with a latitude, longitude.
type location struct {
    lat, long float64
}

// coordinate in degrees, minutes, seconds in a N/S/E/W hemisphere.
type coordinate struct {
    d, m, s float64
    h       rune
}

// newLocation from latitude, longitude d/m/s coordinates.
func newLocation(lat, long coordinate) location {
    return location{lat.decimal(), long.decimal()}
}

// decimal converts a d/m/s coordinate to decimal degrees.
func (c coordinate) decimal() float64 {
    sign := 1.0
    switch c.h {
    case 'S', 'W', 's', 'w':
        sign = -1
    }
    return sign * (c.d + c.m/60 + c.s/3600)
}

func main() {
    spirit := newLocation(coordinate{14, 34, 6.2, 'S'}, coordinate{175, 28,
➥21.5, 'E'})
    opportunity := newLocation(coordinate{1, 56, 46.3, 'S'}, coordinate{354,
➥28, 24.2, 'E'})
    curiosity := newLocation(coordinate{4, 35, 22.2, 'S'}, coordinate{137,
➥26, 30.12, 'E'})
    insight := newLocation(coordinate{4, 30, 0.0, 'N'}, coordinate{135, 54,
➥0, 'E'})
    fmt.Println("Spirit", spirit)
    fmt.Println("Opportunity", opportunity)
    fmt.Println("Curiosity", curiosity)
    fmt.Println("InSight", insight)
}
```

Experiment: distance.go

```go
package main

import (
    "fmt"
    "math"
)

// location with a latitude, longitude.
type location struct {
    lat, long float64
}

// coordinate in degrees, minutes, seconds in a N/S/E/W hemisphere.
type coordinate struct {
    d, m, s float64
    h       rune
}

// newLocation from latitude, longitude d/m/s coordinates.
func newLocation(lat, long coordinate) location {
    return location{lat.decimal(), long.decimal()}
}

// decimal converts a d/m/s coordinate to decimal degrees.
func (c coordinate) decimal() float64 {
    sign := 1.0
    switch c.h {
    case 'S', 'W', 's', 'w':
        sign = -1
    }
    return sign * (c.d + c.m/60 + c.s/3600)
}

// world with a volumetric mean radius in kilometers
type world struct {
    radius float64
}

// distance calculation using the Spherical Law of Cosines.
```

```go
func (w world) distance(p1, p2 location) float64 {
    s1, c1 := math.Sincos(rad(p1.lat))
    s2, c2 := math.Sincos(rad(p2.lat))
    clong := math.Cos(rad(p1.long - p2.long))
    return w.radius * math.Acos(s1*s2+c1*c2*clong)
}

// rad converts degrees to radians.
func rad(deg float64) float64 {
    return deg * math.Pi / 180
}

var (
    mars  = world{radius: 3389.5}
    earth = world{radius: 6371}
)

func main() {
    spirit := newLocation(coordinate{14, 34, 6.2, 'S'}, coordinate{175, 28,
21.5, 'E'})
    opportunity := newLocation(coordinate{1, 56, 46.3, 'S'}, coordinate{354,
28, 24.2, 'E'})
    curiosity := newLocation(coordinate{4, 35, 22.2, 'S'}, coordinate{137,
26, 30.12, 'E'})
    insight := newLocation(coordinate{4, 30, 0.0, 'N'}, coordinate{135, 54,
0.0, 'E'})
    fmt.Printf("Spirit to Opportunity %.2f km\n", mars.distance(spirit,
opportunity))
    fmt.Printf("Spirit to Curiosity %.2f km\n", mars.distance(spirit,
curiosity))
    fmt.Printf("Spirit to InSight %.2f km\n", mars.distance(spirit, insight))

    fmt.Printf("Opportunity to Curiosity %.2f km\n", mars.distance(opportunity,
curiosity))
    fmt.Printf("Opportunity to InSight %.2f km\n", mars.distance(opportunity,
insight))

    fmt.Printf("Curiosity to InSight %.2f km\n", mars.distance(curiosity,
insight))

    london := newLocation(coordinate{51, 30, 0, 'N'}, coordinate{0, 8, 0, 'W'})
```

```
    paris := newLocation(coordinate{48, 51, 0, 'N'}, coordinate{2, 21, 0, 'E'})
    fmt.Printf("London to Paris %.2f km\n", earth.distance(london, paris))

    edmonton := newLocation(coordinate{53, 32, 0, 'N'}, coordinate{113, 30, 0,
➥'W'})
    ottawa := newLocation(coordinate{45, 25, 0, 'N'}, coordinate{75, 41, 0,
➥'W'})
    fmt.Printf("Hometown to Capital %.2f km\n", earth.distance(edmonton,
➥ottawa))

    mountSharp := newLocation(coordinate{5, 4, 48, 'S'}, coordinate{137, 51, 0,
➥'E'})
    olympusMons := newLocation(coordinate{18, 39, 0, 'N'}, coordinate{226, 12,
➥0, 'E'})
    fmt.Printf("Mount Sharp to Olympus Mons %.2f km\n",
➥mars.distance(mountSharp, olympusMons))
}
```

Lesson 23

Experiment: gps.go

```
package main

import (
    "fmt"
    "math"
)

type world struct {
    radius float64
}

type location struct {
    name       string
    lat, long float64
}

func (l location) description() string {
    return fmt.Sprintf("%v (%.1f°, %.1f°)", l.name, l.lat, l.long)
}
```

```go
type gps struct {
    world       world
    current     location
    destination location
}

func (g gps) distance() float64 {
    return g.world.distance(g.current, g.destination)
}

func (g gps) message() string {
    return fmt.Sprintf("%.1f km to %v", g.distance(),
➥g.destination.description())
}

func (w world) distance(p1, p2 location) float64 {
    s1, c1 := math.Sincos(rad(p1.lat))
    s2, c2 := math.Sincos(rad(p2.lat))
    clong := math.Cos(rad(p1.long - p2.long))
    return w.radius * math.Acos(s1*s2+c1*c2*clong)
 }

func rad(deg float64) float64 {
    return deg * math.Pi / 180
}

type rover struct {
    gps
}

func main() {
    mars := world{radius: 3389.5}
    bradbury := location{"Bradbury Landing", -4.5895, 137.4417}
    elysium := location{"Elysium Planitia", 4.5, 135.9}

    gps := gps{
        world:       mars,
        current:     bradbury,
        destination: elysium,
    }

    curiosity := rover{
```

```
        gps: gps,
    }
    fmt.Println(curiosity.message())
}
```

Prints 545.4 km
to Elysium
Planitia (4.5°,
135.9°)

Lesson 24

Experiment: marshal.go

```go
package main

import (
    "encoding/json"
    "fmt"
    "os"
)

// coordinate in degrees, minutes, seconds in a N/S/E/W hemisphere.
type coordinate struct {
    d, m, s float64
    h       rune
}

// String formats a DMS coordinate.
func (c coordinate) String() string {
    return fmt.Sprintf("%v°%v'%.1f\" %c", c.d, c.m, c.s, c.h)
}

// decimal converts a d/m/s coordinate to decimal degrees.
func (c coordinate) decimal() float64 {
    sign := 1.0
    switch c.h {
    case 'S', 'W', 's', 'w':
        sign = -1
    }
    return sign * (c.d + c.m/60 + c.s/3600)
}

func (c coordinate) MarshalJSON() ([]byte, error) {
    return json.Marshal(struct {
```

```go
        DD  float64 `json:"decimal"`
        DMS string  `json:"dms"`
        D   float64 `json:"degrees"`
        M   float64 `json:"minutes"`
        S   float64 `json:"seconds"`
        H   string  `json:"hemisphere"`
    }{
        DD:  c.decimal(),
        DMS: c.String(),
        D:   c.d,
        M:   c.m,
        S:   c.s,
        H:   string(c.h),
    })
}

// location with a latitude, longitude in decimal degrees.
type location struct {
    Name string     `json:"name"`
    Lat  coordinate `json:"latitude"`
    Long coordinate `json:"longitude"`
}

func main() {
    elysium := location{
        Name: "Elysium Planitia",
        Lat:  coordinate{4, 30, 0.0, 'N'},
        Long: coordinate{135, 54, 0.0, 'E'},
    }

    bytes, err := json.MarshalIndent(elysium, "", "  ")
    if err != nil {
        fmt.Println(err)
        os.Exit(1)
    }

    fmt.Println(string(bytes))
}
```

Capstone 25

```go
package main

import (
    "fmt"
    "math/rand"
    "time"
)

type honeyBee struct {
    name string
}

func (hb honeyBee) String() string {
    return hb.name
}

func (hb honeyBee) move() string {
    switch rand.Intn(2) {
    case 0:
        return "buzzes about"
    default:
        return "flies to infinity and beyond"
    }
}

func (hb honeyBee) eat() string {
    switch rand.Intn(2) {
    case 0:
        return "pollen"
    default:
        return "nectar"
    }
}

type gopher struct {
    name string
}
```

```go
func (g gopher) String() string {
    return g.name
}
func (g gopher) move() string {
    switch rand.Intn(2) {
    case 0:
        return "scurries along the ground"
    default:
        return "burrows in the sand"
    }
}
func (g gopher) eat() string {
    switch rand.Intn(5) {
    case 0:
        return "carrot"
    case 1:
        return "lettuce"
    case 2:
        return "radish"
    case 3:
        return "corn"
    default:
        return "root"
    }
}
type animal interface {
    move() string
    eat() string
}
func step(a animal) {
    switch rand.Intn(2) {
    case 0:
        fmt.Printf("%v %v.\n", a, a.move())
    default:
        fmt.Printf("%v eats the %v.\n", a, a.eat())
```

```
        }
    }

    const sunrise, sunset = 8, 18

    func main() {
        rand.Seed(time.Now().UnixNano())

        animals := []animal{
            honeyBee{name: "Bzzz Lightyear"},
            gopher{name: "Go gopher"},
        }

        var sol, hour int

        for {
            fmt.Printf("%2d:00 ", hour)
            if hour < sunrise || hour >= sunset {
                fmt.Println("The animals are sleeping.")
            } else {
                i := rand.Intn(len(animals))
                step(animals[i])
            }

            time.Sleep(500 * time.Millisecond)

            hour++
            if hour >= 24 {
                hour = 0
                sol++
                if sol >= 3 {
                    break
                }
            }
        }
    }
```

Unit 6

Lesson 26

Experiment: turtle.go

```go
package main

import "fmt"

type turtle struct {
    x, y int
}

func (t *turtle) up() {
    t.y--
}

func (t *turtle) down() {
    t.y++
}

func (t *turtle) left() {
    t.x--
}

func (t *turtle) right() {
    t.x++
}

func main() {
    var t turtle
    t.up()
    t.up()
    t.left()
    t.left()
    fmt.Println(t)        // Prints {-2 -2}
    t.down()
    t.down()
    t.right()
    t.right()
    fmt.Println(t)        // Prints {0 0}
}
```

Lesson 27

```go
package main

import (
    "fmt"
)

type item struct {
    name string
}

type character struct {
    name     string
    leftHand *item
}

func (c *character) pickup(i *item) {
    if c == nil || i == nil {
        return
    }
    fmt.Printf("%v picks up a %v\n", c.name, i.name)
    c.leftHand = i
}

func (c *character) give(to *character) {
    if c == nil || to == nil {
        return
    }
    if c.leftHand == nil {
        fmt.Printf("%v has nothing to give\n", c.name)
        return
    }
    if to.leftHand != nil {
        fmt.Printf("%v's hands are full\n", to.name)
        return
    }
    to.leftHand = c.leftHand
    c.leftHand = nil
    fmt.Printf("%v gives %v a %v\n", c.name, to.name, to.leftHand.name)
```

```
}
func (c character) String() string {
    if c.leftHand == nil {
        return fmt.Sprintf("%v is carrying nothing", c.name)
    }
    return fmt.Sprintf("%v is carrying a %v", c.name, c.leftHand.name)
}
func main() {
    arthur := &character{name: "Arthur"}

    shrubbery := &item{name: "shrubbery"}
    arthur.pickup(shrubbery)

    knight := &character{name: "Knight"}
    arthur.give(knight)

    fmt.Println(arthur)
    fmt.Println(knight)
}
```

Prints Arthur picks up a shrubbery

Prints Arthur gives Knight a shrubbery

Prints Arthur is carrying nothing

Prints Knight is carrying a shrubbery

Lesson 28

Experiment: url.go

```
u, err := url.Parse("https://a b.com/")

if err != nil {
    fmt.Println(err)
    fmt.Printf("%#v\n", err)

    if e, ok := err.(*url.Error); ok {
        fmt.Println("Op:", e.Op)
        fmt.Println("URL:", e.URL)
        fmt.Println("Err:", e.Err)
    }
    os.Exit(1)
}
fmt.Println(u)
```

Prints parse https://a b.com/: invalid character " " in host name

Prints &url.Error{Op:"parse", URL:"https://a b.com/", Err:" "}

Prints Op: parse

Prints URL: https://a b.com/

Prints Err: invalid character " " in host name

Capstone 29

Experiment: sudoku.go

```go
package main

import (
    "errors"
    "fmt"
    "os"
)

const (
    rows, columns = 9, 9
    empty         = 0
)

// Cell is a square on the Sudoku grid.
type Cell struct {
    digit int8
    fixed bool
}

// Grid is a Sudoku grid.
type Grid [rows][columns]Cell

// Errors that could occur.
var (
    ErrBounds     = errors.New("out of bounds")
    ErrDigit      = errors.New("invalid digit")
    ErrInRow      = errors.New("digit already present in this row")
    ErrInColumn   = errors.New("digit already present in this column")
    ErrInRegion   = errors.New("digit already present in this region")
    ErrFixedDigit = errors.New("initial digits cannot be overwritten")
)

// NewSudoku makes a new Sudoku grid.
func NewSudoku(digits [rows][columns]int8) *Grid {
    var grid Grid
    for r := 0; r < rows; r++ {
        for c := 0; c < columns; c++ {
```

```
            d := digits[r][c]
            if d != empty {
                grid[r][c].digit = d
                grid[r][c].fixed = true
            }
        }
    }
    return &grid
}

// Set a digit on a Sudoku grid.
func (g *Grid) Set(row, column int, digit int8) error {
    switch {
    case !inBounds(row, column):
        return ErrBounds
    case !validDigit(digit):
        return ErrDigit
    case g.isFixed(row, column):
        return ErrFixedDigit
    case g.inRow(row, digit):
        return ErrInRow
    case g.inColumn(column, digit):
        return ErrInColumn
    case g.inRegion(row, column, digit):
        return ErrInRegion
    }

    g[row][column].digit = digit
    return nil
}

// Clear a cell from the Sudoku grid.
func (g *Grid) Clear(row, column int) error {
    switch {
    case !inBounds(row, column):
        return ErrBounds
    case g.isFixed(row, column):
        return ErrFixedDigit
    }
```

```
        g[row][column].digit = empty
        return nil
}

func inBounds(row, column int) bool {
    if row < 0 || row >= rows || column < 0 || column >= columns {
        return false
    }
    return true
}

func validDigit(digit int8) bool {
    return digit >= 1 && digit <= 9
}

func (g *Grid) inRow(row int, digit int8) bool {
    for c := 0; c < columns; c++ {
        if g[row][c].digit == digit {
            return true
        }
    }
    return false
}

func (g *Grid) inColumn(column int, digit int8) bool {
    for r := 0; r < rows; r++ {
        if g[r][column].digit == digit {
            return true
        }
    }
    return false
}

func (g *Grid) inRegion(row, column int, digit int8) bool {
    startRow, startColumn := row/3*3, column/3*3
    for r := startRow; r < startRow+3; r++ {
        for c := startColumn; c < startColumn+3; c++ {
            if g[r][c].digit == digit {
                return true
            }
        }
```

```go
        }
    }
    return false
}

func (g *Grid) isFixed(row, column int) bool {
    return g[row][column].fixed
}

func main() {
    s := NewSudoku([rows][columns]int8{
        {5, 3, 0, 0, 7, 0, 0, 0, 0},
        {6, 0, 0, 1, 9, 5, 0, 0, 0},
        {0, 9, 8, 0, 0, 0, 0, 6, 0},
        {8, 0, 0, 0, 6, 0, 0, 0, 3},
        {4, 0, 0, 8, 0, 3, 0, 0, 1},
        {7, 0, 0, 0, 2, 0, 0, 0, 6},
        {0, 6, 0, 0, 0, 0, 2, 8, 0},
        {0, 0, 0, 4, 1, 9, 0, 0, 5},
        {0, 0, 0, 0, 8, 0, 0, 7, 9},
    })

    err := s.Set(1, 1, 4)
    if err != nil {
        fmt.Println(err)
        os.Exit(1)
    }

    for _, row := range s {
        fmt.Println(row)
    }
}
```

Unit 7

Lesson 30

Experiment: remove-identical.go

```go
package main

import (
    "fmt"
)

func main() {
    c0 := make(chan string)
    c1 := make(chan string)
    go sourceGopher(c0)
    go removeDuplicates(c0, c1)
    printGopher(c1)
}

func sourceGopher(downstream chan string) {
    for _, v := range []string{"a", "b", "b", "c", "d", "d", "d", "e"} {
        downstream <- v
    }
    close(downstream)
}

func removeDuplicates(upstream, downstream chan string) {
    prev := ""
    for v := range upstream {
        if v != prev {
            downstream <- v
            prev = v
        }
    }
    close(downstream)
}

func printGopher(upstream chan string) {
    for v := range upstream {
```

```
        fmt.Println(v)
    }
}
```

Experiment: split-words.go

```go
package main

import (
    "fmt"
    "strings"
)

func main() {
    c0 := make(chan string)
    c1 := make(chan string)
    go sourceGopher(c0)
    go splitWords(c0, c1)
    printGopher(c1)
}

func sourceGopher(downstream chan string) {
    for _, v := range []string{"hello world", "a bad apple", "goodbye all"}
    {
        downstream <- v
    }
    close(downstream)
}

func splitWords(upstream, downstream chan string) {
    for v := range upstream {
        for _, word := range strings.Fields(v) {
            downstream <- word
        }
    }
    close(downstream)
}

func printGopher(upstream chan string) {
```

```
    for v := range upstream {
        fmt.Println(v)
    }
}
```

Lesson 31

Experiment: positionworker.go

```go
package main

import (
    "fmt"
    "image"
    "time"
)

func main() {
    go worker()
    time.Sleep(5 * time.Second)
}

func worker() {
    pos := image.Point{X: 10, Y: 10}
    direction := image.Point{X: 1, Y: 0}
    delay := time.Second
    next := time.After(delay)
    for {
        select {
        case <-next:
            pos = pos.Add(direction)
            fmt.Println("current position is ", pos)
            delay += time.Second / 2
            next = time.After(delay)
        }
    }
}
```

Experiment: rover.go

```go
package main

import (
    "image"
    "log"
    "time"
)

func main() {
    r := NewRoverDriver()
    time.Sleep(3 * time.Second)
    r.Left()
    time.Sleep(3 * time.Second)
    r.Right()
    time.Sleep(3 * time.Second)
    r.Stop()
    time.Sleep(3 * time.Second)
    r.Start()
    time.Sleep(3 * time.Second)
}

// RoverDriver drives a rover around the surface of Mars.
type RoverDriver struct {
    commandc chan command
}

// NewRoverDriver starts a new RoverDriver and returns it.
func NewRoverDriver() *RoverDriver {
    r := &RoverDriver{
        commandc: make(chan command),
    }
    go r.drive()
    return r
}

type command int

const (
```

```go
    right = command(0)
    left  = command(1)
    start = command(2)
    stop  = command(3)
)

// drive is responsible for driving the rover. It
// is expected to be started in a goroutine.
func (r *RoverDriver) drive() {
    pos := image.Point{X: 0, Y: 0}
    direction := image.Point{X: 1, Y: 0}
    updateInterval := 250 * time.Millisecond
    nextMove := time.After(updateInterval)
    speed := 1
    for {
        select {
        case c := <-r.commandc:
            switch c {
            case right:
                direction = image.Point{
                    X: -direction.Y,
                    Y: direction.X,
                }
            case left:
                direction = image.Point{
                    X: direction.Y,
                    Y: -direction.X,
                }
            case stop:
                speed = 0
            case start:
                speed = 1
            }
            log.Printf("new direction %v; speed %d", direction, speed)
        case <-nextMove:
            pos = pos.Add(direction.Mul(speed))
            log.Printf("moved to %v", pos)
            nextMove = time.After(updateInterval)
```

```
        }
    }
}
// Left turns the rover left (90° counterclockwise).
func (r *RoverDriver) Left() {
    r.commandc <- left
}

// Right turns the rover right (90° clockwise).
func (r *RoverDriver) Right() {
    r.commandc <- right
}

// Stop halts the rover.
func (r *RoverDriver) Stop() {
    r.commandc <- stop
}

// Start gets the rover moving.
func (r *RoverDriver) Start() {
    r.commandc <- start
}
```

Capstone 32

Experiment: lifeonmars.go

```
package main

import (
    "fmt"
    "image"
    "log"
    "math/rand"
    "sync"
    "time"
)

func main() {
    marsToEarth := make(chan []Message)
```

```
        go earthReceiver(marsToEarth)

        gridSize := image.Point{X: 20, Y: 10}
        grid := NewMarsGrid(gridSize)
        rover := make([]*RoverDriver, 5)
        for i := range rover {
            rover[i] = startDriver(fmt.Sprint("rover", i), grid, marsToEarth)
        }
        time.Sleep(60 * time.Second)
}

// Message holds a message as sent from Mars to Earth.
type Message struct {
    Pos        image.Point
    LifeSigns int
    Rover      string

}

const (
    // The length of a Mars day.
    dayLength = 24 * time.Second
    // The length of time per day during which
    // messages can be transmitted from a rover to Earth.
    receiveTimePerDay = 2 * time.Second
)

// earthReceiver receives messages sent from Mars.
// As connectivity is limited, it only receives messages
// for some time every Mars day.
func earthReceiver(msgc chan []Message) {
    for {
        time.Sleep(dayLength - receiveTimePerDay)
        receiveMarsMessages(msgc)
    }
}

// receiveMarsMessages receives messages sent from Mars
// for the given duration.
func receiveMarsMessages(msgc chan []Message) {
    finished := time.After(receiveTimePerDay)
```

```
    for {
        select {
        case <-finished:
            return
        case ms := <-msgc:
            for _, m := range ms {
                log.Printf("earth received report of life sign level %d from
%s at %v", m.LifeSigns, m.Rover, m.Pos)
            }
        }
    }
}
func startDriver(name string, grid *MarsGrid, marsToEarth chan []Message)
*RoverDriver {
    var o *Occupier
    // Try a random point; continue until we've found one that's
    // not currently occupied.
    for o == nil {
        startPoint := image.Point{X: rand.Intn(grid.Size().X), Y: rand.Intn(
grid.Size().Y)}
        o = grid.Occupy(startPoint)
    }
    return NewRoverDriver(name, o, marsToEarth)
}

// Radio represents a radio transmitter that can send
// message to Earth.
type Radio struct {
    fromRover chan Message
}

// SendToEarth sends a message to Earth. It always
// succeeds immediately - the actual message
// may be buffered and actually transmitted later.
func (r *Radio) SendToEarth(m Message) {
    r.fromRover <- m
}

// NewRadio returns a new Radio instance that sends
```

```go
// messages on the toEarth channel.
func NewRadio(toEarth chan []Message) *Radio {
    r := &Radio{
        fromRover: make(chan Message),
    }
    go r.run(toEarth)
    return r
}

// run buffers messages sent by a rover until they
// can be sent to Earth.
func (r *Radio) run(toEarth chan []Message) {
    var buffered []Message
    for {
        toEarth1 := toEarth
        if len(buffered) == 0 {
            toEarth1 = nil
        }
        select {
        case m := <-r.fromRover:
            buffered = append(buffered, m)
        case toEarth1 <- buffered:
            buffered = nil
        }
    }
}

// RoverDriver drives a rover around the surface of Mars.
type RoverDriver struct {
    commandc chan command
    occupier *Occupier
    name     string
    radio    *Radio
}

// NewRoverDriver starts a new RoverDriver and returns it.
func NewRoverDriver(
    name string,
    occupier *Occupier,
```

```
        marsToEarth chan []Message,
) *RoverDriver {
    r := &RoverDriver{
        commandc: make(chan command),
        occupier: occupier,
        name:     name,
        radio:    NewRadio(marsToEarth),
    }
    go r.drive()
    return r
}

type command int

const (
    right command = 0
    left  command = 1
)

// drive is responsible for driving the rover. It
// is expected to be started in a goroutine.
func (r *RoverDriver) drive() {
    log.Printf("%s initial position %v", r.name, r.occupier.Pos())
    direction := image.Point{X: 1, Y: 0}
    updateInterval := 250 * time.Millisecond
    nextMove := time.After(updateInterval)
    for {
        select {
        case c := <-r.commandc:
            switch c {
            case right:
                direction = image.Point{
                    X: -direction.Y,
                    Y: direction.X,
                }
            case left:
                direction = image.Point{
                    X: direction.Y,
                    Y: -direction.X,
```

```
                }
            }
            log.Printf("%s new direction %v", r.name, direction)
        case <-nextMove:
            nextMove = time.After(updateInterval)
            newPos := r.occupier.Pos().Add(direction)
            if r.occupier.MoveTo(newPos) {
                log.Printf("%s moved to %v", r.name, newPos)
                r.checkForLife()
                break
            }
            log.Printf("%s blocked trying to move from %v to %v", r.name,
r.occupier.Pos(), newPos)
            // Pick one of the other directions randomly.
            // Next time round, we'll try to move in the new
            // direction.
            dir := rand.Intn(3) + 1
            for i := 0; i < dir; i++ {
                direction = image.Point{
                    X: -direction.Y,
                    Y: direction.X,
                }
            }
            log.Printf("%s new random direction %v", r.name, direction)
        }
    }
}

func (r *RoverDriver) checkForLife() {
    // Successfully moved to new position.
    sensorData := r.occupier.Sense()
    if sensorData.LifeSigns < 900 {
        return
    }
    r.radio.SendToEarth(Message{
        Pos:       r.occupier.Pos(),
        LifeSigns: sensorData.LifeSigns,
        Rover:     r.name,
```

```go
    })
}

// Left turns the rover left (90° counterclockwise).
func (r *RoverDriver) Left() {
    r.commandc <- left
}

// Right turns the rover right (90° clockwise).
func (r *RoverDriver) Right() {
    r.commandc <- right
}

// MarsGrid represents a grid of some of the surface
// of Mars. It may be used concurrently by different
// goroutines.
type MarsGrid struct {
    bounds image.Rectangle
    mu     sync.Mutex
    cells  [][]cell
}

// SensorData holds information about what's in
// a point in the grid.
type SensorData struct {
    LifeSigns int
}

type cell struct {
    groundData SensorData
    occupier   *Occupier
}

// NewMarsGrid returns a new MarsGrid of the
// given size.
func NewMarsGrid(size image.Point) *MarsGrid {
    grid := &MarsGrid{
        bounds: image.Rectangle{
            Max: size,
        },
        cells: make([][]cell, size.Y),
```

```
    }
    for y := range grid.cells {
        grid.cells[y] = make([]cell, size.X)
        for x := range grid.cells[y] {
            cell := &grid.cells[y][x]
            cell.groundData.LifeSigns = rand.Intn(1000)
        }
    }
    return grid
}

// Size returns a Point representing the size of the grid.
func (g *MarsGrid) Size() image.Point {
    return g.bounds.Max
}

// Occupy occupies a cell at the given point in the grid. It
// returns nil if the point is already occupied or the point is outside
// the grid. Otherwise it returns a value that can be used
// to move to different places on the grid.
func (g *MarsGrid) Occupy(p image.Point) *Occupier {
    g.mu.Lock()
    defer g.mu.Unlock()
    cell := g.cell(p)
    if cell == nil || cell.occupier != nil {
        return nil
    }
    cell.occupier = &Occupier{
        grid: g,
        pos:  p,
    }
    return cell.occupier
}

func (g *MarsGrid) cell(p image.Point) *cell {
    if !p.In(g.bounds) {
        return nil
    }
    return &g.cells[p.Y][p.X]
```

```
}

// Occupier represents an occupied cell in the grid.
type Occupier struct {
    grid *MarsGrid
    pos  image.Point
}

// MoveTo moves the occupier to a different cell in the grid.
// It reports whether the move was successful
// It might fail because it was trying to move outside
// the grid or because the cell it's trying to move into
// is occupied. If it fails, the occupier remains in the same place.
func (o *Occupier) MoveTo(p image.Point) bool {
    o.grid.mu.Lock()
    defer o.grid.mu.Unlock()
    newCell := o.grid.cell(p)
    if newCell == nil || newCell.occupier != nil {
        return false
    }
    o.grid.cell(o.pos).occupier = nil
    newCell.occupier = o
    o.pos = p
    return true
}

// Sense returns sensory data from the current cell.
func (o *Occupier) Sense() SensorData {
    o.grid.mu.Lock()
    defer o.grid.mu.Unlock()
    return o.grid.cell(o.pos).groundData
}

// Pos returns the current grid position of the occupier.
func (o *Occupier) Pos() image.Point {
    return o.pos
}
```

INDEX

Symbols